TEACHER'S BOOK

BARBARA GARSIDE

INTERMEDIATE OUTCOMES

HEINLE
CENGAGE Learning™

Australia • Brazil • Japan • Korea • Mexico • Singapore • Spain • United Kingdom • United States

Outcomes *Intermediate Teacher's Book*
Barbara Garside

Publisher: Jason Mann
Commissioning Editor: John Waterman
Development Editor: Heidi North
Product Manager: Ruth McAleavey
Head of Production: Alissa Chappell
Production Controller: Paul Herbert
Cover and text designer: Studio April
Compositor: Pre-PressPMG

ISBN: 978-1-4240-2801-6

Heinle, Cengage Learning EMEA
Cheriton House, North Way, Andover, Hampshire
SP10 5BE United Kingdom

Cengage Learning is a leading provider of customised learning solutions with office locations around the globe, including Singapore, the United Kingdom, Australia, Mexico, Brazil and Japan. Locate our local office at **international.cengage.com/region**

Cengage Learning products are represented in Canada by Nelson Education Ltd.

Visit Heinle online at **elt.heinle.com**
Visit our corporate website at **cengage.com**

Artwork produced by KJA Artists pp. 69, 94, 129, 139,156.

Printed in Singapore
1 2 3 4 5 6 7 8 9 10 – 12 11 10

CONTENTS

INTRODUCTION

WHAT'S IN *OUTCOMES* STUDENT'S BOOK?

16 Units based round common topics Each unit has three interlinked 'lessons' of 50–90 minutes. The unit contents give clear practical outcomes. The first lesson teaches language leading to *Conversation Practice*. The second and third spreads develop reading or listening and teach more grammar and vocabulary connected with the topic.

8 Writing units The two-page writing units on pp. 120–135 teach different types of writing for everyday life and exams. Each has a model text, *Grammar* or *Vocabulary*, *Keywords for writing* and *Practice*.

4 Review units Each review has a learner training discussion, two pages of games, tasks and pronunciation exercises to revise language and then a two-page test including a listening exercise.

Grammar Thirty-two points of grammar are covered. Each *Grammar* section links to the previous text. An explanation or guided questions teach meaning. Exercises give controlled and freer practice. There's a link to the Grammar reference if you need extra help.

Grammar reference This is on pp. 136–155 at the back of the book. Each section has an expanded explanation, further natural examples of usage and extra controlled practice exercises with a glossary.

Language patterns This is a short translation exercise into the student's own language and back into English. It draws attention to other aspects of syntax and grammar based on a pattern seen in a text.

Vocabulary Vocabulary is carefully chosen to enable students to talk about the topic in the context of English as a lingua franca. Tasks generally move from meaning, to contextualised usage to personalised practice. Other sections focus on word-building.

***Outcomes* Vocabulary Builder** The separate booklet allows students to look up meaning of new language which is key to learn, offers several examples of collocations and usage plus a page of revision practice.

Native speaker English Draws attention to common words or phrases fluent speakers use which students may hear or want to learn.

Keywords Most writing units have a focus on linking words and patterns, which help develop fluent, coherent writing. There's a link to the text, a short explanation and practice exercises.

Developing conversations The sections teach typical questions, responses and patterns common to conversation. An explanation clarifies the focus while exercises give controlled practice.

Conversation practice A task lets students practise social and practical conversations based on their own experience or through role-play.

Speaking These sections give students the chance to exchange ideas. The final speaking task in each unit is a variety of longer tasks that draw the language and / or the themes of the unit together.

Listening These sections are introduced with a short description of the context. There is usually a pre-listening speaking task to generate interest or predict content, followed by tasks to guide students to understand the text and focus on vocabulary.

Reading These sections are introduced with a short description of the context. There is usually a pre-reading speaking task to generate interest or predict content, followed by tasks to guide students to understand the text and focus on vocabulary.

WHAT'S IN *OUTCOMES* TEACHER'S BOOK?

The Teacher's book is organised into three sections: Teacher's notes, Writing lessons and Communication activities. **TEACHER'S NOTES** provide guidance on how to use the 16 units and four **REVIEWS** in the Student's book. Each unit opens with a brief **UNIT OVERVIEW** that allows you to understand the main elements of the lesson very quickly.

Under the same headings as in the Student's book, the notes give clear aims and simple steps to provide a very easy path through the material. Answer boxes and audioscripts embedded in the notes ensure you have everything you need at your fingertips. Suggestions throughout the notes help you with ways to set up activities, check and clarify meaning, monitor, conduct feedback, etc. An icon indicates where you might want to use a **COMMUNICATION ACTIVITY** (see next page). In addition, there's help through four mini features.

The **Tip** feature offers ideas on things such as:
- other ways to check meaning;
- how to adapt material for different groups such as mono or multilingual classes;
- bringing extra material into lessons.

The **Note** feature gives bite-size information about:
- places and people in the text;
- how cultures can differ.

The **Alternatively** feature provides:
- a different way to stage an activity than the one suggested in the Student's book;
- ideas on how to make an activity more or less challenging.

The **Optional activity** suggests:
- ways to extend an activity if students need to do more work.

The **Writing lessons** section opens with a two-page introduction on teaching writing. It explains the approach to writing and suggests ways you can provide feedback to students. The introduction is followed by **Teacher's notes** and the answer key for the eight writing lessons.

The **Communication activities** section contains simple instructions on how to use the 32 photocopiable activities. The activities are designed to revise key grammar and vocabulary from the Student's book in a fun and varied way. There are quizzes, word puzzles, questionnaires, games, information gaps and short role-plays. Each unit has two activities calculated to take between 10–15 minutes of class time.

Other *Outcomes* components

***Outcomes* Workbook** The ***Outcomes* Workbook** thoroughly revises all the language areas that are in the Student's book. Each unit also has:
- a listening and a reading with tasks based on topics loosely connected to the theme of the unit and providing interest and extra challenges to students.
- **Developing Writing** that focuses on types of text students might write in their academic, professional and personal lives and further work on relevant language.

The ***Outcomes* Workbook** also comes with:
- **Audio CD** of recordings of the listening and reading texts.
- **Answer key** and **Audioscript** to aid self-study.

***Outcomes* Exam*View*®** Writing tests to check your students' progress takes a lot of time and work but the **Exam*View*®** CD allows you to create tests and exams in as little as five minutes. What's more:
- all the tests are closely based on the Student's book.
- the software also generates the answer key.
- it provides a variety of exercise types (True / False, Multiple choice, Yes / No, Matching, Short answer, etc.)
- tests can be printed, computer-based, or on the Internet.
- you can easily edit the questions and add your own.
- you can save all tests for another time.
- it is easy to reorder questions to avoid cheating.

My*Outcomes* online resource Every copy of the *Outcomes* Student's book has a unique code at the front of the book which provides access to **My*Outcomes*** online resource where they will find additional work on all the elements of the Student's book. There are:
- over 230 activities practising the grammar, vocabulary, pronunciation and conversations in the 16 units.
- additional listening, reading and speaking practice.
- reviews every four units to test students' progress.

Teachers can also use the online resource if they apply for an access code. Go to **myelt.heinle.com** and request an MyELT instructor account. This will allow you to set specific work for all your students and then receive their results. You can then store these results through the **Grade book**, so both you and your students have a record of their marks and progress.

OUTCOMES INTERMEDIATE

In this introduction we try to answer these questions:
What are the goals of language students?
What is key language for students at this level?
What is key for teachers to help them teach?

Key goals

The Common European Framework of reference (CEF) states that language learning and teaching overall goals should be:
1.1 *to deal with the business of everyday life in another country, and to help foreigners staying in their own country to do so;*
1.2 *to exchange information and ideas with young people and adults who speak a different language and to communicate their thoughts and feelings to them;*
1.3 *to achieve a wider and deeper understanding of the way of life and forms of thought of other peoples and of their cultural heritage.*
(Council of Europe, 2001, p. 3)

These ideas underpin everything we do in the *Outcomes* series. At Intermediate level, we look at can-do statements for B1 and B2 level as a guide to what students might want to achieve.

Business of everyday life You can see the communicative areas that are dealt with in the *how to* sections of the contents and title strip that heads each unit. *Outcomes* has a strong practical thread. For example, students at Intermediate learn the grammar and vocabulary to:
- explain why you're late pp. 12–13.
- help explain a menu to a foreigner pp. 54–55.

For many students passing exams is also the business of everyday life, which is why *Outcomes* has a **Grammar Reference** with exercises on all the grammar you'd expect. Similarly, **Writing** deals with both practical types of writing (emails pp. 122–123) and exam-type writing (essays pp. 130–131).

Communicating thoughts and feelings Practicalities are important, but just as important, and perhaps more motivating, is the ability to communicate in a way which reflects your personality, feelings and opinions. That's why most of the **DEVELOPING CONVERSATIONS** and **CONVERSATION PRACTICE** work towards practising typical conversations we have to establish and maintain friendships.

- talking about feelings pp. 14–15.
- talking about jobs pp. 36–37

This is also why we constantly give students the chance to exchange their ideas, through **SPEAKING**, practice activities in **VOCABULARY** and **GRAMMAR**, the lead-ins to **READING** and **LISTENING** and discussions about the texts.

Understanding other cultures Students will best understand other cultures by talking with other students, which the various speaking activities in *Outcomes* always encourage. However, many classrooms may not have a people from a large mix of backgrounds, which is why we use texts with international contexts and reflecting other cultures throughout the world – including Britain. Students come to realise they share many of the same desires and concerns!

- schooling in Korea pp. 50–51.
- housing around the world pp. 66–67.

Native speaker notes also draw attention to ways fluent speakers express themselves, which may be different to the neutral international language that we generally present.

KEY LANGUAGE

There were five guides to the input at Intermediate level – the communicative outcomes (outlined in *Outcomes Goals*), the frequency of words, 'naturalness' of usage, student autonomy and teacher– student expectations or interest.

For example, to talk about feelings (pp. 114–115) students need to know a number of core adjectives which are presented and practised in **VOCABULARY**. The practice gets them to think of language which might go with these words and the **OVB** provides further help in terms of collocations. **GRAMMAR** looks at linking verbs we typically use when talking about feelings and provides a fuller context for the vocabulary. **LANGUAGE PATTERNS** draws attention to the grammar around the word *expect*. **LISTENING** then gives a model conversation. **DEVELOPING CONVERSATIONS** teaches expressions to respond as a listener in such conversations. **PRONUNCIATION** is based on the phrases they've learnt.

This is typical of the way language input is focused on helping students achieve the stated communicative outcome, but not all language learning can be developed in this way. A lot of vocabulary may be very frequent but not specific to any one topic (e.g. issue, unlike, refer). The language highlighted through texts is largely of this nature. The exercises and **OVB**, then show a range of natural collocations. Similarly, some grammar may not be fundamental to a conversation in the way we saw with 'talking about feelings'. Here, we make the choice based on what students and teachers expect to be covered at this level or have tested in exams. This may be "exam grammar", but we try to give natural sounding examples.

Input is also decided on the basis that students need to learn outside the classroom. The *word families* strand in **VOCABULARY**, the **OVB** language boxes and **READING**, shows students how words are formed. This helps them recognise and learn new words in their own studies. The same motives underlie **LANGUAGE PATTERNS**, but with a focus on grammar.

Finally, students and non-native speaker teachers often express an interest in colloquial language and idioms. The **NATIVE SPEAKER NOTE** provides explanations and examples of this in contrast to the normal input which can be freely used and understood in contexts where English is a lingua franca.

KEY TO LEARN

There are many ways to learn but it seems there are a few essentials:

- Students need to notice.
- Students need to understand.
- Students need to practise – spoken, written, receptive.
- Students need to make mistakes.
- Students need to repeat these steps a lot.

Noticing and understanding Obviously the exercises in **GRAMMAR** and **VOCABULARY** encourage students to notice and understand. Visuals and clear explanations of vocabulary and examples of collocations in the **OVB**, reinforce meaning. The **LANGUAGE PATTERNS** exercise trains students to notice and consider how English compares with their own language. The bold vocabulary in reading texts (pp. 10–10) encourages students to notice and think about them, while follow-up exercises ensure understanding and get students to notice collocations.

Practice Students always have chance to practise language. This goes from very controlled 'remember and test' and gap-fills to freer role-play and personalised speaking. **COMMUNICATION ACTIVITIES** in this Teacher's book provide more practice.

Making mistakes Not all teaching and input can or should be provided by the coursebook. We all know from experience and research that people learn new language when they are struggling to express something and the 'correct' or better word is given. This is also why we have lots of speaking activities. They are not just opportunities for students to practise what they know, they are chances for them to try and say something new, stretch themselves and make mistakes, which you can then correct.

Repetition Seeing a word once is not enough! Some say you need to see and understand vocabulary ten times before you have learnt to use it. Maybe grammar takes even longer. Recycling and Revision is therefore a key part of the design of

Outcomes. For example, the **OVB**, **Workbook** and **Exam*View*®** allow unit-by-unit revision, while **Review** after every four units ensures further revision at a later date.

With grammar, students can revise after the class by using the **Grammar reference** and exercises, the **Workbook** or the **MyOutcomes** *online resource*. Grammar structures are often looked at in several contexts over the course and at various levels. **Review** units test grammar and you can also create tests with **Exam*View*®**.

Apart from this revision we try to repeatedly re-use language from **Vocabulary** in **Listening** and **Reading**; in **Grammar** and **Grammar reference**; in **Developing conversations**; in workbook texts; in exercises and texts in other units of the Student's book and even in other levels of the series. And as we have seen, **Speaking** and **Conversation Practice** allow students to re-use language they've learnt.

In terms of speaking, research suggests that students can improve performance with repetition. Within the first two pages of each unit there are often several opportunities to have conversations around the same topic as we saw with 'talking about feelings' through **Vocabulary** or **Grammar** practice, **Developing conversations** and **Conversation practice**. The **Review** units also encourage students to look back and repeat speaking tasks. There are also more ideas about revision in the **Teacher's notes**.

KEY TO TEACH

Most teachers need or want material which:

- is quick and easy to prepare
- caters for mixed level classes
- motivates students

Quick and easy to prepare A coursebook is easy to use when the relation between input and outcomes is clear and we hope you already see that is the case with *Outcomes*. However, other aspects of the design should help you just pick up the book and teach:

- limited number of sections that appear in all units.
- a regular structure to the units.
- a variety of familiar tasks.
- double-pages can exist as unique lessons but 6-page open units allow you greater flexibility.
- straightforward rubrics in the Student's book fully explain tasks.
- **Grammar** and **Vocabulary** have clear links to texts.
- **OVB** follows the spreads of the book so you and students can easily look up words in class.

Mixed level classes Students often start at different levels within a class and so the input in *Outcomes* Intermediate revises and extends language encountered at Pre-intermediate. However, the exercises and design of *Outcomes* also works for multi-level classes.

- **OVB** The *Outcomes* Vocabulary builder allows weaker students to look up new words, before during and after class, because it follows the spreads of the book. Stronger students benefit from the **OVB** because it gives extra input through collocation lists, extra language boxes and practice exercises.
- **Grammar** The short explanations help weaker students with exercises in the units. The Grammar reference helps weaker students with more examples but stronger students will like the extra information that is always given.
- **Easy to difficult** Whether it is grammar or vocabulary, reading or listening, we usually move from easier to more difficult tasks in each section. For example, reading texts often allow language to be pre-taught, the first tasks are then based on general understanding and further tasks are more detailed.
- **Translation** Several exercises including **Language patterns** encourage students to translate. Translation is particularly important for weaker students who benefit from the support of their mother tongue and bilingual dictionaries. In monolingual classes, especially, it allows stronger students to help others in the class by providing the translations.
- **Test and remember** Tasks like this are comforting for weaker students, but they can also be made more challenging for stronger students by asking them to remember more.
- **Native speaker notes** and **Language patterns** These offer extra input for stronger students and classes. You might consider dropping them for weaker classes.
- **Teachers note's** There are loads more ideas for dealing with multi level classes in this book – particularly through the **Tip** and **Alternatively** features.

Motivating students As a teacher motivating students will be a major part of your job however, we know a coursebook can often work against student motivation by having irrelevant or boring content, unclear, unrealistic or unfulfilled outcomes or simply by a dull design. *Outcomes* helps you motivate students by having:

- outcomes matching students wants and needs.
- a clear menu of input and outcomes at the start of each unit.
- input and tasks that carefully match those outcomes.
- a manageable number of keywords to learn in the **OVB**.
- texts based on authentic sources that we think you'll find by turns informative, funny, even moving.
- a range of speaking tasks that allow for play, humour, gossip as well as serious discussion.
- a fresh design with bright, interesting illustration.

The CEF and Level There is not a direct correlation between publishers' levels and the CEF: completing Pre-intermediate will not mean a student has reached B1 and completing Intermediate is not equivalent to reaching B2. That's because the CEF descriptions of level or the ALTE can-do statements do *not* exactly describe content, but describe someone's *performance* in a language. We have used can-do statements from both B1 and B2 levels at Intermediate as a guide to what tasks and outcomes students want to achieve. However, students' performance in *doing* any of the speaking, reading, listening or writing tasks may be assessed using CEF scales as being A2(+), B1(+) or B2. If students are regularly outside the range of A2+ and B1+ they are probably at the wrong level for this material!

01 MY FIRST CLASS

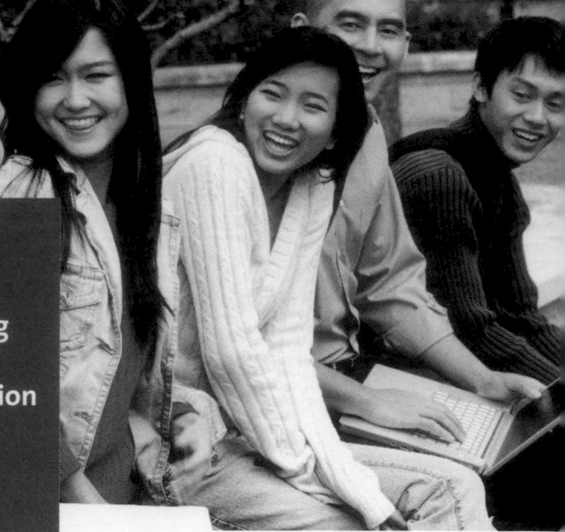

UNIT OVERVIEW
In this unit, students practise asking and answering **common questions** and **maintaining conversations**. They have practice in **talking about language learning experiences** and **telling stories**. They **read** an article about **language teaching policy, listen to** a **conversation** between a **teacher** and **a new student** and a **conversation** between **two classmates**. The main **grammar** aims are **question forms** and **narrative tenses – past simple, past continuous** and **past perfect**.

SPEAKING

Aim
To lead in to the lesson and allow students to introduce themselves to each other.

Step 1 If this is a new class, start by asking students their names. Get them to introduce themselves and say where they are from and why they are here. You might get them to write name cards to help everyone remember. Lead in to the lesson by asking students the questions in exercise A.

Step 2 Put students in pairs and tell them to interview their partner and find out as much as they can about the areas in B. Monitor and note any problems with question formation to focus on when students are doing *Grammar*. Ask them to report back to the rest of the class about their partner at the end. You could round off by asking the whole class to remember one thing about each student.

NATIVE SPEAKER ENGLISH

Write on the board *I'm really into swimming, my sister's really into music*. Ask students what they think this means (to like something very much). Is it formal or informal? (Informal.) Read out the box or ask students to read it. Ask them for some examples of what they are really into.

GRAMMAR Question formation

Aim
To extend and consolidate students knowledge of question forms in different tenses.

Step 1 Lead in by asking students some of the questions they asked in *Speaking* exercise B. Write a few examples of different question types on the board and check students know the form, especially the use of auxiliaries and inversion of subject and verb. Read out the box or ask students to read it and check they understand by eliciting one or two more examples of each type of question given. Direct students to the grammar reference on p. 136 if you think they need more help.

Step 2 Ask students to complete the questions in A with one or more words. Check in pairs then check with the whole group by getting students to ask each other in open pairs.

Answers
1 are you / do you come
2 do you
3 are you
4 Are you
5 Have you
6 have you been
7 do you
8 Have you got
9 are you going to / are you planning to
10 did you

Step 3 Put students in new pairs and get them to take turns to ask each other the questions.

LISTENING

Aim
To hear the target language in context and introduce follow-up questions.

Step 1 Tell students they are going to hear a conversation between an English teacher and a new student. Give them a few seconds to read the questions in A. Then ask them to think about the answers as they listen. Play the recording.

1.1
G = Guy, O = Olga
G: Hi. Come in. Sit down. Take a seat.
O: Thank you.
G: So ... um ... what's your name?
O: Olga.
G: Right, OK. And where are you from, Olga?
O: Russia.
G: Oh OK. Whereabouts?
O: Saratov. It's maybe 500 kilometres from Moscow. Do you know it?
G: No, sorry. I'm afraid I don't. My geography of that area's not great! So how long have you been learning English, Olga?

O: About 10 or 12 years on and off.
G: OK. So have you been to the UK to study before?
O: No, no. In fact this is my first time in an English-speaking country.
G: Really?! That's amazing, because your English is really good. I mean, you haven't got a very strong accent.
O: Thanks. I had really good teachers at school.
G: Yeah? Mine weren't that good, but then I wasn't a very good student either!
O: Yes. I was lucky.
G: So how long are you going to stay here?
O: I'm not sure. I'd like to do a degree here – maybe in business management, but I'll see. It depends on my husband as well. He's looking for work here.
G: Oh OK, So how old are you, if you don't mind me asking?
O: I'd rather not say.
G: Oh right. OK, fair enough. Anyway, I think that's all I need to ask. I'm going to put you in the top class. Is that OK?
O: Fine. Thanks.

Answers
1 She's from Saratov in Russia
2 About 10 or 12 years on and off
3 She's not sure – probably a few years

Step 2 Ask students to complete the sentences in B using the correct word in italics. Then play the recording again for them to check. Perhaps look at the audioscript as they listen as well, especially as this is the first listening. Exploit further, e.g. phrases like *on and off, it depends on, fair enough*.

Answers

1 Come in	3 strong	5 mind
2 kilometres	4 stay	6 top

Language patterns

Aim
To draw students attention to the use of *I'd rather* . . . to talk about preference.

Ask students to read the sentences in the box and tell you what patterns they notice *I'd rather* (+ *not*) + base form = *I would rather*. This is another way of saying *I would prefer (not) to* + base form, to talk about preference.

Speaking

Aim
To exploit the listening by giving students a chance to express their opinions and to give fluency practice.

Step 1 Give students a few moments to read the questions in A and think about how they would answer them.

Step 2 Put students in pairs or small groups to discuss the questions. Conduct brief feedback.

Developing conversations

Asking follow-up questions

Aim
To draw students attention to some common follow-up questions we use in certain situations after a first question has been answered in a certain way.

Step 1 Read out the introduction and ask students if they remember the follow-up questions (i.e. the questions that came next) from *Listening*.

Answers
Whereabouts?
So have you been to the UK to study before?

Step 2 Ask students to look at questions 1–6 in B and match them with a pair of possible follow-up questions a–f. Check in pairs and then play the audio for them to check. Make sure they understand that they will only hear one follow-up question in each case.

1.2
1 A: What do you do?
B: I'm a computer programmer.
A: Oh yeah? Do you enjoy it?
B: Yeah, it's OK. It pays the bills!
2 A: Have you studied here before?
B: No. Never.
A: So where did you learn your English?
B: I lived in Canada for a year and I just picked it up there.
3 A: What do you do when you're not studying?
B: I like going shopping, going out with friends, that kind of thing, but I've also got a part time job in a café.
A: How long have you been doing that?
B: Only about six months.
4 A: Have you got any brothers or sisters?
B: Yeah, seven!
A: Seven! Older or younger?
B: I'm the youngest, so, as they like to remind me, I'm the baby of the family.
5 A: What did you do at the weekend?
B: Nothing much. I went shopping on Saturday, but that's all.
A: Oh right. Did you get anything nice?
B: Yeah, I did actually. I got this really nice T-shirt in the market.
6 A: What are you studying?
B: Media studies.
A: Oh right. What does that involve? I've never heard of that subject.
B: Really? It's quite popular here. You study everything about TV, newspapers and advertising. Some of it's practical, and some of it is more theoretical, almost like philosophy. It's really interesting.

Answers

1 b	2 a	3 f	4 c	5 e	6 d

Step 3 Ask students to look at questions 1–6 again. Elicit possible answers, e.g. 1 *history* and then possible follow-up questions, e.g. *What kind of history?* Repeat the procedure with the other questions to prepare for Step 5.

Step 4 Put students in pairs and ask them to think of one more possible follow-up question for each of the questions 1–6. Check their ideas.

Step 5 Put students in new pairs if possible. Ask them to take turns to ask each other the questions in B with suitable follow-up questions, depending on their partner's answers. Conduct brief feedback at the end.

Conversation practice

Aim
To give further practice of the target language.

Step 1 Ask students to look at the pictures and choose one of them. They are going to 'be' this person and invent an identity. Tell them to think about this and make a few notes.

Step 2 Put students in groups of four or five and get them to ask each other questions and answer in role. They should try to identify the picture in each case.

Alternatively You could conduct this as a mingling activity. Ask students to walk around and introduce themselves – in role – to as many people as they can, as if they were at a party or speed dating session. At the end, conduct brief feedback, including which picture they think each student had chosen.

pp. 10–11

Next class Make photocopies of **1A** p. 128.

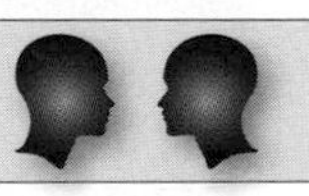

Vocabulary Learning languages

Aim
To introduce some words and phrases commonly used about learning languages.

Step 1 Put students in pairs and ask them to look at the sentences in A and try to guess the meaning of the words / phrases in bold from the context.

Answers
a quite confident and able to speak without too much hesitation; can talk easily about different subjects
b survive / manage
c simple / limited
d speaking two languages equally well, as a native speaker
e don't speak too fast
2 learn through self-study; learn informally

Step 2 Ask students to put the answers in A in order of how well the speaker speaks the language, starting with the most proficient. Check in pairs then check with the whole group.

Answers

1 d	2 a	3 e	4 b	5 c

Step 3 Put students in small groups and ask them to ask each other and answer the questions in A. If they only speak English and their first language, they should think about someone they know and answer the questions about them. Or they could answer for a famous person they know about – or just use their imaginations and make up the answers. Conduct brief feedback at the end.

Reading

Aim
To give students practice in predicting, reading for gist and specific information and responding to text.

Step 1 Tell students they are going to read an article about British people and foreign languages. You could lead in by asking them whether they think British people are good linguists and why this may or may not be the case.

Step 2 Ask students to look at the title and section headings in A and guess what the article is about and what is said in each section. Do not conduct feedback but ask them to read the article quickly to check their ideas.

Answers
- The number of students taking languages at school is falling and this is a disaster because it is bad for trade.
- Students are not motivated because when they go abroad, people speak to them in English.
- Britain is losing trade because British people lack language skills.
- Not everyone thinks the plan to teach languages from an early age (at primary schools) is a good idea.

Step 3 Ask students to read the article in more detail, ignoring the words and phrases in bold. Then look at the statements in C and decide if they are true or false. Check in pairs, then check with the whole group. Ask students to tell you where the evidence for the answers is in the text and to correct the false statements.

Answers

1 F	3 F	5 F	7 F
2 T	4 T	6 F	8 T

Alternatively If you feel students need more help with the vocabulary in the article before they discuss it, you could do exercise E first, before going on to *Speaking*.

Step 4 Put students in pairs and ask them to look at the words / phrases in bold and try to guess the meanings from the context. Point out *pick things up* (learn things) vs *pick it up off the street* (learn informally – as in *Vocabulary* above).

Answers
Well-respected director of a school
desire to do something
the purpose or reason for doing something
Depending on
proof
context, situation
linked progression
learn faster or more slowly
manage
easier to do, offered more widely

Step 5 Ask students to read the text again and put a tick (✓) where they agree, a cross (✗) where they don't agree and an exclamation mark (!) if something surprises them. Put them in pairs or small groups to discuss their ideas.

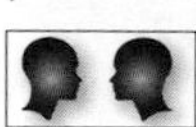
1A see Teacher's notes p. 120.

Speaking

Aim
To exploit the reading text further.

Step 1 Ask students to read the short text about Brian Willis, the language expert from the article and check their overall understanding. Ask some questions like: *Where was Brian Willis? What language do they speak there? What mistake did he make? How did it happen? What is the point of the story? What advice does he give?* (to not be embarrassed about speaking and making mistakes). Have students ever been embarrassed when speaking a foreign language? Ask students to decide whether they agree with the advice he gives. Why / Why not? They could discuss this briefly in pairs or just tell you as a group.

Step 2 Ask students to look at question C and think about how they would answer it. They should write five pieces of advice in answer to question C, using the sentence starters given. Then put students in small groups to discuss the questions. Monitor and feed in language learning vocabulary as necessary and / or encourage students to use vocabulary from the section on learning languages. Conduct brief feedback at the end.

Vocabulary Language words

Aim
To check students know words for different parts of speech and other 'metalanguage' and get them thinking about word formation, collocation and pronunciation.

Step 1 Read out the rubric and put students in threes to answer the questions. Check with the whole group.

Answers
1 fluently, fluency
2 both
3 second syllable
4 forrin
5 about
6 on
7 pick up, get by
8 make
9 language, your English, financial situation, housing, relationships, etc.
10 a strong accent

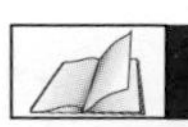
pp. 12–13

Next class Make photocopies of **1B** p. 129.
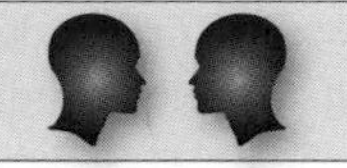

Grammar Narrative tenses

Aim
To revise past simple, past continuous and past perfect as used in story telling.

Step 1 Ask students to look at the examples of the three tenses in the box, or read the examples out to them and elicit two or three more examples of each tense from them.

Step 2 Ask students to try to complete the story about Brian Willis without looking back at it, by choosing the correct tense in each of the gaps. While they do that, write the first example of the past continuous and the second example of the past perfect from the box on the board: *I was chatting to him and he suddenly walked off. I realised I'd left my bag in the restaurant.* Check the exercise in pairs and then check with the whole group. Ask students if they understand why any they got wrong are wrong and use this to lead into Step 3.

Answers
1 was teaching
2 had done
3 was explaining
4 told
5 looked
6 said
7 acted
8 continued
9 had used
10 had actually said
11 didn't / did not stop

Step 3 Draw students' attention to the two sentences on the board and elicit the different tenses and highlight the form and meaning using timelines and concept questions.

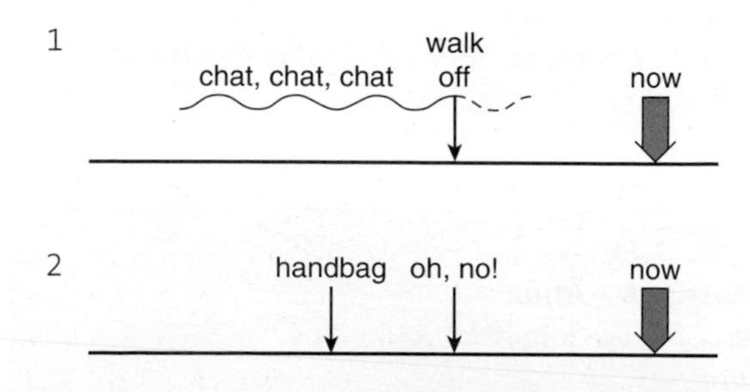

1 *I was chatting to him and he suddenly walked off.*
Tenses: past continuous, past simple
Form: *was / were* + verb + *-ing*, past simple form
Concept questions: 1 Which action is longer? (Chatting.)
2 Which action started first? (Chatting.) 3 Did he interrupt him / her chatting when he walked off? (Yes.)
2 *I realised I'd left my bag in the restaurant.*
Tenses: past simple, past perfect
Form: past simple form, *had* + past participle
Concept questions: 1 Did she leave her bag in the restaurant? (Yes.) 2 Did she realise that before or after she left? (After.)

Step 4 Ask students to look at the tenses in C and the descriptions and match each tense with a description.

Answers
a 2 b 1 c 3

Step 5 Ask students to look at the examples in D and prepare to talk about one of them. They could make a few notes if they wish.

Step 6 Put students in pairs and ask them to tell each other about their experiences.

Step 7 Conduct brief feedback by asking students to report back on what their partner told them.

Listening

Aim
To hear examples of the target language in context and give practice in listening for specific information and retelling a story.

Step 1 Tell students they are going to hear a conversation between Martin and Anna, who are both studying Spanish in Spain. Ask them to look at the questions in A and talk about them in pairs / threes.

Step 2 Ask students to listen and decide why Anna and Martin were both late for class. Play the recording and then check the answers.

Answers
Martin was late because he had left his book at home so he went home to get it, spent ages banging on the door and then missed a train.
Anna was late because she was phoning round a few places looking for a flat before class.

1.3
M = Martin, A = Anna
M: Sorry, but I've forgotten your name.
A: Anna.
M: Oh yeah, sorry. Hi.
A: So what did you do in the first half of the class?
M: I don't know. I missed it as well.
A: Oh dear. Why was that?
M: Well, I was late getting up and then I rushed out of the house to get the train, but when I got to the station, I realised I'd forgotten my book. So I went back home to get it and then I realised I didn't have my keys either! I rang the bell, but my flatmate was sleeping so he didn't answer. I was banging on the door and shouting, but nothing.
A: He must be a really heavy sleeper!
M: It's not that, really. He works nights, so he doesn't get home till five o'clock in the morning.
A: Oh right. So did you get in the house?
M: No, in the end, I stopped trying, but by then I'd missed my train to get here and I had to wait another twenty minutes before the next one came.
A: Oh right. Whereabouts are you living?
M: Moncada. It's only about twenty minutes by train from here, but the trains only run every thirty minutes. So anyway, what about you? What's your excuse?
A: Sorry?
M: What's your excuse for being late?
A: Oh right. Sorry. Well, I'm looking for a flat to rent and I was phoning round a few places this morning before class.
M: Right. So did you have any luck?
A: Not really. I'm going to see one later near the centre of town, but it's quite expensive.
M: Mmm.
A: Actually, Frank – the German guy in class – was telling me that you're looking for another person to share your flat.
M: Yeah, well, we've got a spare room and it'd be good to pay less rent.
A: So how much would it be?
M: I guess about forty euros a week.
A: Really? That's really cheap! So what's the room like?
M: It's all right. It's quite big. The only problem is it's an internal room. I mean, it doesn't have any windows to the outside, so there's no natural light.
A: Oh right. And how many people live there?
M: Oh, just the two of us. Me and this Spanish guy, Pedro.

Tip It is not possible to say *I forgot my book at home.* You can say *I forgot my book* or *I left my book at home.*

Step 2 Put students in pairs and ask them to retell the stories and try to use the three tenses as far as possible. When they have finished, ask them to look at the audioscript on p. 160 and underline the examples of the three tenses. Then compare the audioscript with the way they told the story. Elicit examples of the tenses, especially past continuous and past perfect and ask why they are used in each case.

Step 3 Put students in pairs and ask them to discuss the questions in E. Conduct very brief feedback.

Grammar

Other uses of the past continuous

Aim
To introduce a common use of the past continuous and give practice.

Step 1 Read out the explanation in the box and the examples from the audioscript. Ask students to complete the sentences in A with the past continuous form of one of the verbs in the box. Check in pairs and then check with the whole group. While checking, elicit possible responses to number 3 – ask students to look at B for ideas – and give further practice of this by repeating for numbers 4–6, in preparation for B.

Answers

1 was crying
2 was he doing; were building
3 was chatting
4 was having
5 was sorting out
6 was looking for; was driving

Step 2 Put students in pairs and ask them to take turns saying sorry for being late, using a different excuse each time. The listener should respond with one of the expressions in B. Demonstrate with a strong student, then continue in open pairs, then in closed pairs.

Speaking

Aim
To practise storytelling using the three past tenses.

Step 1 Start off by getting students to describe each picture in the present to check the vocabulary. Get students to pick out which parts of the story refer to a previous past action. Then get the whole class to tell the story together, in the past.

Suggested answer

Steve had a very stressful time trying to get to his exam on time. When he woke up, he was shocked to find he had overslept. He had been studying the night before and had not gone to bed until 3 am. He got up really quickly and went to the bus stop. He waited for a while, but the bus didn't come and so he got a taxi. Unfortunately, the traffic was terrible and they got stuck in a traffic jam. Steve decided to walk but when he looked for his wallet to pay the driver, he realised he had left it at home. The taxi driver was shouting at him but he got out of the taxi and ran to the college. When he arrived at the college, the exam had already started and the other students were all writing. Steve had only written half a page when the invigilator told them to stop.

Step 2 Put students in pairs and ask them to retell the story. Monitor closely and correct their use of the past tenses. Ask them to discuss the questions in B. This could be a pair work or class activity.

Optional Ask students to write the story, either in class or for homework.

Developing conversations

John was telling me . . .

Aim
To introduce the expression . . . *was telling me.*

Step 1 Read out the box and ask students if they can remember an example of this from the *Listening 1.3* (Frank – the German guy in class – was telling me that you're looking for another person to share your flat).

Step 2 Put students in pairs and ask them to have short conversations using the prompts in B. Look at the example with them and check they understand. Ask them to add an answer to the second question to complete the dialogue. For the example it could be: *Only a couple of times a month.* Check with the whole group at the end.

Suggested answers

1 John was telling me you lived in Germany.
Yes, I did.
What were you doing there?
I was studying German.
2 John was telling me you play golf.
Yes, that's right.
Are you any good?
Not bad.
3 John was telling me you've just been on holiday.
Yes, I have.
Where did you go?
Italy.
4 John was telling me you're getting married.
Yes, I am.
Congratulations! When's the big day?
June.
5 John was telling me you're looking for a flat at the moment.
Yes, I am.
Have you had any luck?
No, not yet.

Step 3 Ask students to try to remember some of the things they have found out about other students during the course of the unit. Then put them in new pairs to tell each other what they heard. Ask them to develop conversations, as in the example.

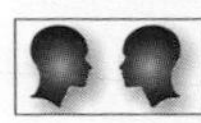
1B see Teacher's notes p. 120.

02 FEELINGS

UNIT OVERVIEW
In this unit, students extend their ability to talk about **feelings** and practise **responding to good** or **bad news**, **making excuses**, using **stress and intonation** more effectively and asking **double questions** and **response questions**. They **read** an article about **an experiment to make people happier** and **listen** to **two conversations** about **how people feel** and one **conversation** about **work**. The main **grammar** aims are ***be, look, seem*, etc. + adjective, *-ing / -ed* adjectives** and revision of **the present continuous**.

VOCABULARY Feelings

Aim
To extend vocabulary and introduce *-ed* adjectives.

Step 1 Lead in by asking students to look at the pictures and describe the scenes / situations. Ask students how one or two people in the pictures are feeling. Then put students in pairs and ask them to describe all the people using the adjectives in the box. Check with the whole group. Drill for pronunciation and elicit and mark the stress on the board. Use dictionaries if necessary to help with the meanings. You could mime or ask students to mime the meanings.

Answers
Picture 1
The child could be exhausted, furious, upset, fed up, in a bad mood; the father could be stressed, furious, annoyed, in a bad mood; the mother could feel terrible, guilty, worried, stressed; the other people could be annoyed, fed up.

Picture 2
The man could be pleased, in a good mood, disappointed (but pretending to be pleased); the other people could be relaxed, pleased (and down, fed up if they wish they were retiring).

Step 2 Ask students in the same pairs to discuss which of the adjectives in A show you are feeling tired (exhausted, stressed), ill (stressed, terrible, down), happy (pleased, in a good mood, relaxed), unsure (confused, worried) angry (annoyed, furious), bad about something you've done (in a bad mood, down, terrible, worried, guilty). Check with the whole group.

Step 3 Ask the whole group which of these feelings they have had today / in the last week / month and why.

GRAMMAR *Be, look, seem* etc.

Aim
To revise verbs *like be, look* etc. + adjective in the context of people's feelings.

Step 1 Read out the introduction and check that students understand the differences in meaning between the verbs. Then ask students to match sentences 1–8 in A with the correct reason a–h. Check in pairs, then check with the whole group, in open pairs.

Answers
1 d 2 b 3 h 4 g 5 c 6 e 7 f 8 a

Step 2 Ask students to write their own responses to the questions in A. Monitor and help students with their writing where necessary.

Step 3 Put students in pairs and ask them to take turns asking and answering with their own responses. Monitor and help with pronunciation where necessary.

Look at the grammar reference on p. 138 if you think students need further explanation at this stage.

LANGUAGE PATTERNS

Aim
To draw students attention to the use *expect* + *to*-infinitives.

Ask students to look at the box and tell you what pattern they notice (*expect* + *to*-infinitive, *expect* + object + *to*-infinitive). You could ask them to translate into their language and notice how the pattern is similar / different. If you don't want them to translate, or in a multilingual class, you could ask if they know any similar patterns (want, ask).

Listening

Aim
To hear the target language in context and give practice in listening for gist and detail.

Step 1 Tell students they are going to hear two conversations, the first about Karim and the second between Belinda and Alisha. Ask them to listen and note down how each of these people are feeling. Play the recording, pausing after the first conversation to allow students time to complete their notes. Check in pairs, then check with the whole group.

Answers
Karim: a bit down, worried, upset; Belinda: fed up, stressed; Alisha: great, pleased.

2.1
Conversation 1
R = Ryan, C = Clara
R: Hey, Clara!
C: What is it, Ryan?
R: Have you seen Karim this week?
C: Yeah, I saw him yesterday. Why?
R: Is he OK? I haven't spoken to him for a while, but the last time I saw him he seemed a bit down.
C: Hmm. I know. I think it's his mum. Apparently, she's quite ill and he's just very worried about her.
R: Oh no. What's wrong with her? Is it very serious?
C: I think it must be. He was quite upset when I spoke to him, and he didn't want to say much.
R: Oh dear. That's awful. I feel a bit guilty now that I haven't rung him, because I had a feeling something was wrong.
C: Why?
R: Well, I met him outside the university with Chris. Chris and I were chatting, but Karim didn't say much. In fact, he hardly said anything at all.
C: Really?
R: And Karim is normally really chatty.
C: I know. Well, he probably isn't in the mood to talk to anyone at the moment.
R: Oh dear. Well, if you see him, tell him I'm thinking of him. Say 'hello' to him from me.
C: Sure.
Conversation 2
B = Belinda, A = Alisha
B: Hello Alisha! How's it going?
A: Great actually, Belinda. I've just finished all my exams!
B: That must be a relief. How did they go?
A: Quite well, I think. I was really pleased with how I did.
B: That's great.
A: Are you all right? You look a bit fed up.
B: Yeah, sorry. It's not you. I'm just having a few problems with my accommodation.
A: Oh dear. What's the problem?
B: Oh, I've just found out I can't continue to stay where I am at the moment.
A: What a pain! How come?
B: I don't really want to explain. Basically, I need to find something else and, to be honest I just don't need the stress.
A: I can imagine. Can I do anything to help?
B: No, it's OK. I'm sure it'll sort itself out, but thanks.
A: Well at least let me buy you a drink.
B: OK. That'd be nice.
A: What would you like?
B: A cappuccino would be good.
A: Anything else? A bit of cake? Go on. It'll cheer you up.
B: Well I have to say that chocolate cake looks very nice.
A: I think I'll join you – to celebrate finishing my exams.

Step 2 Ask students if they can remember why each person feels this way. Play the recording again for them to check if necessary.

Answers
Karim's mother is ill; Belinda has to find somewhere new to live, Alisha has finished her exams.

Native speaker English

Read out the box to students and check they understand. What is another way of saying *How come?* (*Why*?) Is this formal or informal? (Informal.)

Speaking

Aim
To extend and personalise the topic using the target language.

Step 1 Ask students to read the questions and think about how they would answer them.

Step 2 Put students in pairs or small groups to talk about the questions. Conduct brief feedback at the end.

Developing conversations

Response expressions

Aim
To draw students' attention to some typical short responses to people's news.

Step 1 Lead in by telling students some news e.g. I've just won the lottery, I've lost my job etc. and elicit responses.

Step 2 Ask students to look at the short responses in bold in A. Ask them to try to translate them into their own language and see if there are any they can't translate. If you don't want them to translate these put students in pairs and ask them to guess the meanings from the context. Elicit another scenario in which you might give each response.

PRONUNCIATION Responding

Aim
To draw attention to the intonation in responses.

Step 1 Read out the box and demonstrate the wider voice range with a positive response (that's fantastic!) and the narrower voice range with a negative response (oh, that's sad). Ask students if they notice the difference.

Step 2 Ask students to listen to the sentences from *Developing conversations*. Pause the recording after the responses in bold and ask students to repeat after each one, paying particular attention to the intonation.

2.2
1 A: I can't drink at the moment. I'm pregnant.
B: Really? Congratulations! When is the baby due?
2 A: I'm going to Canada to study English.
B: Wow, that's great. How long are you going for?
3 A: I'm afraid I can't meet you tonight.
B: Oh, what a shame. Are you sure?
4 A: My brother's not very well.
B: Oh no! I'm really sorry. I hope it's not too serious.
5 A: I've lost my wallet.
B: Oh no, what a pain! Did it have much in it?
6 A: I've found my wallet!
B: Phew, that's a relief! Where was it?

Step 3 Put students in pairs and ask them to practise the exchanges in *Developing conversations*. They should pay particular attention to the intonation and try to develop the conversations by continuing them. Demonstrate with a strong student, continue in open pairs, then in closed pairs. Monitor and help students with pronunciation where necessary.

pp. 16–17

Next class Make photocopies of **2A** p. 130.
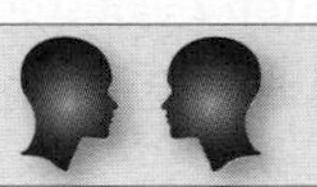

CONVERSATION PRACTICE

Aim
To put the target language in a real personalised context and give further practice.

Step 1 Put students in pairs and ask them to write a short conversation similar to the ones they heard, including some response expressions. When they are ready, they should practise the conversations together. Monitor and correct any mistakes in target language.

Step 2 Round off by asking willing pairs to act out their conversations in front of the class. Give the other students a 'reason to listen', e.g. get them to note down the news in each case and how the speakers felt. Check their ideas at the end.

SPEAKING

Aim
To extend students' vocabulary of parts of the body and associated verbs and lead in to the reading.

Step 1 Ask students to look at the sentences in A and check they understand the words / phrases in bold. If possible, take in monolingual dictionaries for students to check with. If not, check the words with them. The easiest way is to mime / demonstrate. Model and drill for pronunciation.

Step 2 Put students in small groups (mixed nationality if possible) and ask them to discuss the questions in A. Conduct brief feedback.

READING

Aim
To give practice in predicting, reading for gist and specific information and noticing common collocations.

Step 1 Put students in pairs. Ask them to look at the pictures and the title and answer the questions in A. They could also discuss what they think the title means and why he is called Juan Mann. Do not conduct feedback on this.

Step 2 Ask students to read the article quickly and check their ideas in A and decide whether they feel differently about the man afterwards. Check overall understanding with the whole group.

Step 3 Put students in pairs and ask them to try to answer the questions in C, then read the text again to find any answers they are not sure about.

Answers
1 He felt lonely and depressed and wanted to do something different.
2 He felt rather pessimistic and vulnerable.
3 A woman whose dog had died and for whom this was the anniversary of the death of her daughter.
4 He became famous through the Internet site YouTube.
5 He was told at school he could not do this kind of work; he learns from other people's mistakes as well as his own.
6 He thinks many people need someone to listen to and comfort them but are too embarrassed to ask a professional.

Step 4 Ask students to look at the nouns in D and try to remember the adjectives that went with them in the text. They should look at the text again to check. Check in pairs, then check with the whole group. Check the meanings of the phrases and perhaps ask students to make sentences to illustrate each one.

Answers

meaningful connections	*true* identity
desperate attempt	*social* skills
international star	*professional* help
miserable year	*original* plan

VOCABULARY Adjective collocations

Aim
To look at adjectives which frequently collocate with certain nouns and to introduce *-ing* adjectives before contrasting them overtly with *-ed* adjectives.

Step 1 Ask students to look at the groups of words in A and match each group with one of the adjectives in the box. Check in pairs then check with the whole group. Drill for pronunciation and elicit and mark the stress on the board. You could give further practice by asking students prompt questions e.g. How did you feel on holiday? (Relaxed.) How did you feel when they phoned you at 6 am? (Annoyed.)

Answers

1 relaxing	4 inspiring
2 annoying	5 confusing
3 exciting	6 disappointing

Step 2 Ask students to write eight true sentences about themselves using each adjective with one or two of the nouns given in A. Elicit a few examples first, e.g. *I had a really relaxing holiday in Greece.* Put students in pairs to check each other's sentences and develop conversations by asking when, why, etc.

GRAMMAR *-ing / -ed* adjectives

Aim
To contrast *-ing / -ed* adjectives and give practice.

Step 1 Lead in by writing two examples on the board, e.g. *The book was really exciting. I was really excited by the book.* Ask students which one describes my feeling (excited) and which the thing or person (exciting). Read out the explanation in the box or ask students to read it.

Step 2 Ask students to read the sentences in A and choose the correct answer. Check in pairs then check with the whole group.

Answers

1 confused	4 bored
2 interesting	5 embarrassing
3 disappointing	6 scary

Tip Point out that not all adjectives of feeling fit into neat *-ing / -ed* pairs. Ask students for an example from the exercise (*scary / frightened*). They could look back at exercise A on p. 14 and the grammar reference on p. 138 for help with this.

Step 3 Ask students to look at the picture and match each person with one of the sentences in A. Point out that there may be more than one possibility.

Answers

1 girl with yellow T-shirt	4 girl with brown hair
2 girl with black hair	5 boy with glasses
3 boy with green T-shirt	6 blond boy at back

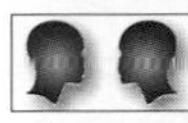
2A see Teacher's notes p. 120.

SPEAKING

Aim
To round off the lesson and give fluency practice.

Step 1 Ask students to look at the questions and think about how they would answer them.

Step 2 Put students in pairs or small groups and ask them to discuss the questions. Conduct brief feedback at the end.

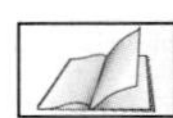
pp. 18–19

Next class Make photocopies of **2B** p. 131.
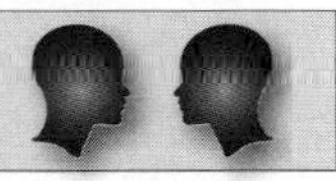

LISTENING

Aim
To introduce the grammar (different uses of the present continuous) in context and give practice in predicting, listening for gist and detail.

Step 1 Lead in by asking students to look at the picture and say where Louise and Sarah are and what they think they are talking about. Tell them to imagine a conversation beginning, 'Hi, how are you? What are you doing here?' and to practise it in pairs. Do not give feedback on this.

Step 2 Tell students they are going to hear to Sarah and Louise's conversation. They should listen and check their ideas from A (step 1) and also decide which adjective(s) from the box in B describe each of the women.

Answers
Louise: stressed, exhausted, shocked
Sarah: mysterious, happy, annoyed

2.3
S = Sarah, L = Lousie
S: Hello Louise!
L: Oh Sarah. All right?
S: How's it going?
L: OK. I'm a bit stressed to be honest. I'm working quite hard at the moment. We're finishing at nine most days!
S: Really? What a pain. You must be exhausted.
L: Yeah I am. So what are you doing here? Are you window shopping?
S: What? No, no. Not really. I'm just meeting a friend here. I'm a bit early.
L: Oh right. Hey listen, Sarah. I've rung you a few times recently, but you always seem to have your phone switched off or you don't answer it.
S: Oh right, yeah, Sorry about that.
L: So why aren't you answering it? Don't you want to talk to me?
S: No, no, it's not that!
L: I mean, you usually answer it on the first ring!
S: I know, I know.
L: So what? Is it work?
S: Sort of.
L: What do you mean, 'sort of'?
S: Well, if you must know, I'm seeing someone from work.
L: Oh right! But why are you being so mysterious about it? It's unlike you. You normally tell me everything.
S: Well, it's just ... well, it's my boss!
L: You're going out with your boss? So how long has this been happening?
S: About three weeks.
L: That's not long.
S: No. That's why I don't want anyone to know for the moment. I've just changed jobs too.
L: Oh really? I didn't know that. What are you doing now? Did you get promoted?
S: No, the new job isn't really a promotion. I'm not getting any more money. I'm just doing something different. It's more marketing than sales.
L: And you studied marketing, didn't you?
S: Yeah, that's right. I prefer marketing, so it's a good change. I'm really enjoying it.
L: Well, with your boss, it sounds like you're having a great time!
S: But I didn't get the new job because of my boss. I was promoted by Head Office.
L: Oh right.
S: But you see, this is why I don't want people to know about the relationship! They'll think I've got the job because I'm going out with the boss. It's really annoying.
L: OK, OK, I'm sorry. It was a stupid thing to say. Listen, what are you doing on Friday? Do you fancy meeting? It'd be nice to hear more of your news.
S: I'm afraid I can't. I play badminton on Fridays. And this Friday we're going for a meal afterwards.
L: Oh right. That's a shame. Maybe next week sometime.
S: Yeah ... yeah.
L: So ... when am I going to meet your boss?
S: Er ... Um ... er ... now. There – coming towards us.
L: Wait! That's your boss?!

Step 3 Ask students if they remember why the women have each of the feelings given in B. Play the recording again if they need to check.

Answers
Louise: stressed and exhausted because of working long hours; shocked when she hears Sarah's going out with her boss (and when she sees him).
Sarah: mysterious because she doesn't want to talk about her new boyfriend / boss; happy because she loves her new job. Annoyed because people think she got the job because of her relationship with the boss.

GRAMMAR Present continuous

Aim
To revise different uses of the present continuous.

Step 1 Ask students to look at the sentences in A and complete them using verbs in the present continuous. Do the first example with them. Check in pairs, then check with the whole group.

Alternatively Ask students to look at the audioscript on p. 161 to check their answers. Encourage them to look for other useful language, e.g. *promoted, promotion, to be honest, what a pain*.

Answers
1 am working / are finishing
2 are you doing? Are you window shopping?
3 I'm (just) meeting
4 I'm seeing
5 are you being
6 I'm not getting; I'm (just) doing
7 are you doing
8 we're going

Step 2 Put students in pairs and ask them to answer the questions in B. Check with the whole group.

Answers
1 a 1, 2, 5, 6 b 3, 4, 7, 8
2 5 – because *being* means *behaving / acting* in this case
See grammar reference p. 138

GRAMMAR Present continuous / present simple questions

Aim
To draw students' attention to the way we often ask 'double questions' (one question straight after another); to give practice in present continuous and present simple questions.

Tip It might be useful to check students' understanding of stative verbs here. Elicit some examples (*want, like, understand, know,* etc.) and ask what is unusual about them (they are not normally found in the continuous form). This should help them to choose the correct form in A. Go to the grammar reference on p. 139 for notes on this, including verbs that can be stative and dynamic. Point out that *love* is becoming more commonly used in the continuous form, as in *I'm loving it.*

Step 1 Read or ask students to read out the box. Ask them which tense is used in each question and why? (Present continuous to talk about an activity happening around now, present simple because *fancy* is a stative verb.) Ask students to create 'double questions' in the present continuous and / or the present simple, using the prompts in A. Do the first example with them to check they understand. Check in pairs, then check with the whole group.

Answers
1 How is your course going? Are you still enjoying it?
2 What are you doing now? Do you fancy going for a coffee?
3 What is your sister doing these days? Is she still studying?
4 Are you working this weekend? Do you want to go for a picnic?
5 Do I need a coat? Is it still raining outside?
6 What are you doing here? Do you work near here? (or, Are you working near here?)
7 What are you doing? Are you waiting to be served?
8 What is the matter with her? Why is she shouting at me?

Step 2 Ask students to match the pairs of questions in A with a suitable response in B. Check in open pairs by getting one student to ask one of the questions in A and another to answer with the correct response.

Answers
1 g 2 e 3 f 4 a 5 b 6 h 7 d 8 c

Step 3 Put students in pairs and ask them to have conversations, making 'double questions' by adding their own question to the one already there. Demonstrate with a strong student, then in open pairs, then continue in closed pairs. Monitor closely and take notes for a correction slot at the end.

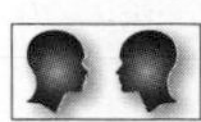 **2B** see Teacher's notes p. 120.

DEVELOPING CONVERSATIONS Making excuses

Aim
To give more practice of the grammar in the context of making excuses.

Step 1 Read or ask students to read out the introduction. Then ask students to prepare a suitable response to the questions in A, using either the present simple or the present continuous.

Step 2 Put students in pairs and ask them to take turns asking the questions and responding with their own ideas. Monitor and correct their responses where necessary.

Answers
Many possibilities, as long as they are using a suitable verb in the present continuous or present simple.

SPEAKING

Aim
To round off the lesson and give fluency practice.

Step 1 Ask students to look at the pictures and ask what they can see (skiing holiday, beach holiday) and whether they would like / dislike these holidays and why. Check they understand heaven (something I love) and hell (something I hate) in this context.

Step 2 Ask students to read the text. Put students in pairs and ask them to discuss which they agree / disagree with and why, and which is their favourite comment and why. Conduct brief feedback.

Step 3 Ask students to write their own idea of both heaven and hell using some of the language from the unit. These should be about 25–30 words each. Monitor as they write and help / correct where necessary.

Step 4 Put students in small groups to discuss their ideas. They could feed back to the whole group by saying whether there were any similar ideas or if they were all very different. You could also ask what was the most surprising / strange / sad, etc. thing each group heard.

03 TIME OFF

UNIT OVERVIEW
The main aims of this unit are to enable students to talk about **holidays** and to **describe interesting places**. They have practice in **asking for and making recommendations** and talking about **holiday problems** and **the weather**. The main grammatical focus is **present perfect questions** and ways of talking about **future plans and predictions, including *will, going to*** and **present continuous**.

SPEAKING

Aim
To lead in and get students immediately involved through personalisation.

Step 1 Tell students to look at the pictures and decide where the places are. Have they been to any of these places and, if so, what were they like? If not, would they like to go? Why / Why not? Do they like going to markets, mosques, castles, ruins? This could be conducted with the whole group or in pairs / threes with brief feedback.

Step 2 Put students in pairs. Ask them to discuss the questions. Check they understand *locally, regionally* and *nationally* by eliciting an example of each. Check a few of their ideas with the whole group.

Tip With a monolingual class, tell students they can include other countries they have visited, to provide more variety. In a multilingual class, pair students in mixed nationalities. Get them to tell each other as much as they can about their chosen places.

VOCABULARY Places of interest

Aim
To present / check key vocabulary.

Step 1 Ask students to fill in the gaps in sentences 1–10 using the correct word from the boxes. They could do this in pairs or individually and then check in pairs.

Step 2 Elicit answers from individual students. Check all students have the right answers. If there are problems with meaning, elicit examples of each item which students are familiar with, to check the concept. Model and drill the words for pronunciation. Write on the board, elicit and mark the stress.

Answers

1 lake	5 galleries	9 ruins
2 market	6 castle	10 mosque
3 square	7 theme park	
4 palace	8 old town	

Step 3 Ask students to look back at the sentences. Elicit the prepositional phrases. Model and drill for pronunciation / stress.

Answers

a outside of town	c down by the river
b out in the west	d all along the coast

Step 4 Model the dialogue with a strong student. Then model a few examples in open pairs. Draw students' attention to *there's a / an* vs *there are some.*

Step 5 Students individually write down five interesting places they've been to. These could be in their country or in the rest of the world.

Step 6 If possible, put students in new pairs here. Students ask each other the questions, following the model in C. Provide an alternative model if students answer 'yes' to the first question, e.g.

A Have you ever been to . . . ?
B Yes, I have.
A What do you think of it?
B Oh, it's great. There are some . . .

Monitor closely and note down correct usage and any errors in the target vocabulary. Conduct brief feedback on this at the end.

LISTENING

Aim
To introduce the language of asking for and giving recommendations. To give students practice in listening for gist and for specific language in context.

Note Krakow is one of the most visited cities in Poland, although it is not the capital (Warsaw is). It is famous for its well-preserved streets and buildings, many of which date back to medieval times.

Step 1 Ask students where Krakow is and if they know anything about it. Tell them to look at the guide to Krakow and ask them to discuss in pairs or threes which they would like to visit and why.

Check vocabulary: *Medieval, concentration camp, mines, World Heritage site, location, live music, lively, sixteenth century.*

Tip Students in Krakow could discuss which of the places they would recommend to a visitor and why.

Step 2 Tell students they are going to listen to a conversation between a tourist, Claire and a hotel receptionist in Krakow. They should tick the places on the guide which they mention and identify what Claire decides to do. Play the recording once and then ask them to check in pairs. Check with the whole group.

Answers
Discussed: St Mary's Church, Auschwitz, Kazimierz, Nowa Huta.
Claire decides to take the 2 o'clock tour of Nowa Huta.

3.1
C = Claire, R = Receptionist
C: Hello there. I wonder if you can help me. I'm thinking of going sightseeing somewhere today. Can you recommend anywhere good to go?
R: Well, it depends on what you like. There are lots of places to choose from. What kinds of things are you interested in?
C: I don't know. Erm ... something cultural.
R: Oh right. OK. Well, quite close to here is St Mary's Church. It's Kraków's most famous church – and very beautifully decorated. You can walk there in five or ten minutes.
C: OK. I'm not really a big fan of churches, to be honest.
R: That's OK. I understand. Of course, the most visited place near here is Auschwitz. There's a day tour leaving soon.
C: Actually, we're planning on going there later in the week.
R: Well, in that case, you could try Kazimierz, the old Jewish Quarter, where Steven Spielberg filmed some of *Schindler's List*. It's actually quite a lively area now. There are lots of good bars and restaurants round there.
C: Oh, so that might be nice for this evening, then.
R: Yes, maybe. Let me know if you want more information about places to eat or drink there. Erm ... Then, if you'd prefer something a bit different, how about a guided tour of Nowa Huta – the old communist district? They'll show you what life was like in the old days there.
C: Oh, that sounds interesting. How much is that?
R: About €40. I can call and book a place for you, if you want.
C: What times does that leave?
R: Every two hours from outside the hotel – and the tours last around 90 minutes. They leave at 10 o'clock, 12 o'clock, 2 o'clock and 4 o'clock.
C: OK, that's great. Can you book me onto the 2 o'clock tour? Then I can do some shopping in the main square in town beforehand.
R: Sure.

Step 3 Ask students to try to fill in the gaps in the sentences from memory. They could do this individually and then check in pairs. Tell them you do not expect them to remember many of the words, but it would be good for them to have a try.

Step 4 Tell students they are going to hear the recording again to check their answers. Play the recording straight through, then check the answers with the whole group. If students have problems, you could pause the recording after each answer to help them. You could drill each answer as you check them.

Answers
1 wonder
2 thinking
3 recommend
4 on what – it depends on what you like
5 fan – a big fan of
6 could – you could try ...
7 How about ...
8 book / place – I can call and book you a place

Optional extra Ask students what these sentences have in common (they are asking for or giving recommendations). Elicit which phrases are used to ask (*I wonder if ... I'm thinking of ... Can you recommend ...*) and to make recommendations (*you could try ... how about? ...*).

DEVELOPING CONVERSATIONS

Recommendations

Aim
To allow students to see ways of requesting / giving recommendations. To provide controlled practice of these and a model for the role-play.

Step 1 Let students read the lines quickly and check any vocabulary they are not sure of.

Step 2 Students individually put the lines in the correct order in the two conversations. Check in open pairs. Correct any mistakes they make with pronunciation e.g. *recommend, sightseeing, department stores, bargains, museums.* Ask students which expressions they can see in both dialogues.

Answer

A I'm thinking of doing some shopping today. Can you recommend anywhere?
B Well, you could try Oxford Street. There are lots of big department stores there.
A To be honest, I'm not really a big fan of department stores.
B Oh, OK. Well, in that case, how about Portobello Road? It's a really big street market. You can find lots of bargains there.
A Oh, that sounds great. I love that kind of thing. Is it easy to get to?
B Yes, very. Here. I'll show you on the map.

A I'm thinking of doing some sightseeing today. Can you recommend anywhere?
B Well, you could try the local museum. That's quite close to here. They've got lots of interesting things in there.
A Right. I'm not really into museums, to be honest.
B That's OK. In that case, how about going to the Roman ruins down by the lake? There are also some nice cafes and you can swim there.
A Oh, that sounds better. Is it expensive to get into?
B No, it's quite cheap. It should be only about $10.

Step 3 Students practise the dialogues in closed pairs. Monitor closely and correct any mistakes. Conduct a brief correction slot at the end.

CONVERSATION PRACTICE

Aim
To personalise the language and give freer practice.

Step 1 Students work individually and think about what they are going to say.

Step 2 Put students in pairs – new pairs if possible. Students practise the conversations. Monitor closely and conduct a correction slot at the end.

 **pp. 22–23**

VOCABULARY Holiday problems

Aim
To introduce and give practice in vocabulary related to holiday problems.

Step 1 Students look at the pictures and discuss what is the problem in each one. This could be done with the whole group or in pairs / threes, followed by brief feedback.

Step 2 Check students understand the vocabulary in the exercise, e.g. *arguing, stuck, upset, threw up, ripped off, spoilt, poured.* Concept check the difference between *missed* and *lost*. The vocabulary could be elicited / pre-taught using the pictures. Drill for pronunciation.

Step 3 Students complete the sentences in pairs. Do the first example with them, then check with the whole group.

Answers

1 missed, lost
2 stole, spoilt
3 crowded, space
4 poured, windy
5 upset, threw up
6 ripped off, charged
7 arguing, angry
8 stuck, hours

Step 4 Ask students to work on their own and think about holiday problems they have had, or someone they know has had. Tell them to make a few notes.

Step 5 Put students in groups of three or four to discuss the holiday problems. Tell them to try to use the target vocabulary. Monitor closely and conduct a brief correction slot at the end.

READING

Aim
To develop the skills of reading for specific information and responding to ideas in a text.

Step 1 Tell students they are going to read an article about public holidays and holiday entitlement.
Check that students understand *bank holidays* and also *holiday entitlement*. Ask how much this is for different jobs they know about.

Step 2 Put students in pairs to discuss the questions.
In a multilingual group, make sure pairs are of different nationalities. Conduct very brief feedback.

Step 3 Ask students to read the Holiday facts and decide if they find anything surprising. Elicit reactions from the whole group. Check they can say the numbers, e.g. 10.8, 17.5. Point out that we use *point* with decimals, not *comma* e.g. *ten point eight, seventeen point five*. Check by writing examples on the board and getting students to say them.

Step 4 Ask students to read the article and find the answers to the questions in C as quickly as they can. Check in pairs, then with the whole group. Check they understand the title: *bank on* = rely on, assume something will happen.

Alternatively Before Step 4 ask students to read the first paragraph of the article and ask which problems from *Vocabulary* are mentioned (to recycle the vocabulary), then go on to Step 4.

Answers

1 Because it is the busiest weekend of the year and there are problems: traffic, delays, overcrowding and stress / arguments.
2 Unions are complaining that there are not enough public holidays in the UK, compared with other countries and that many workers are not getting their legal holiday entitlement.

3 The Union wants the government to declare three new public holidays.
4 *Karoshi* is Japanese for dying from overwork. It is mentioned because many Japanese workers do not take their full holiday entitlement because they have too much work on.
5 The high number of holidays in Puerto Rico cause higher costs, higher unemployment and higher prices, according to businesses.

Step 5 Put students in pairs to find what the numbers refer to. Alternatively, you could make this a race between the whole group.

Answers
millions: people stuck in traffic
eight: bank holidays
20 days of holiday entitlement
One: holiday cancelled in France
16: public holidays in Slovenia
three: amount of new public holidays union wants
hundreds: people getting sunburnt
twenty-one: government workers holidays in Puerto Rico

Step 6 Put students in groups of three or four to discuss the questions in E. In a multilingual class, make sure each group has a mix of nationalities.

SPEAKING

Aim
To extend the reading topic and give fluency practice.

Step 1 Put students in threes – A, B and C. With an odd number, you could have one or two groups of four and double up one of the roles. Ask students to turn to the relevant page and read their role. Tell them to take turns asking and answering the questions.

Step 2 When they finish, tell them to discuss the questions in their threes. Monitor closely during these two phases and note down any mistakes they make or problems they have. Conduct a brief correction slot at the end.

GRAMMAR Present perfect questions

Aim
To give practice in the present perfect simple, contrasted with the past simple, to ask and talk about past experience.

Step 1 Ask students to look at the box and read it quickly. Model the conversation with one or two students. Check students understand when the present perfect simple is used and when the past simple is used and why. (use present perfect in the first question to ask about recent experience but with unspecified time. Use past simple in the answer because the time is now specified or implied.) Direct students to the grammar reference on p. 140 if they are unsure.

Step 2 Ask students to complete the phrases with *yes* or *no* at the beginning of each. Check in pairs then check with the whole group. Drill the responses by asking students about various places and getting them to choose an appropriate response. Practise in open pairs.

Step 3 Ask students to write six names of places they have been to on a piece of paper. Put students in pairs and get them to swap papers and ask each other about the places. Monitor closely and conduct a brief correction slot at the end, focusing on the use of tenses.

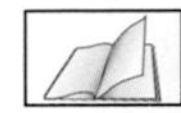

pp. 24–25

Next class Make photocopies of **3A** and **3B** pp. 132–133.

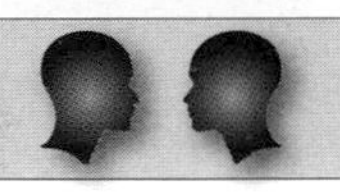

VOCABULARY Weather

Aim
To present / consolidate vocabulary, especially adjectives, about the weather. To introduce future forms for making predictions and plans.

Step 1 Introduce the idea of the weather forecast. Ask what this is, where you can hear / see it, whether they watch / listen to it and why / why not? In a multilingual class, you could ask about the weather in different students' countries, whether it is very changeable or not and whether it affects people's plans much.

Step 2 Ask students individually to match the sentence halves. Do the first example with them. Do not pre-teach the vocabulary as the idea is that they should work it out from the context, but ask if anyone remembers *windy* or *pours* from earlier. When they finish, check in pairs, then with the whole group. Drill the difficult weather words for pronunciation and concept check the vocabulary: *Humid, windy, freezing, boiling hot, to pour down, warm, cloudy, minus 10, 36 degrees, storm, chilly, clear up.* You may also want to check *parasol, blow away, suntan.*

Answers

1 c	3 f	5 b	7 h
2 d	4 a	6 e	8 g

Step 3 Ask students to read through the matched sentence halves and try to memorise them. Put students in pairs and get them to 'test' each other. Student B should close his / her book. Student A should say the sentences and Student B should supply the correct sentence ending. Then they could swap.

Step 4 Put students in new pairs if possible, or threes. In a multilingual class, make sure they are grouped in different nationalities. Ask them to discuss the questions. Monitor and conduct brief feedback at the end.

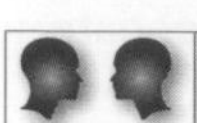

3A see Teacher's notes p. 121.

LISTENING

Aim
To develop the skills of prediction and listening for specific information. To introduce the future forms in context.

Step 1 Put students in pairs. Ask them to discuss why people might describe the weather as annoying or worrying. Do not conduct feedback here. Ask students to listen to the recording to check their predictions. Check with the whole group. Who said what and why?

3.2
C = Christina, A = Andrew
C: Oh I don't believe it!
A: What's up?
C: I'm just checking the weather forecast for next week!
A: Oh right. Is it going to be bad?
C: Well, not here. Apparently, it's going to be boiling here: 27 degrees on Monday!
A: Really? That's great!
C: Great for you, but I'm not going to be here. I've got a week off work. I'm going to Italy and apparently it's going to pour down most of the week!
A: Oh dear. I forgot you were going away. Whereabouts are you going?
C: Sicily. I mean, it's in the south! It's supposed to be really sunny at this time of year. I was hoping to go to the beach and get a suntan, you know.
A: Oh no. Well, it'll probably clear up later in the week. It's not going to be wet for long.
C: I hope not, because I don't think there will be much to do there.
A: Why, where are you staying?
C: Some little village on the coast. We're also thinking of going to Palermo for a couple of days. It depends on the weather.
A: Well, maybe you could go to Palermo first? There'll probably be museums you could visit if it's wet.
C: I suppose so. I prefer the beach, though.
A: Oh, OK. Well, maybe the forecast will be wrong and it'll turn out really sunny.
C: Mmm. So what you are you doing over the Easter holiday? Have you got any plans?
A: Well, I've got to work on Saturday, and I'm having lunch with my parents on Sunday, but apart from that ... I don't know. I don't usually do much on bank holidays, but if it's going to be hot, I might go for a picnic in the park. I might even go to the beach. I guess it depends what time I get up on Monday! But honestly – 27 degrees! That's mad for this time of the year! It's actually a little but worrying, really.
C: Or annoying!

Answers
Andrew said it was worrying – probably because it is unnatural for the weather to be so hot at this time of year (Easter) and this is probably the result of global warming. Cristina said it was annoying because she is going to miss it. She will be in Italy where the forecast is not good.

Step 2 Students could work in pairs to try to complete the table from memory. Then listen again to check / add to their tables. Check in pairs, then with the whole group.

Answers	Cristina	Andrew
Plans	Italy, Sicily, holiday, beach, suntan, village on coast, Palermo	Work, lunch with parents, picnic, beach
Weather	Pour down, wet.	Hot, sunny, 27 degrees

LANGUAGE PATTERNS

Aim
To draw students' attention to some common patterns used in the context of the weather.

Warning (!) Possible confusion between *weather* and *whether*.
Depends on NOT ~~*depends of*~~ ...

Step 1 Ask students to read the examples in the box. Draw their attention to the constructions: it depends ***on*** ... it depends ***on whether*** ... it depends **on *how long it takes*** (notice the word order change here and highlight the use of *on*, not *of*). Drill some examples by giving prompts e.g. What are you doing tonight, next weekend, next summer? Are you going to work, for a picnic? etc.

Speaking

Aim
To give fluency practice around the topic of holidays.

Alternatively Omit this stage and go straight on to *Grammar* to avoid interruption between *Listening* and *Grammar*. Then use this speaking activity to round off the unit. Or you could use it as a lead-in to this lesson, i.e. before the *Vocabulary*.

Step 1 Ask students what else is important for them when choosing a holiday, apart from the weather. Ask them individually to rank the items 1–8 in order of importance for a successful holiday (8 = the most important).

Step 2 Put students in pairs or small groups. Tell them to discuss their rankings and try to reach a consensus. Alternatively conduct this as a 'pyramid discussion', i.e. pairs – fours – eights, reaching a consensus each time. Conduct brief feedback.

Grammar The future

Aim
To revise / consolidate different ways of talking about future plans or predictions.

Step 1 Remind students of *Listening* – What was it about? Who was speaking? (If doing this after the speaking activity, you might want to use the audioscript here to make the link with the listening more explicit and begin by asking students to underline the examples given here in the audioscript.)

Step 2 Ask students individually to match the grammar explanations with the example, by writing the correct letter in each box. Point out that some letters are used more than once. Check in pairs, then check with the whole group.

Answers
1 a 2 a 3 b 4 d 5 a, c 6 a 7 b, d

Step 3 Concept check when we use *going to* + base form (for a definite plan / intention – in this case); *will + base form* (for something possible or probable – in this case); *present continuous* or *I've got + a / an / some* (for an arrangement); *I'm thinking of* + gerund or *I might + base form* (to talk about vague or possible plans for the future, plans which are not yet confirmed); *I've got to + base form* (for an obligation). Direct students to the grammar reference on p. 141 if they are still unsure.

Step 4 Tell students to fill in the gaps individually. Do the first example with them. Check in pairs, then with the whole group.

Answers

1 thinking	4 meeting	7 going to
2 'll	5 's got	8 've got to
3 might	6 might	

Tip Students may have problems with 4 as this is an indefinite arrangement. Point out that the present continuous can also be used with *probably* and that *probably* comes after *to be*.

Native speaker English

Ask students to read the box and check they understand. Concept check: Can I use *at some point* with different tenses? (Yes.) Does it mean I know when something will happen / happened or I'm not sure? (Not sure.)

Step 5 Ask students to read through the questions in D and think about how they would answer them.

Step 6 Put students in new pairs (if possible) or small groups. Get them to discuss the questions. Monitor closely and take notes for a correction slot at the end.

Alternatively Ask each group to appoint a secretary who takes notes and reports back at the end on some of the more interesting things said by their group.

Speaking

Aim
To draw together all the language used in the unit and give fluency practice.

Step 1 Set the scene by eliciting what this is (a calendar) and asking students to read the instructions in A. Check they understand. Give them two minutes to complete their calendars individually. Tell them to think about other things they might do and when they might do them.

Step 2 Put students in new pairs to role-play the conversation. Monitor closely and conduct a correction slot at the end.

Alternatively Conduct this as a 'mingling' activity. Ask students to get up and move around and ask different students about their plans. They should try to find two or three other students to share some of their activities and write their names next to them. Conduct brief feedback / have a correction slot at the end.

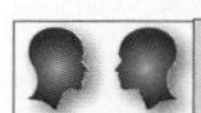
3B see Teacher's notes p. 121.

04 INTERESTS

UNIT OVERVIEW
The main aims of this unit are to enable students to talk about **free-time activities** especially **sports (including sports-related problems) and music** and to give them practice **pronouncing groups of words**. They also have practice in **talking about frequency** in the **present** and the **past** and **duration**, using the **past simple and present perfect continuous**.

SPEAKING

Aim
To lead in to the topic and to get students immediately involved through personalisation.

Step 1 Ask students to look at the picture and think about the answers to the questions. Also point out the main unit photo and pre-teach / check any vocabulary you think they may not know, e.g. fly a kite, go roller-blading, go jogging. Remind students of *-ing* form following *like, enjoy, interested in*, etc.

Step 2 Put students in groups of four / five. Ask them to talk about the questions. Conduct brief feedback and help them with any vocabulary problems.

VOCABULARY

Evening and weekend activities

Aim
To give students exposure to common collocations used to talk about activities / interests.

Step 1 Ask students to decide which four endings are possible for each sentence. Do the first one with them. They could do this in pairs or individually. Check in pairs, then check with the whole group. Get them to say the whole sentence each time to help 'fix' the expressions.

Answers
1 I stayed in and studied / took it easy / tidied up. Concept check *took it easy* = relaxed.
2 I played on the computer / golf / tennis.
3 I went clubbing / cycling / walking in the country. Concept check *clubbing* = going out to nightclubs / discos, usually involving drinking and dancing.
4 I went for a meal / a ride on my bike / a swim.
5 I went to the cinema / Karen's house for dinner / a bar to watch the football.

Elicit which answer is not correct and why, i.e.
1 played football (not possible – I was in the house)
2 roller-blading (used with *go* not *play*, should be I *went roller-blading*)
3 I went a run (should be I went *for a run*)
4 I went for a gym (should be I went *to the gym*)
5 I went to shopping (should be *I went shopping*)

Step 2 Put students in pairs to think of at least two more endings for each example. Elicit answers.

Possible answers
1 I stayed in and watched TV / listened to music / the radio / read a book / sent some emails / made some phone calls / cooked dinner, etc.
2 I played cards / chess / poker / volleyball / basketball, etc.
3 I went shopping / jogging / swimming / running / sightseeing, etc.
4 I went for a drink / a sandwich / a coffee / a run, etc.
5 I went to the theatre / a restaurant / the gym / my friend's, etc.

Point out *go for a swim / run / walk = go swimming / running / walking*.

LISTENING

Aim
To listen for gist and detail and to hear the target vocabulary in context.

Step 1 Tell students they are going to hear four short conversations. They listen and note down what the second speaker did and when for each conversation. Play the recording. Students check in pairs, then check with the whole group.

Answers
1 B stayed in and went to bed early – last night.
2 D went shopping – on Saturday (at the weekend).
3 F went to the cinema and saw *The Lives of Others* (a German film) – after seeing E.

4.1

Conversation 1

A: So what did you do last night? You didn't come to Gary's party.

B: No. I was too tired. I just stayed in and went to bed early.

A: Oh right. Are you OK?

B: Yeah, I'm fine. I just had a really busy week and I didn't feel like going out.

Conversation 2

C: Did you have a nice weekend?

D: Yeah, it was OK. I didn't do that much. I went shopping on Saturday and that was all, really.

C: Oh right. Did you get anything nice?

D: No, I didn't see anything I liked.

Conversation 3

E: So what did you do after we left you?

F: We went to the cinema.

E: Oh right? What did you see?

F: *The Lives of Others*. It's a German film.

E: Oh yeah? I've been thinking about going to see that. Is it any good?

F: Yeah. It's brilliant.

Conversation 4

J = Jason, M = Mohammed

J: So did you have a nice weekend?

M: Yeah, it was OK. Nothing special really.

J: No? What did you do?

M: Well, I went round to a friend's for dinner on Saturday, which was nice.

J: Yeah.

M: And then on Sunday I played football.

J: Really? I didn't know you played football. Where do you do that?

M: Oh, I play for a local team in a Sunday league.

J: Oh yeah. So are you any good?

M: I'm OK. I'm quite good in defence, but I'm useless at shooting. I think the last time I scored a goal was about three years ago.

J: So how long have you been playing?

M: Well, in this team, about five years, but I played at school before that. Do you play at all?

J: No, I'm rubbish at football. I do a bit of swimming, though.

M: Yeah? How often do you go?

J: Well, not as often as I used to. Since I started this job I haven't had much time. I actually went on Saturday, but I think that was the first time in about three weeks. I used to go three or four times a week.

Step 2 Ask students to listen again and write down the questions they hear. Pause the recording after each one to help them. Ask students to check in pairs, then check with the whole group.

Step 3 In pairs ask students to use the questions to help them role-play the conversations. It doesn't matter if there are slight variations. Then ask them to cover up the questions and role-play similar conversations from memory.

Alternatively To give more support, students could read the audioscript on p. 162 before Step 3. Or, before going into pairs in Step 3, elicit what the answers to the questions are and then put students in pairs.

PRONUNCIATION Connected speech

Aim

To make students more aware of two features of connected speech: catenation (when a final consonant sounds as if it is added to the following word, if this begins with a vowel sound) and elision (when one of two adjacent consonant sounds appears to be omitted, particularly /t/ and /d/).

Step 1 Read out the box. Emphasise the features of connected speech.

Step 2 Tell students they are going to hear the conversation between Jason and Mohammed again.
Play the first part of 4.1 then pause the recording. Elicit the sentence and write it on the board. Elicit examples of catenation / elision and show how to mark these. They should then read the rest of the audioscript as they listen and mark the examples of catenation and elision. Check in pairs, then with the whole group. Drill the examples of catenation / elision.

Step 3 Students work in pairs and read out the conversation, paying particular attention to pronunciation. Monitor closely and help / correct where necessary.

GRAMMAR Frequency (present and past)

Aim

To draw students' attention to ways of asking and talking about frequency / habit in the present and the past.

Step 1 Read out what is in the grammar box. Get a student to supply an example for each verb and then drill with that example. Get students to ask each other in open pairs, using different verbs.

Step 2 Ask students to complete the sentences with the words in the box. They could do this in pairs or individually and then check in pairs. Check with the whole group, possibly in open pairs.

Answers

1 all 2 every 3 quite 4 that 5 hardly 6 'd 7 used to

Step 3 Ask students which sentences compare the past and the present (numbers 5–7). Ask them which tenses are used to talk about frequency in the present (present simple) and the past (past simple or *used to* + base form). Direct them to the grammar reference on p. 142 if they are unsure.

Step 4 Ask students to underline the frequency expressions. Check in pairs, then with the whole group.

If you don't want students to translate the expressions, concept check and drill some of them, e.g. at least a book / film a week; at least twice a month; nearly every day / week / month; quite a lot / quite a bit / quite often; not that often; hardly ever; not as much as I'd like to / I used to / I did. **Note** *Much* can only be used in questions and negative answers.

1 A So, do you read much?
B Yeah, all the time. I read at least a book a week.
2 A Do you go swimming a lot?
B Yeah, nearly every day, unless I'm really busy.
3 A Do you go to the cinema much?
B Yeah, quite a lot. I probably go once every two weeks.
4 A How often do you play games on the computer?
B Not that often, actually. It's not really my kind of thing.
5 A So how often do you go to the gym?
B Hardly ever now, to be honest. Today was the first time in ages. I used to go more often.
6 A Do you ever watch your favourite team play?
B Yeah, but not as much as I'd like to.
7 A Do you eat out a lot?
B Not as much as we used to. Before we were married we went out all the time.

Language patterns

Aim
To introduce how *unless* is used – often to qualify a response about how frequently we do things.

Step 1 Ask students to read the examples in the box. Ask them to translate into their own language and notice differences. Alternatively, if you prefer not to use translation, ask students which tenses are used after *unless* (present simple, present continuous or past simple). Drill a few examples, by asking students *How often do / did you...?* and they reply using *unless*.

Step 2 Model the conversation, by asking students some of the questions from A, then continue in open pairs. Make sure students use a variety of the frequency expressions in their answers and try to include *unless*. Put students in groups of three or four to ask and answer the questions in A. Monitor closely and note down errors in the target language for a correction slot at the end.

Developing conversations

Are you any good?

Aim
To draw students' attention to ways of asking and talking about abilities using *are you (any) good at* + noun / gerund and suitable responses.

Step 1 Ask students to read the exchange from *Listening*. Concept check *Are you any good at...?* = Can you do this well? *I'm useless at shooting* = I can't shoot very well at all. Draw their attention to *good / quite good / OK / not bad / not very good / no good / useless at* + noun / gerund. Drill a few examples.

Step 2 Ask students what sport was being referred to in the conversation (football). Tell them to look at sentences 1–8 and identify the sport in each case. Do not pre-teach the vocabulary here but tell them to try to work out the answers from the context / a process of elimination. They could do this in pairs or individually and then check in pairs. Check with the whole group. Ask how they guessed and concept check *court, net, breaststroke, front crawl, backwards, black runs, free throws.*

Answers

1 tennis	5 table tennis
2 football	6 judo
3 swimming	7 skiing
4 roller-blading	8 basketball

Step 3 Model the conversation by asking students. *Are you (any) good at...?* And then getting them to ask each other in open pairs. Put them in new pairs if possible and get them to ask each other about their abilities. Monitor closely and note down errors in the target language. Conduct a correction slot at the end.

Conversation practice

Aim
To give further practice of the target grammar and vocabulary and to personalise the language.

Step 1 Ask students individually to read the conversation on p. 157 (file 6) and think about what they would say in answer to the questions, using two different sports or activities.

Step 2 Put students in pairs and ask them to practise the conversation, taking turns to ask and answer the questions. Monitor and note down errors in the target language. Conduct a correction slot at the end.

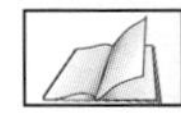
pp. 28–29

Next class Make photocopies of **4A** p. 134.
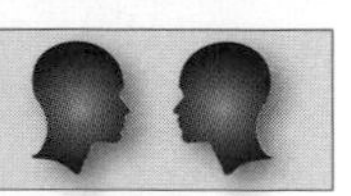

Listening

Aim
To give students practice in listening for gist and specific information.

Step 1 Put students in pairs and ask them to discuss the questions in A. Concept check *martial arts* = a technique of self-defence that comes from the far East. Conduct brief feedback and check forms of martial arts, *judo, karate, tae-kwon-do, kung fu*, etc.

Step 2 Tell students they are going to hear a conversation between Rika and Ian. Ask them to read the questions in B and think about the answers as they listen. Play recording 4.2 then check the answers.

4.2
I = Ian, R = Rika
I: Am I imagining things, Rika, or did that guy just ask you for your autograph?
R: You saw that? Oh, I'm embarrassed now, Ian!
I: Why? How come he knew you?
R: You won't believe me when I tell you!
I: Go on! What?
R: Well, in my other life, away from selling books, I'm kind of famous! I do judo and last week I was on TV and that guy recognised me from there. That's why he wanted my autograph.
I: Seriously? That's amazing!
R: Oh, it's no big deal. I didn't even win the tournament. I lost in the semi-finals, but at least the girl who beat me went on to win the whole thing, so it wasn't too bad!
I: So you got to the semi-finals! I can't believe it! You don't look big enough to fight – if you don't mind me saying.
R: Well, that's why I love judo. It's nothing to do with how big you are. It's all about balance. You learn how to take advantage of your opponent's strength and size and to throw them off balance.
I: Oh right. I see. So how long have you been doing that, then?
R: Ever since I was a kid. I used to get into fights when I was at school because I was so small. The big kids used to bully me, so my dad suggested I started doing a martial art and that was it, really.
I: You've kept very quiet about it all the time I've known you!
R: Yeah, well, I don't like to talk about it. People might think I'm being big-headed. I don't really feel like it's connected to what I do at work.
I: So how often do you have to train?
R: Oh, well, I usually practise all the techniques for at least an hour a day – once I get home in the evening – and then two or three times a week I go to a special judo school to spar, you know, to practise fighting.
I: I'm speechless, Rika, I really am!
R: Yeah, well. There you go!
I: And this tournament the other week ... what was it exactly? Was it a big thing?
R: Um ... Yeah ... It was the women's national final!
I: No!
R: Yeah, honestly! I'm actually quite annoyed. I think I had a chance of winning it, but I hurt my back quite badly last year fighting in a competition. I didn't warm up properly before the fight, so my body wasn't really ready for it, and when I fell I injured myself a bit. I didn't fight for a couple of months after that and it took me a while to get used to competing again.
I: I can imagine!
R: Yeah, but I've been doing quite a lot of yoga for the last few months, and that has really helped a lot.

Answers
1 Because she was in a judo tournament which was shown on TV.
2 She practises every day.
3 Because Rika doesn't like talking about it – she is too modest.

Step 3 Put students in pairs and tell them to try to answer the true / false questions from memory. Check *boasts* = talks about something proudly in a way which could be annoying. Play the recording again for them to check. Check with the whole group.

Answers
1 T 2 F 3 F 4 T 5 F 6 F 7 T 8 F

Step 4 Ask students to look at the questions in D and think about how they would answer them. Check they understand *bully* = to use your strength or power to hurt or frighten someone, also a noun and *big-headed* = having an excessively high opinion of oneself.

Step 5 Put students in groups of three to discuss the questions. Conduct brief feedback with the whole group.

NATIVE SPEAKER ENGLISH

Draw students' attention to this use of *kind of* (i.e. not the same as *what kind of sports do you like?*). Get them to read the box and check they understand. Can *kind of* be used with different parts of speech? (Yes.) Elicit a few more examples.

VOCABULARY Problems and sports

Aim
To extend the topic further by introducing injuries and other problems often associated with sports.

Step 1 Elicit what problem Rika had when fighting in a competition (she hurt her back). Draw students' attention to the pictures and ask what problems they can see and what was the sport in each case (broken leg – skiing; pulled muscle – running).

Step 2 Ask students individually to complete the sentences with the correct word from the box. Do not pre-teach the vocabulary, but try to get them to guess from the context. Check in pairs then with the whole group. Check concept (point out the woman's leg in plaster in the picture) and pronunciation. Ask students to make up their own examples, using the target vocabulary in different contexts.

Answers			
1 unfit	3 pulled	5 broke	7 bloody
2 stiff	4 beat	6 banged	8 fell

Step 3 Ask the whole group the questions in B.

GRAMMAR Duration

Aim
To draw students' attention to ways of talking about duration and give practice.

Step 1 Ask students to correct the mistakes in the sentences in A. Do the first example with them. They could do this in pairs or individually and then check in pairs.

Answers
1 Rika usually practises all the techniques **for** at least an hour a day.
2 After her injury, Rika didn't fight **for** a couple of months.
3 She's **been** doing quite a lot of yoga for the last few months.
4 She used to get into fights **when** she was at school.
5 She's been doing judo **ever since** she was a kid.

Step 2 Ask students to look at the sentences in A again and the audioscript on pp. 162–163 then complete the rules in B. Check in pairs, then with the whole group.

Answers
for, since, present perfect (continuous), past

Concept check the difference between *for* (with a period of time) and *since* (with a point in time).

Tip Make sure that students understand that *during* is used with a noun, e.g. *during the week, during the lesson, during the film, during the night.*

Step 3 Put students in pairs and ask them to choose the correct answer to complete the sentences in C. Do the first example with them. Check with the whole group at the end. Drill the phrases of duration.

Answers	
1 since; for	4 were you
2 for	5 have you been; Since
3 ever since; I've been	6 did you do; Until

Step 4 Put students in pairs and get them to have conversations about sport and practise the expressions of duration. Model the conversation first with you and a student, then in open pairs. Monitor their conversations and correct any mistakes you hear in the target language.

4A see Teacher's notes p. 121.

PRONUNCIATION Auxiliaries

Aim
To draw students' attention to weak forms of auxiliaries and give practice in the context of duration.

Step 1 Read out the comment under *Pronunciation*. Play the recording and get students to repeat after each phrase.

4.3
1 How long was your flight delayed?
2 How long do you want to stay?
3 How long were you waiting?
4 How long did it take you to get home?
5 How long are you going to go for?
6 How long will it take to repair?
7 How long have you been seeing Dan?
8 How long does it take you to get here?

Step 2 Play the recording again and ask students to write down the questions. Check in pairs, then with the whole group. Try to get them to use the weak forms.

SPEAKING

Aim
To practise asking and talking about duration.

Step 1 Ask students to read the instructions and the example and think about what they will say.

Step 2 Model the conversation with a strong student, then in open pairs. Put students in groups of three or four to have the conversations. Monitor closely and take notes for an error correction slot at the end.

pp. 30–31

Next class Make photocopies of **4B** pp. 135.
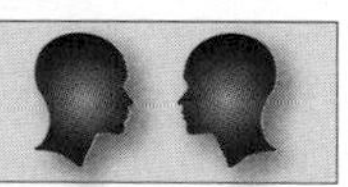

DEVELOPING CONVERSATIONS
Music, films and books

Aim
To further extend the topic, give personalised practice and lead in to the reading.

Step 1 Briefly introduce the topic by asking students what kind of books / films / music they like. Check they understand R&B (Rhythm and Blues). Put students in pairs and ask them to put the conversation in A in the right order. Play the recording for them to listen and check. Drill the expressions in bold and check the concept.

4.5 / Answer
A: Do you listen to music much?
B: Yeah, all the time.
A: What kind of music are you into?
B: All sorts really but mainly pop music and R & B.
A: Oh right. Anyone in particular?
B: Erm, I don't know ... Girls Rock!, Soul Train, stuff like that.
A: So have you bought anything good recently?
B: Well, I downloaded this great song by K Boy. It's fantastic.
Stuff like that = that kind of thing
All sorts = every kind
Mainly = mostly, especially
Anyone in particular? = (Do you like) one group or musician / singer especially?
Have you bought anything good recently? = Have you bought a good single / album / CD recently?
What kind of music are you into? = Do you like?

Step 2 Model the conversation with a strong student, using their own answers, then model in open pairs. Encourage them to use the expressions in bold. Put students in pairs to have similar conversations. Monitor and correct any mistakes they make with the target vocabulary.

VOCABULARY Music

Aim
To introduce ways to describing types of music.

Step 1 Check students understand all the types of music in the box. Elicit examples. Drill for pronunciation.

Step 2 Ask students to think about which type of music they associate with each of the descriptions, then put them in pairs to discuss it.

Suggested answers

1 pop	6 pop, R&B
2 hip-hop, techno, heavy metal, R&B	7 blues, folk, classical
3 heavy metal	8 any
4 classical, jazz	9 pop, salsa, classical, R&B
5 pop, blues	10 blues

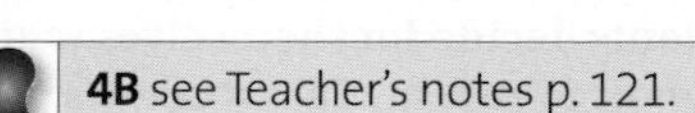 **4B** see Teacher's notes p. 121.

READING

Aim
To give practice in reading for gist and detail.

Step 1 Put students in pairs and ask them to talk about the songs in A. Do they know any of them? Do they like them?

Step 2 Ask students to read the magazine article and find out if the people in the texts liked the songs or not and why. Check *playlist* = a set of songs you choose for a particular reason.

Answers
- The first person liked *Hey Jude* because it's good to sing along to and he learnt English through the Beatles; *Love Phantom* because they were great live.
- The second person liked *A Little Less Conversation* because it reminds her of her time in Amsterdam.
- The third person likes *The Four Seasons* – though parts are sad – because it reminds him of life; *Limón Y Sal* because it cheers him up.
- The fourth person likes *I Wanna Be Like You* because it makes her brother laugh; *Underneath* because her sister likes it.
- The fifth person does not like *My Heart Will Go On* because it is commercial and sentimental; he dislikes *The Birdie Song* because it's catchy and annoying.

Step 3 Put students in pairs and ask them to answer the questions in C together. Check with the whole group.

Answers

1 Natalia	3 Corina	5 Natalia
2 Kevin	4 Toshi	6 Kari, Kevin

Step 3 Ask students to correct the words in italics. Tell them to use the text to help them. Do the first example with them. Check in pairs, then with the whole group.

Answers

1 along	4 comes / is put	7 do
2 live	5 match	8 sentimental
3 reminds	6 background	9 done

SPEAKING

Aim
To personalise the topic with fun fluency practice.

Step 1 Individually students choose three of the categories and write down a playlist of three songs and their reasons for choosing them.

Step 2 Put students in pairs to explain their playlists to each other. Conduct brief feedback at the end – the funniest, strangest, etc. one they heard.

Next class Make photocopies of **5A** p. 136.
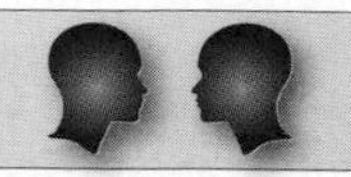

01 REVIEW

OVERALL AIMS

It is rarely enough to meet and use 'new' language and skills once. In reality, people learn these things by being exposed to them and activating them again and again. Therefore, each of the four review units are designed to revise material covered in the previous four units. They also introduce a *Learner training* section (helping students to become more aware of their learning style / strategies and enabling them to learn more effectively). The first two pages are designed to revise the material in a fun, interactive way. The second two pages are more traditional listening, grammar and vocabulary exercises, which could be given as a progress test. In addition, these test pages expose students to exam-type questions they are likely to meet in common English exams.

LEARNER TRAINING

Overview

Research has shown that effective language learners develop strategies for dealing with a range of situations from making sense of unknown language to recording and reviewing language. The *Learner training* feature encourages students to review their own strategies, whether implicit or explicit, as well as developing new strategies so they become more effective language learners and users.

Aim

To get students thinking about the way they make and use notes and to encourage them to adopt more efficient ways of doing this.

Step 1 Put students in threes and ask them to discuss the questions. They could make notes of their discussion and then compare the different ways they have done this.

Step 2 Ask each group to use the sentence heads to write some recommendations. An effective way to do this would be to get each group to use the sentence starters as the basis for a poster and display these on the wall. Then students could walk round and look at each other's posters. Alternatively, you could elicit their recommendations and write them on the board. Conduct brief feedback.

GAME

Overview

Games are valuable for language learners because as they become involved in the activity they become less self-conscious about speaking in a foreign language and less worried about making mistakes. In addition, games help develop classroom dynamics and they are fun – it's important to enjoy learning!

Aim

To recycle some of the language covered in the units in a fun, student-centred way.

Step 1 Put students in A / B pairs. Ask student A to look at the questions in the green squares and student B to look at the questions in the yellow squares. They should find the answers in the units and try to memorise them. They may need longer than five minutes for this.

Step 2 Tell students to play the game in pairs. They should take turns to throw a coin and move one of their squares for heads and two of their squares for tails. They should answer the question on the square they land on. Their partner should check the answer in the relevant part of the book. If they get the answer right, they move forward one square (but don't answer that question until their next turn). If they get the answer wrong, their partner tells them the answer and they miss a turn – and use the coin again for their next turn. The first one to reach their last square is the winner. Students could then swap colours and play again.

CONVERSATION PRACTICE

Overview

In this activity students decide for themselves which conversation they want to repeat. Two students perform the task in front of a third, who acts as 'judge'. Having an audience normally means students perform better. The judge also has to listen carefully because they have the responsibility for marking their classmates. This whole process has the added advantage of promoting learner autonomy.

Aim

To give fluency practice and also to raise students' awareness of their speaking ability by asking them to observe and assess each other.

Step 1 Put students in threes. They can refer to the *Vocabulary builder* if they wish. They should take turns to be a pair of speakers and an observer. Each pair should choose one of the topics, look back at the relevant part of the book and take a few minutes to prepare. They then conduct the conversation while the third student listens and takes notes. At the end, the observer gives a mark out of 10 to each person in the pair and explains the mark (1 = poor, 10 = excellent). It would be useful if they could also use their notes to give more detailed feedback on strengths and weaknesses / errors. Then swap. You can monitor and prompt / help where necessary and also give some overall feedback at the end.

Act or draw

Overview
This is an enormously popular game amongst people the world over because it is so much fun. The gap between the actor / artist's performance and the 'guesser's' ideas leads to a lot of laughter and a lot of language use as well.

Aim
To revise vocabulary in a fun way.

Step 1 Put students in groups of three and ask them to take turns to act or draw the words / phrases in the box, chosen at random. They should not speak while they are acting or drawing. Their partners should guess the word / phrase. Then swap.

Quiz

Overview
This game is best played in teams of two or three in order to promote speaking. It's a good idea to give students a realistic time limit. The pressure also increases energy levels and makes the game more exciting.

Aim
To revise some of the other vocabulary from the units.

Step 1 Put students in pairs / threes and ask them to answer as many of the questions as possible. You could conduct this as a race so the first pair / three to finish with the correct answers is the winner.

Alternatively You could conduct this as a 'pub quiz' with you reading out each question and groups of three or four students quietly conferring on the answers. You could then check with the whole group at the end and see which group is the winner.

Answers

1. A head teacher runs a school.
2. Holding hands: what couples or a parent and child do. Shaking hands: what people do when they meet.
3. You can sort out problems, your finances, a mess, etc.
4. You feel annoyed / cheated when you get ripped off because someone is stealing from you or overcharging you.
5. You would be in a rush (hurry) because you are late / short of time. You would rush someone to hospital after an accident / if they are at risk.
6. No, it isn't good to get sunburnt – it means *over-exposed to the sun.*
7. You would ignore someone you didn't like – you would avoid or not speak to them.
8. People boast about their achievements, their qualifications, their children, their jobs, their salaries, etc.
9. Cars, marriages, relationships and boilers can break down.
10. You need to warm up before exercise or sport.
11. You get promoted to a better job or higher position.
12. You can't hurt a car – you can damage it. You can only hurt people or animals.
13. To practise is to try to improve at something by doing it or parts of it. To play is to actually do it, often in competition with others.
14. You might need cheering up if you were sad, depressed or upset.
15. Bills or payments can be due, library books can be due, assignments can be due.

Collocations

Overview
Collocations are words which usually go together such as, *do me a favour,* and *a pressing problem.* Until relatively recently the concept of collocation was not an area that was covered in vocabulary teaching. However, computational linguistics has shown how important a force collocation is in language. This activity helps to develop students' awareness of the importance of collocation in natural language generation.

Aim
To revise some common collocations from the first four units and give students practice in using the *Vocabulary builder.*

Step 1 Put students in pairs and ask them to take turns to test each other on collocations. One should look at unit 1 of the *Vocabulary builder* and read out a collocation, with a 'gap' where there is a '~'. They should say 'blah' for the gap, and their partner should say the missing word. They could do 6–8 and then swap.

PRONUNCIATION

Overview
These activities encourage students to be reflective about sounds and to develop their 'inner ear'. The main aim is not to make students native-speaker like but to develop their ability to understand spoken English as well as to improve their own intelligibility when speaking to other non-native and native English speakers.

Aim
To revise vowel sounds.

Step 1 Ask students to listen to the recording and repeat the words. Play the recording.

R 1.1
1 At least you're here now.
2 Fair enough.
3 I'm sure it'll sort itself out.
4 I think I'll join you.
5 It's not worth it.
6 Apart from that.
7 Not as much as I should.
8 Whenever I get the chance.
9 Ten years, on and off.
10 On in the background.
11 I can't get it out of my head.
12 It doesn't do anything for me.

Step 2 Ask students to put the words from the box in the correct space according to the underlined sound. They could do this individually and then check in pairs.

Step 3 Ask students which sounds they find most difficult and drill some of these individually.

Answers

cheek – relief	hurt – confirm
rip – skills	sort – exhausted
pull – bully	bang – accent
boots – due	hum – wonder
upset – therapist	spa – marks
gallery – attempt	loss – mosque

CONNECTED SPEECH

Aim
To revise features of connected speech, namely elision and catenation.

Step 1 Ask students to listen to the recording and repeat the sentences, paying particular attention to pronunciation and the stressed sounds. Play the recording.

R 1.2
1 At least you're here now.
2 Fair enough.
3 I'm sure it'll sort itself out.
4 I think I'll join you.
5 It's not worth it.
6 Apart from that.
7 Not as much as I should.
8 Whenever I get the chance.
9 Ten years, on and off.
10 On in the background.
11 I can't get it out of my head.
12 It doesn't do anything for me.

Step 2 Ask students to look at the sentences and mark them. They could write **e** for elision (where the sound disappears) and **c** for catenation (where the consonant of one word appears to join the following vowel sound).

Step 3 Play the recording again for them to check. They could also look at the audioscript on p. 163 to check.

Answers
e = elision, c = catenation
1 At least-e, least you're-c
2 Fair enough-c
3 sure it'll-c, sort itself-c, itself out-c
4 think I'll-c, join you-c
5 not worth-e, worth it-c
6 Apart from-e
7 Not as-c, as I-c
8 Whenever I-c, get the-e
9 Ten years-c, on and-c, and off-c
10 On in-c
11 can't get-e, get it-c, it out-c
12 it doesn't-e

Note *Listening* and the rest of the review unit could be used as the basis of a Progress test. The suggested scores are given below each exercise. Alternatively, these exercises could be done in pairs or individually then checked in pairs, or you could conduct them as a quiz / competition, with students in teams. If students have problems with any of the exercises, refer them to the relevant pages in the grammar reference or the *Vocabulary builder*.

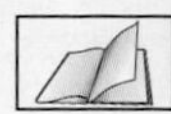

pp. 34–35

Listening

Aim
To give practice in listening for gist.

A Answers
a 2 b 3 c 4 d - e 1

B Answers
a 2 b 3 c 1 d e 4

Grammar

Answers

1 look	11 fell
2 since	12 had
3 do	13 go
4 used	14 at
5 started	15 are
6 been	16 going
7 had	17 to
8 happened	18 will
9 got / arrived	19 might / could / may
10 running	20 call / ring / text / email / contact

Present perfect questions and answers

1 walked round
2 'm meeting / am meeting
3 'll probably / will probably stay
4 've been / have been
5 's / is supposed to be

-ing / *-ed* adjectives

Answers
1 disappointed
2 scary; terrified
3 fascinating
4 moving
5 depressing; uplifting

Developing conversations

Answers
1 f
2 a
3 g
4 h
5 d
6 b
7 c
8 e

Collocations

Answers
1 e
2 g
3 f
4 b
5 j
6 c
7 i
8 a
9 d
10 h

Forming words

Answers
1 accommodation
2 response
3 loss
4 heat
5 entitlement

Language patterns

1 How much did that cost, if you don't mind me asking?
2 I'd rather not sit in the front row, if you don't mind.
3 We didn't expect to have such / so much difficulty finding the place.
4 I only brought a T-shirt as I expected that it would be warmer.
5 It depends on my dad whether I can go out or not.
6 It depends how much it costs.
7 She goes swimming every day – if she isn't busy / unless she's busy.
8 I never managed to win – not even once!

Vocabulary

Answers
1 beaten
2 lost
3 attempting
4 set
5 highlight
6 evidence
7 increases
8 linked
9 making

05 WORKING LIFE

UNIT OVERVIEW
The aims of this unit are to enable students to talk about **jobs, work places** and **activities** involved in certain jobs. The main **grammatical focus** is ***must be*** + **adjective** as used in **sympathetic responses,** ***have to / don't have to*** to talk about **rules** and ***be / get used to*** for talking about **habits** and **routines**.

VOCABULARY Jobs

Aim
To lead into the unit and revise / extend vocabulary related to jobs.

Step 1 Start by asking students what jobs they have / have done / would like to do. Ask students to look at the pictures and label the jobs they can see. Elicit the first example with them. They could do this in pairs or individually, then check in pairs. Check with the whole group. Drill for pronunciation. Concept check the words in the box.

Answers

estate agent	labourer
security guard	electrician
plumber	surgeon

Step 2 Tell students to look at the sentences and work out the meanings of the words in bold from the context. Do the first example with them. Check in pairs then with the whole group. Drill for pronunciation and check the concepts. You could also ask about opposites in some cases.

Tip In a multilingual class, or if you don't want students to translate, get them to try to define the words or give an example.

Answers
- competitive = lots of people want it / try to get it
- well-paid = it has a good salary
- rewarding = makes you feel you are doing something worthwhile or useful
- insecure = could suddenly come to an end
- responsibility = duty to take charge or deal with something
- creative = having the ability to invent original or new ideas
- stressful = causing stress or anxiety
- physically demanding = requiring a lot of physical energy or strength
- varied = having a lot of different aspects
- paperwork = documents, reports and forms that need completing

Step 3 Give students a chance to read the questions in C and think about how they would answer them. Put the students in groups of four or five – in a multilingual group, make sure you have a mix of nationalities – and ask them to discuss the questions. Monitor closely and note down any errors in the target vocabulary. Conduct a brief correction slot at the end.

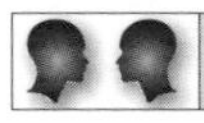
5A see Teacher's notes p. 122.

LISTENING

Aim
To give practice in listening for specific information and specific language.

Step 1 Tell students they are going to hear a conversation between Ivan and Amanda about jobs. Give them a few seconds to read the questions and tell them to note down the answers as they listen. Check in pairs then check with the whole group.

Alternatively As the questions are quite detailed, you could set a gist question first and play the recording once for students to answer it, e.g. *how do the two speakers feel about their present occupations?* (Amanda likes it but it can be boring and stressful, Ivan feels his future will be more secure.)

Answers
1 Amanda works as a graphic designer for a mobile phone company, Ivan is a student
2 Ivan worked for a law firm before, Amanda worked for a company that designed websites
3 Ivan wants to be a civil servant (as it's a job for life)
4 Amanda is 33, Ivan 30

5.1

I = Ivan, A = Amanda

I: So what do you do, Amanda?
A: I work for a mobile phone company.
I: Oh yeah. Doing what?
A: I work in the design department. I'm involved in designing what you see on the screen of the phone. You know, all the graphics and icons.
I: Oh right. Sounds interesting. How did you get into that?
A: Well I studied graphic design. After I graduated, I worked for a company that designed websites. Then one day I saw Vodafone were recruiting people so I applied and I got a job. They gave me some training and I just got into it that way.
I: So how long have you been working there?
A: It must be seven years now. Wait! No, eight! I was 25 when I joined. Time goes so fast!
I: You must enjoy it.
A: Yeah, I do generally. It's quite varied because they're constantly changing the phones and designs, and of course it's quite a creative job, which is nice. But, you know, it's like any job. It has its boring moments and the hours can be quite long.
I: Really? How long?
A: Well, it depends if we have a deadline to meet, but sometimes I do something like fifty or sixty hours a week.
I: Really? That must be stressful.
A: Yeah, it can be, but you get used to it. In fact, I sometimes need that stress to work well, you know. I sometimes work better under pressure.
I: Really? I can't work like that.
A: So what do you do?
I: Oh, nothing! At the moment, I'm just studying.
A: Really? How old did you say you are?
I: Thirty.
A: Really? You look younger.
I: Thanks.
A: So were you working before?
I: Kind of. I worked in a law firm two years ago, but it was really insecure. They said I would get a permanent contract, but then it never happened and it was really badly paid. I got almost nothing.
A: That's terrible!
I: Yeah, but you know, it happens quite a lot. Anyway, now I'm preparing for government exams, so I can get a civil service job. It's much more secure. It's almost a job for life.

Step 2 Ask students to look at the sentences and try to guess the correct word from memory or prior knowledge. Play the recording again for them to check. Elicit the answers.

Answers

1 in	3 applied	5 meet	7 stressful
2 get into	4 moments	6 something	8 under

Step 3 Give students a few seconds to read the questions and think about them. Check *a job for life*. Put them in pairs / threes to discuss the questions.

Language patterns

Aim

To draw students' attention to the way we often use *which* to refer back to a whole clause, especially when we are adding a comment about something.

Step 1

Ask students to read the examples in the box and check they understand. Ask them to translate into their own language and notice any differences. Alternatively, if you prefer not to use translation, ask checking questions e.g. what does *which* refer to here? (The previous clause or the whole idea.) You could drill this by giving prompts for them to complete with *which*, e.g. I went to Paris at the weekend, I often see my niece these days, I don't work on Fridays, etc.

Vocabulary Workplaces and activities

Aim

To extend the topic with work-related vocabulary.

Step 1

Draw students' attention back to the pictures. Ask questions about the pictures e.g. Which one works in a hospital? (Picture 6 – surgeon.) Who deals with property? (Picture 1 – estate agent.) Which one is responsible for maintenance / making sure things are in good condition? (Picture 4 – engineer) etc. Ask students to match a sentences 1–5 with sentences a–e. Do the first example with them. Check in pairs, then check with the whole group. Check the vocabulary for pronunciation and concept: *warehouse, marketing, accounts department, human resources, campaigns, recruitment, rep, admin.*

Answers

1 c	2 e	3 d	4 b	5a

Native speaker English

Ask students to read the box and check they understand before they go on to B.

Step 2 Model the conversation in B with a strong student, then continue in open pairs. Put students in pairs to practise similar conversations. Students without jobs should invent something.

DEVELOPING CONVERSATIONS

That must be . . .

Aim

To introduce a common use of *must* + base form to give a sympathetic response.

Step 1 Ask students to look back at sentences 6 and 7 in *Listening* exercise B. Ask them what kind of response this is (sympathetic) and what *must* means here (I'm sure it is). Ask students to read the box and check they understand. Ask students to respond using further examples of *that must be + adjective* by giving prompts, e.g. I work really long hours, I have 12 weeks holiday, I'm on my own in the office, etc.

Step 2 Start off exercise A in open pairs, then get students to continue in closed pairs. Monitor closely and correct any mistakes you hear.

Step 3 Tell students they are going to listen to six short conversations. They should write down the three responses to the examples with *that must be*.... Check in pairs, then check with the whole group.

Answers
It can be (yes / but . . .)
Not really
Yeah, it is

5.2

1
A: I'm the sales manager for Europe. I'm in charge of thirty reps.
B: That must be quite stressful.
A: It can be, but I like the responsibility and my own manager is quite supportive if there are any big problems.

2
C: I travel a lot round Europe and the Middle East.
D: That must be really interesting.
C: Not really. A lot of the time all you see is the hotel. You get fed up with it quite quickly.

3
E: I care for people who are dying.
F: That must be quite upsetting.
E: It can be, yes. Er... but when you work as a nurse you have to get used to working in emotional situations.

4
G: Basically, I just sit in front of a TV screen all day.
H: Yeah? That must be quite boring.
G: It can be, but I read quite a lot, which is good.

5
I: I often can't explain myself clearly in English.
J: That must be really frustrating.
I: Yeah, it is. I often get quite annoyed with myself.

6
K: I really see the kids develop and improve.
L: That must be really rewarding.
K: Yeah, it is. I wouldn't do any other job.

Step 4 Put students in pairs to practise the conversations. Monitor closely and correct any mistakes you hear in target language.

Alternatively If you think Step 4 is too hard, ask students to read the audioscript on p. 164 first and try to memorise the conversations. Then put them in pairs to practise.

CONVERSATION PRACTICE

Aim

To give further practice of language about jobs and to end the lesson on a fun note.

Step 1 Model the activity by describing one of the jobs in the lesson in great detail. Ask students to try to guess it. If they are not sure, they could ask yes / no questions.

Step 2 Put students in pairs and tell them to take turns to choose a job from the lesson (preferably) or a different job and describe it, using some of the language they have practised. Their partner should guess the job. Then they swap. Monitor closely and note down any errors you hear in the target language. Conduct an error correction slot at the end.

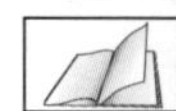

pp. 38–39

Next class Make photocopies of **5B** p. 137.

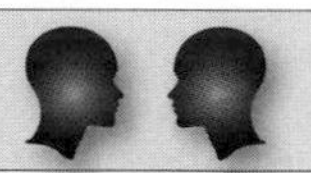

GRAMMAR *Have to, don't have to, can*

Aim

To revise and practise *have to / don't have to* and *can* to talk about rules in the work place.

Step 1 Lead in to the lesson by eliciting from students some examples of things they *have to / don't have to do* and *can do* at work / university / school. Ask them to read the sentences in exercise A and check any vocabulary they aren't sure about e.g. *supportive* = helpful and understanding. Do the first example with them, then ask them to complete the exercise. Check in pairs, then check with the whole group. Drill the correct answers.

Tip Check students know the negative of *have to* is *don't have to*, not *haven't to*.

Answers
1 have to
2 don't have to
3 can
4 have to
5 can
6 don't have to
7 have to
8 can
9 have to

Step 2 Ask students to read the box and check they understand. Tell them to read the grammar reference on p. 144 if they are still unsure. Ask them to go back to exercise A and tick the sentences which are true for them. Then think of three more sentences that are true for them, if possible one with *have to*, one with *don't have to* and one with *can*. Put them in pairs / threes to discuss their examples. Try to get them to develop conversations, with responses and follow-up questions. Monitor closely and correct mistakes in target language.

Step 3 Draw students' attention to the pictures. Elicit the names of the jobs, model and drill.

Answers

1 lifeguard
2 optician
3 vet
4 farmer
5 tour guide
6 firefighter

Elicit a few examples about picture 1 to model the next activity, e.g. – *If you are a lifeguard you have to be a good swimmer. You don't have to work in an office. You can sometimes choose your own hours,* etc. Put students in new pairs / threes to talk about the jobs. Monitor closely and make notes on errors in the target language for a correction slot at the end.

LISTENING

Aim

To extend the topic, hear the target language in context and focus on some lexical phrases or chunks associated with the work place.

Step 1 Ask students to look at the sentences in A. Check the vocabulary e.g. *a hard hat* = a helmet worn for protection, especially on a building site, *surf the web* = look for information on the Internet. Put them in pairs to briefly discuss the questions.

Step 2 Tell students they are going to hear three conversations about the workplace. They should listen and identify which rule from A is being talked about in each conversation. Check in pairs, then check with the whole class.

5.3

Conversation 1

D = Dom, L = Laura

D: Did you hear about Patrick?
L: No. What?
D: Apparently, he's been reprimanded.
L: You're joking! What for?
D: He was going on the Internet all the time to buy concert tickets and book holidays. And he was always sending personal emails.
L: No! But everyone does that, don't they?
D: Yeah, well, you're not supposed to use the company computers like that. Not in his company, anyway.
L: That's a bit unfair, isn't it?
D: I know. Actually, I think the problem was that he visited some site and got a computer virus and then it infected the whole system. Apparently, the company have had to spend over £20,000 to sort out the problem.
L: Oh right. I can see why they might be a bit angry then!

Conversation 2

F = Francesca, J = Jade

F: Are you thinking of buying that?
J: Yeah, what do you think?
F: Very smart. I don't usually see you wearing stuff like that.
J: No, I know, but I've got this new job working in a law firm.
F: Oh really? That's great news! What are you going to be doing there?
J: Just admin work really, but they have a strict dress code – you're not even allowed to wear smart trousers. You have to wear skirts!
F: You're joking! Is that legal?
J: I guess. They can do what they want, can't they?
F: You think?
J: Well, anyway, I need the job, and I've been looking for ages so I'm not going to complain!

Conversation 3

A = Adam, B = Bill

A: Bill, sorry to interrupt, but can I have a quick word?
B: Yes, of course. What's up?
A: Listen, I need to take the day off on Friday. My son's performing in a school concert.
B: Friday? I'm afraid that's impossible.
A: Are you sure?
B: Sorry, Adam. It wouldn't be a problem normally, but we've got a bit of a crisis. Vicky's off sick and we really need to complete this order by Saturday.
A: Can't someone else help? My son will be so disappointed if I don't watch him play. And I do have some holiday left for this year.
B: I'm sure. But if we're late with this order, we might lose the whole contract.
A: I see.
B: You should really arrange time off with me a month in advance, you know.
A: I know, I know. It's just I've asked you at short notice before and it hasn't been a problem.
B: Well, as I say, normally it isn't.
A: Well, I guess that's all. I don't know what I'll tell my son.
B: I'm sorry. You'll be really helping me and the company.

Answers

1 7 2 1 3 3

Step 3 Put students in pairs. Ask them to match the words used in each conversation from the bubbles, as they remember them from the recording. Do the first example with them. Then play the recording again for them to check. Check with the whole group.

Answers
send personal emails
get a computer virus
infect the whole system
work in a law firm
have a strict dress code
wear smart trousers
have a quick word
perform in a school concert
ask at short notice

Alternatively If you think this is too hard for students, they could try matching items in box two and box three first, then add items from box one, or let them read the audiocript on p. 164 and underline the phrases.

Step 4 Give students a few minutes to think about how they feel about each of the rules. Then put students in small groups to discuss the rules. They could talk about all the rules in A rather than just those in B if you want to extend the speaking practice.

GRAMMAR Talking about rules

Aim
To introduce *be allowed to, be supposed to, should really* + base form to talk about rules.

Step 1 Go back to sentence 8 in exercise A on p. 38. Ask students if they know another way of saying this (I am usually allowed to take time off if I need to). Ask them to read the box and check they understand. Get them to read the grammar reference on p. 144 if they seem unsure. Check the concept of *be allowed to* = it is possible to / have permission to and *be supposed to / should really* = have to (but not quite as strong) – especially used when rules have been broken.

Step 2 Ask students to choose the correct answer to complete the sentences. Do the first example with them. They could do this in pairs or individually, then check in pairs. Check with the whole group.

Answers
1 You're not allowed to
2 I'm supposed to
3 I have to / I'm allowed to
4 supposed to
5 We are allowed to
6 shouldn't really
7 I should really
8 You're not really supposed to

Step 3 Ask students to look at the pictures and decide which rules are being broken. Elicit possible answers with *not supposed to / shouldn't really / not allowed to.*

Answers
- You're not allowed to carry a knife / anything sharp / liquid in your hand luggage. You're not allowed to bring in / smuggle in anything illegal.
- You shouldn't really / you're not supposed to lie on the grass / to take your dog on the grass.
- You're not allowed to come in wearing trainers. You should really wear smart clothes.

Step 4 Give students a few minutes to think about the questions, put them in small groups to discuss them. Monitor closely and note down errors in the target language for a correction slot at the end.

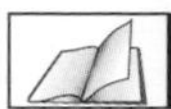
pp. 41–42

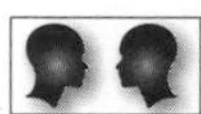
5B see Teacher's notes p. 122.

READING

Aim
To develop the skills of predicting, reading for gist and detail and responding to text.

Step 1 Lead in by eliciting examples of terrible jobs students have done or heard about. Why were they terrible? Ask students to read the opening quickly and answer the questions. Check in pairs, then with the whole group. Don't tell students the answer to question 2 – tell them they will find the answer by reading.

Tip Elicit from students which word is omitted in the title / headline (are). Ask them what kinds of words are often omitted in headlines and why (articles, auxiliaries – to make headlines shorter / punchier). Give another example, e.g. *Queen in hospital* – the Queen is in hospital. *Famous rock star missing since yesterday* – a famous rock star has been missing since yesterday.

Answers
1 The author wrote the article because of a television programme starting about terrible jobs in the 19th century.
2 The rest of the article gives examples and details of terrible jobs in the present.

Step 2 Put students in pairs to discuss the examples in B. Check they understand the vocabulary e.g. *dust* = small particles of dirt, *disease* = serious illness, *bend over* = move top part of the body forwards, *abuse* = cruel or violent treatment.

See if students can match with jobs that have come up earlier in the unit, e.g. labourer with 4, 6, 8 (and possibly 7).

Step 3 Ask students to read the rest of the article and decide which jobs go with which example in B. Make sure they understand there may be more than one possibility each time. Tell them not to worry about the phrases in bold for the time being.

Answers
Human guinea pigs 2, 3
Embalmers 4, 6, 8
Call centre workers 5, 7 and possibly 4 – though this is not explicitly stated
Recycling plant worker 1, 3

Check students understand the jobs by asking concept questions. Check *plant* in *recycling plant worker* = industrial site.

Step 4 Put students in new pairs or threes to discuss the questions. Check with the whole group.

Answers
- Human guinea pigs – can be quick and easy way of making money, helping science
- Embalmers – rewarding, families are grateful
- Call centre workers – good money, hard to find jobs in Mumbai
- Recycling plant worker – likes colleagues, has a laugh

Step 5 Ask students to complete the sentences with a suitable word from the article, without looking at it. Check by getting students to refer to the bold phrases in the article and point out that only one word from each phrase is needed for the answers. Do this in pairs, then check with the whole group.

Answers

1 get	5 grateful
2 cramped	6 wage
3 way	7 effects
4 slammed	8 average

Step 6 Ask students individually to rank the jobs in order of preference and to think about their reasons.
Put them in groups of three / four to discuss their decisions.

VOCABULARY *Be used to, get used to*

Aim
To introduce / revise and contrast two ways of talking about habit.

Step 1 Put the two sentences in the box on the board. Elicit the difference between *be used to* and *get used to* (*be used to* = something has become normal for me, *get used to* = be in the process of adapting to something new except, *I've got used to it* = I am used to it). Draw students' attention to form *be / get used to* + noun / pronoun or *-ing* form. Elicit a few examples from students. Let them read the box to consolidate. Ask them to look at the article and find one example of each.

Answers
I'm even used to the smell now (embalmer)
I even got used to being dirty all the time (recycling plant worker)

Step 2 Ask students to put the phrases in order to complete the sentences. Do the first example with them. Check in pairs, then check with the whole group.

Answers
1 I'm used to it
2 I'm slowly getting used to it / getting used to it slowly
3 I'll just have to get used to it
4 took me a while to get used to it
5 I'm totally used to it now
6 I don't think I'll ever get used to

Step 3 Ask students to underline the expressions with *be / get used* to in the sentences and to translate them into their own language. Is the language structure similar or very different? Alternatively, if you don't want students to translate, ask them to paraphrase the expressions instead, e.g. *I'm used to it* = It's normal for me.

Step 4 Put students in pairs and ask them to practise the conversations. They should take turns to be A and B.

SPEAKING

Aim
To give freer practice of *be / get used to.*

Step 1 Introduce the context. Tell students to imagine they have a new job in Britain or America. Ask them to work individually and invent a profile. Check students understand the questions in A. They could use them to help them think about what they are going to say.

Step 2 Put the students in new pairs to discuss the questions. They should make this a natural conversation rather than 'question and answer', but they should try to use at least two examples with *be / get used to*. Monitor closely and note down errors, especially in the use of *be / get used to*. Conduct a brief correction slot at the end.

06 GOING SHOPPING

UNIT OVERVIEW
The main aims of this unit are to revise / consolidate vocabulary related to **shopping** and **things you buy**, including **clothes** and **mobile phones** and to talk about ways of **comparing products**. Students also practise **describing souvenirs and presents**. The main grammatical aim is revision and extension of ***must*** to talk about both **deductions, strong recommendations** and **obligation**.

VOCABULARY

Describing souvenirs and presents

Aim
To introduce three different kinds of adjectives used to describe things, especially souvenirs and presents.

Step 1 Lead in to the topic by asking students to describe a memorable souvenir they bought or a present they received. This could be something wonderful, strange or awful. You could model this first by telling them about something of yours. Check *souvenir* = something you buy on holiday, usually to remember the place by or to give to other people. Similar to *memento*.

Step 2 Ask students to classify the adjectives in three groups: 1 opinion, 2 how things are produced, 3 material. They could do this in pairs or individually then check in pairs. Check with the whole group, model, drill and ask concept questions.

Answers

Opinion	how things are produced	material
Beautiful	hand-made	clay
Lovely	hand-printed	leather
Gorgeous	hand-painted	silk
Horrible	machine-woven	wooden
Cute	carved	plastic
Tacky		

Tip Note that the table shows the usual order of adjectives. Stronger students could also be encouraged to add colour adjectives, which would normally come after opinion, when describing the pictures.

Step 3 Put students in pairs / threes and ask them to describe the things they can see in the pictures using some of the words. Conduct brief feedback, paying special attention to adjective order and pronunciation.

Step 4 Ask students to complete the sentences using the correct phrase from the box. Check in pairs then check with the whole group.

Answers
1 beautiful hand-printed silk
2 tacky plastic
3 nice clay
4 really cute
5 lovely hand-painted
6 lovely silver
7 traditional hand-carved
8 little hand-woven

Step 5 Ask students to think about three souvenirs they have bought or been given and how to describe them. They could make a few notes.

Step 6 Put students in new pairs / threes and ask them to describe souvenirs they have bought or been given. Monitor and correct any mistakes in the target vocabulary.

LISTENING

Aim
To hear some of the target vocabulary in context and to develop the skills of predicting and listening for specific information. To lead in to further, fun practice.

Note in some countries and situations it is customary to bargain or haggle (negotiate) over prices, e.g. Turkey, the Middle East, India, street markets, flea markets. In others, it is not, e.g. supermarkets, department stores.

Step 1 Put students in pairs / threes and ask them to talk about the questions. Don't conduct any feedback on this.

Step 2 Ask students to listen to the recording and note down the reasons the tourist gives and the reasons the seller gives. Play the recording.

6.1

A: Do you like it? OK.
B: Yeah, it's nice. How much is it?
A: Five hundred.
B: Five hundred! That's really expensive.
A: It's very good quality. Feel it.
B: Yeah, I know.
A: Real silk and it's hand-woven. You see here, it's a bit uneven, whereas this one, it's machine-woven, so it's all the same.
B: Uh huh.
A: This one, the colour, it'll last longer.
B: Sure. It's nice. But five hundred?
A: How much do you want to pay?
B Well, I was thinking one hundred dollars.
A: One hundred! Come on!
B: OK, one fifty.
A: You're insulting me. I won't make any money like that. Listen, I'll give it to you for four hundred.
B: Two. I've seen similar ones for that price.
A: Similar, but not as good. Go then! Go and buy it. You're wasting my time... OK. I tell you what, I'll give you it for three fifty.
B: Three hundred. I don't have much money left.
A: No. Three hundred and fifty. Final offer. Take it or leave it. Three fifty. I'm giving it away. I have children. Look, feel it. It's beautiful.
B: It is nice ... OK three fifty.
A: Three fifty. You are a difficult man. It's a very good price, eh. My wife, she'll kill me! You want anything else? Very nice plates, hand-painted...

Answers

- Tourist – expensive, has seen similar ones for less money, hasn't got much money left
- Seller – good quality, real silk / hand-woven, it will last, he won't make any money, he has children, his wife will kill him

PRONUNCIATION Intonation

Aim
To draw students' attention to the use of intonation used when negotiating prices.

Step 1 Try to elicit how the speakers in *Listening* sound when they want to express surprise. Try to get the idea of a rise and a wider voice range to express suprise or a fall and a narrower voice range to make an alternative offer, or to agree. Illustrate by modelling contrasting examples from the recording e.g. *five hundred*! versus *OK, one fifty*. You could take another example from the audioscript and write it on the board. Elicit / show how to mark with arrows in preparation for Step 2.

Step 2 Ask students to read the audioscript p. 164 while they listen to the conversation again and notice where the numbers rise and fall. They could mark these with arrows going up or down. Check some of their answers.

Step 3 Ask students to work in pairs and practise the conversation. Monitor closely and correct their pronunciation, especially the intonation.

Step 4 Put students in new pairs, A and B. A should choose an item from one of the pictures and ask the price. They then have a similar conversation to the one on the recording, paying particular attention to the intonation. They could then swap roles. You could ask a few pairs to act out their conversation in front of the class. If you do decide to do this, give the others a 'reason to listen' each time, e.g. ask them to listen for the item and the prices in each case.

DEVELOPING CONVERSATIONS

Avoiding repetition

Aim
To introduce a way of avoiding repetition using *this / that one, these / those ones.*

Step 1 Put students in pairs. Ask them to get out their mobile phones and describe them to their partners. They should say how long they've had it, what special features it has, why they chose it and why they like / don't like it.

Step 2 Ask students in pairs to match a sentence beginning 1–6 with a sentence ending a–f. Do the first example with them (1 c). Focus on *one/s* at this point as well as *whereas*. Check they understand *whereas* – demonstrate with objects in the room, e.g. *this pen is green whereas that one is black.* Don't pre-teach the other vocabulary – tell students to try to work it out together. Check vocabulary, *megabytes, lithium battery, nickel cadmium battery, store, MP3 player,* by asking students about their mobile phones.

Answers

1 c	2 b	3 a	4 f	5 e	6 d

Step 3 In the same pairs as before students compare their mobile phones using *whereas*. Join two pairs together for further practice in groups. Monitor and correct any mistakes in target language.

LISTENING

Aim
To practise listening for specific information.

Step 1 Tell students they are going to hear a conversation in a mobile phone shop. They should listen and complete the table.

6.2
A: Can I help you?
B: Yeah, I'm thinking of changing phone companies.
A: Who are you with at the moment?
B: Blue, but I'm looking to see if there are any better deals around.
A: I'm sure we can find you something. What phone have you got now?
B: This one, but they've offered to upgrade it to the S620.
A: OK, that's a nice phone. And what are your monthly payments?
B: £20 a month.
A: OK, well, I think we could offer you something better. For example, this one – the N5703.
B: All right. What's the difference? They look pretty similar.
A: Well, with this one, the N5703, you get greater functionality, like email, and on the whole it's much better quality. For example, this has a lithium battery, whereas the other phone uses a nickel cadmium one, which isn't as good. The lithium one lasts a lot longer.
B: Oh, OK.
A: And then the camera is almost twice as powerful. So this one is 3 mega-pixel and it has a digital zoom, whereas the one on the S620 is just 1.7.
B: Right. And how many pictures can the N5703 store?
A: Well, on the phone itself, not that many, but it comes with a memory card which stores up to 700 photos and 250 songs, whereas the S620 doesn't have a memory card – I guess because there's no MP3 – so you can only store about 15 photos.
B: OK, so this one has an MP3 player as well.
A: Yes, of course.
B: I'm sure the sound quality isn't as good as my normal MP3 player, though.
A: Maybe not, but it is good quality. I use my phone all the time now to listen to music. It's maybe slightly worse than your MP3, but it's a lot more convenient. I mean, you've got everything in one package. You don't really want to carry round a separate phone, MP3 and camera all the time, do you?
B: No, I suppose not. What about calls and text messages? How many can you offer me?
A: Well, for £20 a month we could give you 150 free minutes and 100 texts.
B: 150! That's quite a lot less than Blue are offering me.
A: Well, I'm not sure we can give much more for that phone. What do you get with them?
B: 200 free minutes and 150 texts.
A: OK. Well, we could probably match that and still give you the better phone.

Answers

Features	N5703	S620
Kind of battery?	Lithium	Nickel cadmium
Camera (mega-pixels)?	Yes-3	Yes-1.7
Comes with memory card?	Yes	No
Comes with MP3?	Yes	No
Minutes: free calls?	150	200
Number of free text messages?	100	150

Step 2 Ask students to check in pairs, then check with the whole group.

Step 3 Ask the whole group the question in B.

Step 4 Ask students to read the sentences and correct the information in italics. Then play the recording again for them to check. They could read the audioscript on pp. 164–165 at the same time, or with a stronger group, they could listen first, then use the audioscript to check their answers.

Answers
1 The N5705 is much better quality.
2 The lithium battery lasts a lot longer than the other one.
3 The camera on the N5705 is almost twice as powerful.
4 With the memory card the N5705 stores far more photos than the S620.
5 The sound quality of the MP3 is slightly worse than on a normal player.

CONVERSATION PRACTICE

Aim
To practise some of the language used in *Listening*.

Step 1 Tell students they are going to role play a similar conversation to the one they heard on the recording. Ask students to read the audioscript on pp. 164–165 and underline any useful expressions they might use. Tell them to check any pronunciation they are not sure about with you.

Step 2 Divide students into A / B pairs. Tell As to read File 2 on p. 156 and Bs to read File 8 on p. 158. When they are ready, they should act out the conversation. Monitor closely and note down errors in target language for a correction slot at the end.

pp. 44–45

Next class Make photocopies of **6A** p. 138.

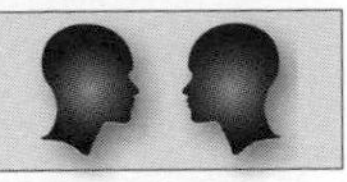

VOCABULARY Clothes and accessories

Aim

To consolidate and give practice in vocabulary related to clothes and accessories.

Step 1 Lead in by asking students what other students are wearing today, what kind of clothes and accessories they like, etc. Check they understand the difference between clothes – something you *wear* – and *accessories* – something you *carry* (apart from *jewellery,* which are *accessories* which you *wear*). We also use *wear* for glasses and belts. Elicit some examples of *clothes*: trousers, shirt, shoes and *accessories*: handbag, shoulder bag, belt, bracelet, chain, etc.

Step 2 Ask students to decide which the odd one out is. Check they understand *odd one out* by demonstrating e.g. apple, orange, potato, banana. Potato is the odd one out because it's different from the others – it's a vegetable. Green, blue, big, red. Big is the odd one out because it isn't a colour. Check the vocabulary in the exercise and model and drill e.g. *earrings, bracelet, tracksuit bottoms, high heels, sandals, woolly hat, thick jumper, scruffy, trendy, stripy, tight, checked.* Ask them to check in pairs and justify their choices, then check with the whole group, eliciting their reasons.

Answers
1 belt – the others are all jewellery
2 skirt – the others are all tops
3 earrings – the others are all clothes
4 socks – the others are all footwear (socks go under them)
5 T-shirt – the others are all things you wear when it's cold
6 scruffy – the others are all positive
7 tight – this is about fit but the others are all about pattern, colour or design

Step 3 Check, model and drill the expressions in italics. *Fit* = to be the right size, *suit* = to look good on someone, *match / go with* = to be of the same material or to look good together. Practise with some examples from the class.

Put students in pairs and ask them to talk about the people in the pictures. Elicit a few examples from them at the end.

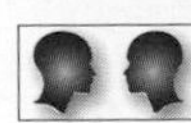

6A see Teacher's notes p. 122.

READING

Aim

To put the vocabulary into context and to give practice in finding out the meanings of new words / phrases, reading for detail and speaking.

Step 1 Divide the class into two equal groups – As and Bs. These groups could then be sub-divided into fours or twos. Ask them to look at their list of words / phrases and help each other with the meanings. If no one knows – or if they want to check – tell them to check in the *Vocabulary builder*. Monitor closely and check they have the correct meaning and pronunciation – but don't help them too much with meaning, as this task is about peer teaching (getting students to explain things to each other).

Step 2 Put students into A / B pairs. Tell them to read through the questionnaire together, asking each other the questions and helping each other with any words or phrases they do not know. They should circle the best answer for themselves.

Step 3 Ask students to look at File 4 on p. 157 and work out their scores. Tell them to read the appropriate description and discuss with their partner whether they think it is true and why / why not. Conduct brief feedback with the whole class.

LANGUAGE PATTERNS

Aim

To draw students' attention to the pattern *it's not worth* + noun / -ing form.

Step 1 Ask students to look at the sentences in the box and translate them into their language. What similarities / differences do they notice? Alternatively, if you prefer not to use translation, start with a simple example, e.g. *how much do you think my watch / ring is worth?* = *What is its value*? Elicit a few more examples. Ask students to look at the box and find one example where *worth* relates to money (the last one). Then notice the way *not worth* is used in the other examples. Check they understand it means *it is a waste of time.*

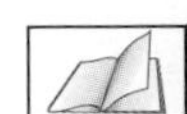

pp. 46–47

Next class Make photocopies of **6B** p. 139.

LISTENING

Aim
To extend the topic and to give practice in listening for specific information.

Step 1 Ask students what is happening in the pictures. Elicit *rock concert / gig*. Ask where you buy tickets for these events (at the box office, over the phone, on the Internet). Put students in pairs / threes to discuss the questions. Conduct very brief feedback and check *venue* = the place where a concert is on, *online auction* = website where people buy and sell things – usually the person who makes the highest bid wins, e.g. eBay, *ticket tout* = someone who buys lots of tickets for a concert or sports event then sells them at a profit, often outside the venue.

Step 2 Tell students they are going to hear a conversation between Leo and Noel about buying concert tickets. Give them time to read the questions and check any vocabulary they are not sure about e.g. *sold out* = there are no tickets left, the concert is fully booked. Ask them to listen and note down the answers.

6.3
L = Leo, N = Noel
L: Hey Noel, can you remind me later? I must try and book some tickets for a gig next week.
N: Yeah, of course – assuming I remember myself, that is! Who are you thinking of seeing?
L: Oh, it's a German group called *The Brain Police*. I don't know if you know them.
N: Yeah, of course I do! They're great. I've been into them for ages. I've already got tickets for the gig next week, as it happens.
L: Oh really? How much did you pay for them?
N: Twenty each, but I'm pretty sure they've sold out now.
L: What? But they've only been on sale for a day.
N: Yeah, but you know what it's like, Leo. Things sell out so quickly. I had to queue for an hour to get mine.
L: Oh no! I was going to take my girlfriend as a birthday present! She would've loved it. She's a huge fan. I don't suppose you want to sell yours, do you?
N: No chance! Nice try, though. Why don't you look online? You must be able to get tickets somewhere. Try looking at one of the auction sites – like eBay or something.
L: Yeah, but things cost a fortune on there.
N: Well, not necessarily, and anyway what other options have you got?
L: No, I guess you're right.
N: And if you really can't find anything on the Internet, then I suppose you could go down to the venue next week. Hang around outside for a while and try and buy tickets from someone. There are sometimes people outside selling spare tickets they've bought.
L: What? You mean buy them from a ticket tout? Isn't that a bit risky? I mean, I don't want to buy a ticket and then not get in because it's a fake or something.
N: Well it's up to you. I'll tell you what, though, if you like *The Brain Police*, you must go and see *Spook Train*. They're brilliant and they're playing next week. I'm sure you'd be able to get tickets for them. Maybe you'd be better just trying that instead.

Answers
1 *The Brain Police*
2 Yes
3 Because they've only been on sale for a day.
4 Because he wants to take his girlfriend, who is a big fan.
5 Try an online auction e.g. eBay or a ticket tout outside the venue.
6 Negatively: the online auction tickets may be expensive and the tout's tickets may be fake.

Step 3 Give students time to read the questions and think about their answers. Then put them in pairs and ask them to discuss the questions.

GRAMMAR *must*

Aim
To revise different uses of *must*.

Step 1 Ask students to look at the sentences in the box. Use these examples to check the concept i.e. which example goes with which description in A? Get students to give their own examples too. Ask students if they remember how *must* was used in Unit 05 (*That must be* + adj) and which rule that use goes with (1).

Answers
1 b 2 c 3 a

Alternatively You could make an explicit link between *Listening* and *Grammar* by asking students to look at the audioscript on p. 165 and underline the examples with *must*. Then do Step 1.

Step 2 Ask students to match the uses – or meanings – in A with an example in B. Do the first example with them. They could do this in pairs or individually and then check in pairs.

Answers		
1 b, d, f	2 a, g, h	3 c, e, i

Step 3 Ask students to complete the sentences with *must* or *mustn't*. They could do this in pairs or individually and then check in pairs.

Answers	
1 must	6 must
2 must	7 mustn't
3 mustn't	8 mustn't
4 mustn't	9 must
5 must	10 mustn't

Step 4 Ask students to work on their own and make a list of the items in E. Then put them in pairs to discuss their ideas. Tell them to try and develop conversations by asking why, etc.

Step 5 Ask students to look at the pictures. Model the conversation with a strong student, using the first picture as an example. Put them in pairs to have similar conversations. Remind them to use *must* and to explain their guesses.

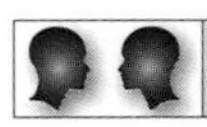

6B see Teacher's notes p. 122.

Native speaker English

Step 1 Ask students to look back at the examples with *want* used as a recommendation. Elicit these: *You don't want to do that, he doesn't want to miss the plane*. Read out the box and check they understand. Point out that this is a very informal way of making recommendations. Check students remember (from Unit 03) *ripped off* = overcharged / robbed (colloquial).

Developing conversations

Responding to recommendations

Aim
To show students ways of offering alternative suggestions and to give practice.

Step 1 Ask students to read the conversation in the introduction and check they understand it.

Step 2 Look at A and make sure students understand that there are two conversations with three speakers in each. They should read the conversations and number the lines in the correct order. Ask students to find the expression in Conversation 2 that is similar in meaning to *You don't want to do that* (I wouldn't do that). They could do this in threes then practise the conversations when they've checked.

Answers

Conversation 1

A I'm thinking of trying to get tickets for the match tonight.
B It's totally sold out. You've got no chance. I guess you could go and hang around outside the stadium and buy them from a ticket tout.
C You don't want to do that. It's illegal. You might get arrested. I'd try the Internet instead.
A No, it's too late for that. They won't be able to deliver the tickets in time.

Conversation 2

A I want to get a present for my girlfriend before I go back.
B Just get something at the airport in Duty Free.
C No, I wouldn't do that! It's more expensive. You'd be better getting something in town.
B There isn't time! He doesn't want to miss the plane!
A It's OK. My flight's not till three. I think I've got time. Where's the best place to go?

Step 2 Put students in threes to read the conversations aloud.

Speaking

Aim
To give further practice in recommending and responding to recommendations.

Step 1 Read out the instructions. Demonstrate with two strong students. Put students in groups of three to act out the conversation. They could then swap roles and repeat the activity. Monitor closely and note down errors in target language for a brief correction slot at the end.

07 SCHOOL AND STUDYING

UNIT OVERVIEW
The main aims of this unit are to enable students to talk about **courses, schools, students and teachers**. They also have practice in **forming words** and **talking about future plans**. The main **grammatical focus is zero and first conditionals** and **adverbial time clauses** with ***when, once*** and ***after***.

SPEAKING

Aim
To lead in and to get students immediately involved.

Step 1 Tell students to look at the pictures and think about what the people are doing. In pairs ask students to discuss the questions in B. Check with the whole group and check / feed in vocabulary, e.g. *graduation ceremony* – the people in the main picture have just *graduated*. They are wearing *gowns* and *mortarboards* and holding their *degree certificates*. Picture two is a *judo class*. Picture three is a *diving* or *scuba diving lesson*. Picture four is a *childcare course*.

Step 2 Pre-teach / check the vocabulary in B, e.g. *a postgraduate course* = a course leading to a second or Master's degree (compared with *undergraduate* – studying for a first or Bachelor's degree), *a training course* = a course which prepares you for a profession, e.g. teacher training, *a first-aid course* = a course which teaches you to help people in emergencies or after accidents, *an online course* = a course where you study via the Internet, *an IT course* = a course which teaches you computer skills. In pairs ask students to discuss the questions about the courses in the box. Check a few of their ideas with the whole group.

VOCABULARY Describing courses

Aim
To present collocations used to talk about education.

Step 1 Ask students to add the correct noun from the box to the correct group of words. Do the first example with them. Point out that generally the nouns go after the words listed, but not always. They could do this in pairs, or individually and then check in pairs. Check with the whole group and model, drill and concept check.

Answers

a essay	d seminar	g deadline
b tutor(s)	e lecture	h modules
c exams	f workload	

Step 2 Ask students individually to think about a course they have done, or one of the courses discussed in *Speaking* exercise B and choose five of the collocations to describe it. Put students in pairs to tell each other about their courses. Monitor closely and correct any mistakes in the target vocabulary.

DEVELOPING CONVERSATIONS

How's the course going?

Aim
To focus on ways of answering questions about courses and to give practice.

Step 1 Ask students to look at the sentences. Explain to them that two of the words have swapped position. Ask them to either underline the two words or re-write the sentences in the correct order. Do the first example with them. They could do the exercise in pairs or individually and then check in pairs. Check with the whole group.

Answers
1 I've had a few ups and downs of course, but the tutors have been very helpful and supportive.
2 Quite well, actually. The lectures can be quite boring but the seminar work in groups is great.
3 OK, but I've got my final exams next week, so I'm having to do lots of revision at the moment.
4 OK, but I'm really busy. I have to hand in an essay next week – and if I miss the deadline I'll fail.
5 Actually I'm struggling at the moment. I just can't cope with the workload. It's really demanding.
6 To be honest, I'm finding it really difficult. The modules I'm doing this term are really hard!

Step 2 Put students in pairs. Ask them to take turns asking, *How's the course going?* and replying using answers from exercise A. Demonstrate with a strong student, then in open pairs, then continue in closed pairs. Monitor and help students with their pronunciation.

LISTENING

Aim

To hear the target vocabulary in a natural context and to give practice in listening for detail.

Step 1 Ask students to read the questions. Ask them what the conversation is about (a course). Tell them to listen and complete the questions as they listen. Check in pairs, then with the whole group.

Tip With stronger students, let them predict what goes in the gaps, then listen to check their answers.

7.1

D = Daniel, P = Paulina

D: So how's the course going? Are you enjoying it?

P: I am, yeah, but it's hard work. I have to go in to college almost every day for a lecture or a seminar or just to use the library, so I've been pretty busy lately.

D: Wow! It sounds quite demanding.

P: Yeah, it is, but it's also really interesting. The course is pretty flexible, so there's a wide range of different modules we can take, which is great. I've just started doing a module in Marketing Psychology, which is fascinating.

D: It sounds it. So what does that involve, then? I mean, what kind of things do you have to study?

P: Well, we have to look at different kinds of shoppers, the relationship between advertising and shopping, that kind of thing. It's brilliant.

D: Oh, that's great. I'm glad it's going well. And what are the other students like? Do you get on with them OK?

P: Yeah, they're mostly really nice and friendly.

D: Mostly?

P: Well, there are one or two guys that never really talk to anyone or help, but generally everyone's very supportive. I mean, we're all in the same situation, so ...

D: Sure. And what about the tutors? What are they like?

P: They're great. They're all so helpful and dedicated. I feel really lucky to have such knowledgeable people teaching me.

D: It sounds great. So how long does the course last? When do you finish?

P: Not for another few months yet. The final exams are next April. I've got plenty of work to do before then!

D: I bet! And what are you going to do once the course has finished? Have you decided yet?

P: Well, actually the first thing I'm going to do is take a long holiday. I think I deserve it.

D: Right. Where are you thinking of going?

P: Well, I'm going to fly to India and then travel through Asia to Australia. When I'm there, I might look for a job.

D: Doing what?

P: Oh I don't know. Bar work or something. Whatever I can get. And then after I get back from Australia, I'll just start looking for a proper job.

Answers

1 enjoying it	4 like
2 kind of things	5 do you finish
3 get on with	6 you decided

Step 2 Tell students to listen again and make notes in answer to each of the questions. Check in pairs, then check with the whole group.

Answers

1 It's hard work but she's enjoying it.
2 Different kinds of shoppers and the relationship between advertising and shopping.
3 Mostly really nice and friendly (one or two guys who never talk to anyone or help).
4 Great – helpful and dedicated.
5 In April.
6 Take a long holiday and go travelling in India, Asia and Australia.

LANGUAGE PATTERNS

Aim

To draw students' attention to an expression often used in responses.

Step 1 Ask students to look at the phrases in the box and notice what they have in common (I'm glad...) Ask them to translate them into their own language and notice any differences.

Alternatively If you prefer not to use translation, ask a few checking questions, e.g. What does this mean? (I'm happy or pleased (to hear / see) ... .) Note that *to hear / see* could be used in the first four sentences and *that* could be used in the last two. When do we use this? (When we want to give a positive or encouraging response to what someone has told us).

GRAMMAR *After, once* and *when*

Aim

To introduce / revise ways of talking about the future using *when, after, once* + present simple or present perfect.

Step 1 Put the three sentences on the board (to save time do this while the students are doing the previous exercise). Ask them questions about form and concept, e.g. Are we talking about the present or the future? (Future.) Which tense is used in the main clause? (*Going to* + base form, *might* + base form, *will* + base form.) Which tense is used in the time clause? (Present simple or present perfect.) How are these different? (The present perfect emphasises completion of the action or situation.) Ask students to read the box and check they understand. Direct them to the grammar reference on p. 146 if they are still unsure.

Step 2 Ask students to re-write the sentences, beginning with the word given. Check in pairs, then check with the whole group. Drill the responses.

Step 3 Ask students to look at the questions and think about what they might ask in various situations. Put them in pairs to practise asking and answering the questions. Monitor closely and correct any mistakes in target language, particularly tense use.

CONVERSATION PRACTICE

Aim
To give further practice and draw the lesson together.

Step 1 Ask students to think about another course they have done or an imaginary one. They should look back at the pairs of questions in *Listening* exercise A and make notes in response to them.

Step 2 Put students in new pairs to ask each other about their courses. Ask them to start each conversation with *How's the course going? Are you still enjoying it?* Monitor closely and note down any errors in target language for a brief correction slot at the end.

 **pp. 50–51**

SPEAKING

Aim
To lead in to the reading and personalise the topic.

Step 1 Ask students to read the short text quickly and answer the questions: what is *Tongjon*? (A special kind of education in Korea where pupils choose what they want to study.) What did Nan-Joo choose to study? (Goats.)

Step 2 Put students in pairs to talk about the questions in A. Conduct brief feedback.

Optional activity Ask students what they think about *Tongjon* – in what ways do they think this might help pupils? What would they choose if they had this in their school?

READING

Aim
To extend the topic and to give practice in reading for specific information and responding to text.

Step 1 Ask students to read the questions in A, then to read the text fairly quickly and find the answers. Tell them to ignore the words in bold for the moment. Check in pairs, then with the whole group.

Answers
1 Reading the book *Affluenza* and thinking about her daughter's behaviour.
2 Because she is concerned that her education is making her unhappy and obsessed with grades or results.
3 Because that is something she learnt at school that she no longer remembers.
4 Because this covers some of the more practical things the writer would have liked to have learnt at school but did not.
5 Because it is an example of students taking responsibility for their own learning and development.
6 Because Pushkin said that an important aspect of learning any subject was inspiration or being inspired.

Step 2 Put students in pairs to discuss the meanings of the words in bold. Check with the whole group. Model and drill the words and check the stress / pronunciation.

Answers
go through = look at and read again
thick = not very intelligent
pushy = strongly encourage someone to do something
bright = very intelligent, smart
points to = shows something as an example
relevant = important to the topic
recite = say something back
parenthood = to be a mother or father
core (in core subject) = a main subject
rigid = unbending

Step 3 Ask students to read the article again and find examples of each thing in exercise C. Put them in pairs to talk about it and about their response to the article in general. Have a group feedback and discussion if students' level of interest is high and time permits.

NATIVE SPEAKER ENGLISH

Step 1 Ask students to look at the sentence at the beginning of the second to last paragraph of the article, *Such ideas are not really what Oliver James has in mind.* Ask them for another way of saying *has in mind* (is thinking about).

Step 2 Ask students to read the examples in the box, then ask for another way of saying each of the sentences listed. *Are you planning to go anywhere in particular for your next holiday? I'm considering three candidates for the new job. What are you thinking of / what's your idea? I'll remember you if I hear of any opportunities for work.* Check the difference between *What have you got in mind?* = What are you thinking about? And *What's on your mind?* = What's bothering you?

VOCABULARY Forming words

Aim
To extend students' vocabulary and to give practice in word formation.

Step 1 Ask students to read the box. Elicit more examples from them e.g. What is the noun and adjective from imagine? *Imagination, (un)imaginative.* Advise? *Advice, (un / in)advisable create, (un)creative*, etc.

Step 2 Ask students to complete the table with nouns and verbs. Tell them that one of each pair of words is in the article, so they could look back at it to help them. The words are in the same order in the article. They could do the exercise in pairs or individually, then check in pairs. Elicit and mark the stress.

Answers

Education, educate	Appreciation, appreciate
Failure, fail	Encouragement, encourage
Achievement, achieve	Inspiration, inspire
Calculation, calculate	

Step 2 Ask students to look at the questions and think about how they would answer them. Put them in pairs / threes to discuss the questions. Conduct brief feedback.

Next class Make photocopies of **7A** p. 140 and **7B** p. 141.

pp. 52–53

SPEAKING

Aim
To extend and personalise the topic.

Step 1 Ask students what they can see in the pictures and how they are similar / different.

Step 2 Put students in pairs and ask them to talk about the advantages and disadvantages of the different schools.

VOCABULARY
Schools, teachers and students

Aim
To build on students' vocabulary and lead into the listening.

Step 1 Put students in pairs and ask them to decide whether each example in A describes a school, a teacher or a student and whether it is positive or negative. Conduct feedback, model, drill and check concept.

Answers
1. teacher – could also be student – positive; *patient* = calm, not easily annoyed
2. school – negative; *rough* = unpleasant, difficult, dangerous
3. student – positive; *studious* = hardworking
4. teacher – positive
5. school – positive; *reputation* = what people think or say about it
6. teacher – negative; *traditional* (here) = old-fashioned
7. teacher – positive; *he really pushes us* = he makes us work hard
8. student – negative; *she never pays attention* = she doesn't show any interest
9. school – positive; *discipline* = strictness, practice of making people obey rules
10. student (or teacher) – negative; *she thinks she knows it all* = she has a high opinion of herself
11. school – positive – *headmaster* = head of school (male) *headmistress* – female. Both now usually called *head teacher*.
12. teacher – positive; *encouraging* = gives you hope or confidence about your achievements
13. student – positive; *bright* = intelligent
14. student – negative; *skip classes* = miss classes
15. teacher – positive; *lively* = dynamic
16. school – negative; *facilities* = buildings, equipment or services

Step 2 Ask students to look at the points in B and think about what they could say about them. Put students in pairs / threes to discuss. Tell them to try to use the vocabulary from A. Conduct brief feedback.

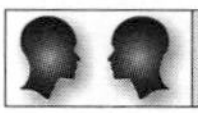

7A see Teacher's notes p. 123.

LISTENING

Aim
To give students practice in listening for gist and specific information, extend the topic and practise fluency.

Step 1 Ask students to read the instructions in A. Tell them they are going to hear four conversations about education. They should listen and identify the speaker in each case. One of the possibilities is not used. Check in pairs, then check with the whole group.

Answers
Conversation 1: b
Conversation 2: d
Conversation 3: c
Conversation 4: a

7.2

Conversation 1

A: How's the class?

B: Awful! They just don't pay attention. If I try to explain something, they sit whispering to each other. It's so rude! And then there's one boy who always walks in 20 minutes late. He doesn't apologise. He just puts his mobile on the table, takes off his iPod and his Armani sunglasses – and then he sits there looking bored, because he thinks he knows it all. He's got no pen, no paper, nothing. It's really annoying!

A: I think you need to set some rules. If they talk, send them to the headmaster or give them a detention.

B: Maybe. I don't want to be too strict.

A: But you have to be! If you're strict from the start, you'll gain their respect. Obviously, you need to be fair as well.

Conversation 2

C: Are you OK? You look a bit fed up.

D: I've just got the results of my English test.

C: Oh dear. What did you get?

D: A 6. And I needed a 6.5 to do a Master's.

C: Oh no! I'm sorry. But you worked so hard. I was sure you'd get at least a 7.

D: I know. I was so stupid. I misread one of the questions. That probably lowered my score.

C: Oh dear. So what are you going to do now?

D: It depends. I'm going to ring the course leader and see if they'll accept me with a 6. If they don't accept me on the course, I'll either re-take the test or I might look for another Master's.

Conversation 3

E: Right, there are a number of things I need to tell you about assessment. Firstly, 50% of your final marks are based on your essays during the course. Because of that, we're very strict on deadlines. If you miss a deadline that your tutor has set, you will be given a zero. No arguments! Secondly, er . . . yes.

F: Yes, sorry to interrupt, but what if you have a family crisis or something?

E: Well, obviously we'll make an exception for certain cases affecting your immediate family. Also, we won't accept any excuses to do with illness unless you produce a doctor's certificate within two days of the deadline. Does that answer your question? Good. I should say, while we're on the subject, that if you have any problems which are affecting your coursework, you should contact the student counselling service. Their number is . . .

Conversation 4

G: So how's Angela doing at her new school?

H: Oh, much better, thanks. I'm so glad we decided to move her to St James's. The teachers seem a lot better prepared. And they push the kids. I think Angela was just a bit bored at her last school.

G: Well, she's a bright kid.

H: And that other school was quite rough. I was always hearing about fights in the playground and kids skipping classes.

G: Well, St James's has a very good reputation.

H: Yes. Discipline is very good there. And I think they look so much smarter in a uniform.

G: Mmm.

Step 2 Ask students to read exercise B and try to answer the questions from memory. Play the recording again for them to check.

Answers

1 She is annoyed because her pupils behave badly. She is advised to be strict but fair.
2 She is unhappy because she didn't get the score she wanted in her English test (probably IELTS), which she needed to start a Master's course. She is going to ask if they will accept her with a 6 instead of 6.5.
3 The lecturer explains that students cannot miss deadlines unless there is a family crisis affecting close family members, or the student is ill and has a doctor's certificate.
4 The parent is happy because her daughter is doing much better at her new school than she was at her old one.

Step 3 Put students in pairs and ask them to try to remember which verb was used with each of the nouns / noun phrases in C. Ask them to check with the audioscript on p. 146 or you could play the recording again for them to check. Check with the whole group and model, drill and concept check.

Answers

1 don't *pay* attention; *whispering* to each other; *gain* their respect
2 *misread* one of the questions; *lowered* my score; *re-take* the test
3 *miss* a deadline; *make* an exception; *accept* any excuses
4 *push* the kids; *skipping* classes; *has* a very good reputation

Step 4 Give students one or two minutes to read the questions and think about how they would answer them. Put students in pairs or threes to discuss the questions. Conduct very brief feedback at the end.

GRAMMAR Zero conditionals and first conditionals

Aim
To give practice in zero and first conditionals.

Step 1 Ask students to look at the sentence from *Listening* and try to complete them. Play the audio to check. Check in pairs, then check with the whole group. Ask students which sentences refer to the present and which to the future and which verb form is used in each part of the sentence.

7.3
1 If I try to explain something, half of them just sit there whispering to each other.
2 If they talk, just send them to the headmaster or give them a detention.
3 If they don't accept me on the course, I'll either re-take the test or I might look for another Masters.
4 If you miss a deadline that your tutor has set, you will be given a zero.
5 If you have any problems which are affecting you're coursework, you should contact the student counselling service.

Answers
1 If I try to explain something, *they sit whispering to each other.*
present; *if* clause: present simple,
main clause: present simple
2 If they talk, *send them to the headmaster.*
could refer to present i.e. whenever they . . . or future i.e. next time they . . . *if* clause: present simple, main clause: imperative
3 If they don't accept me on the course, *I'll either re-take the test or I might look for another Master's.*
future; *if* clause: present simple negative, main clause: *will* + base form, *might* + base form
4 If you miss a deadline that your tutor has set, *you will be given a zero.*
could refer to present i.e. whenever they . . . or future i.e. next time they . . . *if* clause: present simple, main clause: *will* + base form
5 If you have any problems which are affecting your coursework, *you should contact the school counselling service.*
future; *if* clause: present simple, main clause: *should* + base form

Step 2 Read out the grammar box and ask if students have any questions. Check whether they have any questions. Direct them to the grammar reference on p. 146 if they still seem unsure.
Give some initial oral practice by conducting a chain drill – you: *If it's cold I always wear a coat.* Student 1 continues: *If I wear a coat, I . . .* and so on round the class. Then conduct a chain drill for the first conditional in the third person, to help students remember the 's', e.g. *If he works hard, he'll pass his exams – if he passes his exams, he'll...* etc.

Step 3 Ask students to complete the sentences using the correct form of the verbs in brackets. They could do this in pairs or individually and then check in pairs. Check with the whole group. Model and drill the answers (just the conditional part). Draw students' attention to the way a first conditional question can be reduced to 'What if...?' e.g. *What if you don't? What if you haven't?*

Answers
get / I'll probably do; have / I'll go; I'll have to

Step 4 Ask students to look at the sentences in D and check they remember *it depends* from Unit 3. Check they remember the difference when we use it with a noun (we have to use *on*) and a verb (we don't have to use *on*). Ask students to write their own answers to the questions. Monitor and check their sentences for accuracy. Early finishers can check each other's work.

Step 5 Put students in pairs to practise conversations based on what they have written. Make sure they develop conversations by asking *And what if . . . ?* Demonstrate with a strong student, then in open pairs, before continuing in closed pairs. Monitor closely and note down errors for a correction slot at the end.

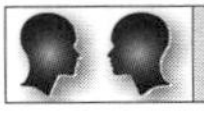 **7B** see Teacher's notes p. 123.

SPEAKING

Aim
To give further practice in conditionals.

Step 1 Lead in by asking students what rules they remember from their schooldays and what they thought of them.

Step 2 Ask students to read the rules and check they understand. Give them time to think about their reactions to each. Check vocabulary, *warning, bullying, victim, suspended, litter, sweep, term, expelled, cheating.*

Step 3 In pairs students discuss the questions in A.

Step 4 Put students in new pairs to invent five new rules for this class. Encourage them to be creative! Monitor and help with ideas and accuracy. They could write these up on posters and display around the class. Ask them to walk round and comment on each other's work.

Optional activity Ask them to read out their favourite two rules then vote for the best three.

08 EATING

UNIT OVERVIEW
The main aims of this unit are to present / revise and practise talking about **food** and **restaurants**. Students describe **dishes and how to cook them** as well as **problems people have with food**. They also practise **ordering in restaurants**. The main grammar aims are **the second conditional** and ***tend to* + base form**.

SPEAKING

Aim
To lead in to the topic and get students immediately involved through personalisation.

Step 1 Lead in by asking students to look briefly at the main unit photo and the illustrations and describe what they can see.

Step 2 Ask students to look at the questions in A and think about how to answer them. Check they understand *adventurous, unadventurous* and *fussy*.

Step 3 Put students in pairs / threes and ask them to discuss the questions as fully as they can. Conduct very brief feedback.

VOCABULARY Describing food

Aim
To build on students' existing knowledge of vocabulary about ways of describing food and methods of cooking.

Step 1 Ask students to look at the pictures in more detail and to match the sections of the picture with the correct verb in the box. Do the first one with them. They could do this exercise in pairs, or individually and then check in pairs. Check with the whole group and drill the collocations, e.g. *stir-frying vegetables*.

Answers
Stir-frying curry / vegetables; slicing courgettes / vegetables; mashing potatoes; steaming fish; grating chocolate; roasting meat; deep-frying chips / fish; boiling broccoli / pasta; marinating chicken.

Tip Point out that verbs are often used in their past participle form to describe food, e.g. *grilled / mashed / steamed / stir-fried /* boiled, but not *roasted*. You could focus on this by asking students how they like their food cooked.

Step 2 Ask students to identify which adjectives go with which of the foods in the picture. Model, drill and concept check.

Answers
1 spicy – curry / stir-fry
2 fattening – mashed potato / deep-fried chips / fish, chocolate cakes
3 tasty – curry, roast meat, kebabs, chocolate
4 greasy – deep-fried chips / fish
5 bland – mashed potato, steamed broccoli
6 filling – cake, mashed potato, chips.

Step 3 Put students in pairs / threes. Ask them to look at the pictures in File 9 on p. 158 and discuss whether anyone they know can't or doesn't eat any of the things illustrated and why not. If they don't know anyone, they could talk about general reasons why people sometimes don't eat these things. Conduct brief feedback.

LISTENING

Aim
To give fluency practice about understanding foreign menus.

Step 1 Tell students they are going to listen to a conversation in a Peruvian restaurant. Ask them if anyone has tried Peruvian food and what they know / imagine about it.

Step 2 Put students in groups of three or four and ask them to talk about the questions in A. Conduct brief feedback, but do not explain the items on the menu. Check *starter, main course, dessert*.

Tip In a multilingual class including Peruvian students, get them to explain the dishes to the other students. With other Spanish speakers they can still guess the meanings as some of the dishes will be unfamiliar to them, but you could still get them to help the other students as they will obviously understand most of the words. If teaching in Peru, ask students how to translate the items into English.

Step 3 Ask students to listen to the conversation and tick the dishes Claes decides to order. Play the recording. Check in pairs then check with the whole group.

Answers
He orders *Ceviche* and *Seco De Cabrito*.

8.1
A = Aurora, C = Claes

A: They don't have an English menu, I'm afraid, Claes – just a Spanish one.
C: That's OK. You'll just have to talk me through it.
A: No problem. Well, for starters they've got *Papa Rellena*. That's balls of mashed potato, stuffed with beef, raisins and olives, and then deep-fried.
C: OK. That sounds very filling for a starter!
A: It can be, yeah. Then there's *Anticuchos*. That's a bit like a Peruvian kebab. It's sliced cow heart, very tender and juicy, grilled on a stick.
C: Right. To be honest, Aurora, I don't really like the idea of eating heart. I don't know why. I just don't.
A: That's OK. No problem. There are plenty of other dishes to choose from.
C: Sorry. Anyway, what's next? What's *Ceviche*?
A: *Ceviche*! That's Peru's national dish. Have you never tried it?
C: No, never.
A: Oh, you really should. It's delicious. It's basically raw fish marinated in lime juice or lemon juice and served with the local kind of potato and corn. You get lots of different kinds of *Ceviche*, using different fish and seafood.
C: OK. Well, I'll go for that, the ceviche. What are you going to have?
A: The *Tallarín Con Mariscos*. It's a kind of spaghetti served with shrimps and prawns and squid.
C: Sounds great. And what about the main courses?
A: Well, the *Bistec Apanado*. That's steak, sliced very thinly and then fried and served with rice.
C: OK.
A: And then there are two rice dishes – *Arroz Con Mariscos*, which is rice with fresh seafood. It's a bit like a Spanish paella, but spicier. Then there's *Arroz Con Pato*, which is rice with duck. The *Lomo Saltado* is a kind of steak dish.
C: Another one? I don't really eat steak very much, to be honest. I tend to find it quite bland.
A: Bland? Not this one. It's cooked with tomatoes and onions and spices and things. It's really good. Honestly!
C: I'll take your word for it, but I don't really feel like steak tonight anyway.
A: OK. Well, finally, there's *Seco De Cabrito*. It's a kind of stew with goat meat in, young goat meat – and they serve it with beans on the side.
C: That sounds very tasty. And quite unusual too. I'll have that.

Step 4 Ask students what they remember about any of the dishes and why he chose / rejected them.

Step 5 Put students in pairs and ask them to try to complete the sentences in D from memory. Play the recording again for them to check. Check with the whole group and concept check the answers.

Answers

1 afraid	4 tender; juicy	7 like; spicier
2 through	5 for	8 kind
3 stuffed	6 thinly; served	9 tasty

DEVELOPING CONVERSATIONS

Describing dishes

Aim
To extend students' ability to describe food and drink, especially strange or exotic items.

Step 1 Ask students to look back at numbers 7 and 8 in exercise D and to notice how Aurora describes the dishes which are unfamiliar to Claes. Ask them to read the box and check they understand. Ask students to describe some of the items in the pictures on p. 54 using *It's a kind of ... It's a bit like ... It's made from ...* .

Step 2 Ask students to think of four different kinds of fruit, vegetable, drinks, dishes, etc. and think about how to describe them, using the phrases from the box.

Step 3 Put students in pairs and ask them to take turns describing their items and guessing what they are. Monitor closely and note down errors in target language. Conduct a brief correction slot at the end.

CONVERSATION PRACTICE

Aim
To further exploit the listening and round off the lesson.

Step 1 Ask students to write an imaginary menu in their own language. This should include three starters, three main courses and three desserts.

Step 2 Put students in pairs (of mixed nationality in a multilingual class). Tell them to take turns being A and B. Student A is a foreign visitor and B lives locally. B talks A through the menu. A rejects at least two things and explains why, then chooses a starter, main course and dessert. Monitor closely and conduct a brief correction slot at the end.

pp. 56–57

Speaking

Aim
To further extend the topic and lead in to the reading.

Tip If students are studying outside their home country, start by asking what food they miss most from home. Ask what – if anything – they can do about it.

Step 1 Ask students to look at the pictures and describe what they can see. Then ask them to read the introduction to the article *Food for thought*. Check they understand *food for thought* = something that makes you think about a topic in a new way or more deeply than before.

Step 2 Put students in pairs and ask them to discuss the questions in A. Conduct very brief feedback.

Reading

Aim
To give students practice in reading for specific information and deducing meaning from context. To encourage them to exchange ideas / information about what they have read by doing a 'jigsaw reading' (where different students read different texts and then discuss them together).

Step 1 Divide the class into two groups, A and B. As should read the texts about Isabella and Ian on the page, while Bs read File 3 on p. 156. Tell them to answer the questions in A as they read.

Step 2 Put students in A / B pairs and tell them to ask each other the questions in exercise A.

Answers
Group A: 1 Spain and America; 2 Isabella – Glasgow, Scotland (studying there), Ian – Taiwan (wife is from Taipei); 3 Isabella likes haggis, the variety of food available; Ian likes street snacks, the variety of veggie (vegetarian) food available, sharing dishes; 4 Isabella misses olive oil; Ian misses splitting the bill; 5 Isabella finds eating times and drinking without eating strange; Ian finds the fact that people are surprised he can use chopsticks annoying; 6 Isabella will never get used to bread and butter with everything, deep fried food; Ian to stinky tofu and men always paying the bill
Group B: 1 Taiwan and Scotland; 2 Ya-Wen – America; Alan – Spain; 3 Ya-Wen likes Taiwanese restaurants, health food shops; Alan likes olive oil on bread, cooking fresh food, eating out, tapas; 4 Ya-Wen misses rice; Alan misses vegetables, food from other countries e.g. curry; 5 Ya-Wen finds big portions strange; Alan finds 'vegetarian' dishes with meat in them strange; 6 Ya-Wen will never get used to steak with blue cheese sauce; Alan to eating so late

Step 3 Ask students to work in the same pairs and help each other to complete the sentences. They should look back at their texts to find the words / phrases. Check with the whole group.

Answers
1 off-putting
2 split
3 starving
4 unadventurous
5 mouldy
6 turn out to be
7 spreading
8 ready

Step 4 Ask students to look at the questions in D and think about how they would answer them.

Step 5 Put students in groups with a mixture of As and Bs. Ask them to discuss the questions. Conduct brief feedback with the whole group.

Tip If students are outside their home country, or have lived in another country in the past, ask which of the four people's experience is / was most like their own.

Language patterns

Aim
To encourage students to notice a pattern frequently used in natural speech.

Step 1 Ask students to read the *Language patterns* box and translate the sentences into their own language. Or, if you prefer them not to use translatation, ask them to tell you what patterns they notice.

Answers
Just because – usually used at the beginning of a sentence or clause, followed by *it doesn't mean (that)*. Check they understand what it means – this is not necessarily a reason or excuse (informal).

Grammar *tend to*

Aim
To draw students' attention to a frequent expression about people's habits, as used in *Reading*.

Step 1 Write the three sentences in the box on the board. Do this while students are looking at the *Language Patterns* box, to save time. Elicit what the three sentences have in common (*tend to*), what this means (generally do / does or is / are) and what form comes after it (base form).

Step 2 Ask students to read the grammar box and check whether they have any problems. If they are still unsure, direct them to the grammar reference on p. 147. Point out the two negative forms.

Step 3 Ask students to re-write the sentences using the correct form of *tend to / tend not to* + base form. Check in pairs then check with the whole group.

Answers
1 My family tends to eat a lot of ready meals, as both my parents work full time.
2 We tend not to (don't tend to) keep food which is left over after dinner.
3 People here tend to eat food with their hands.
4 I tend to skip breakfast during the week unless I have a late start at work.
5 Our family tends not to (doesn't tend to) eat out unless it's a special occasion.
6 People tend not to (don't tend to) leave tips here unless it was an exceptionally good meal.
7 I tend not to (don't tend to) have a dessert when I go out for dinner.
8 People here tend to avoid making any noises while they're eating. It's seen as bad manners.
9 I tend not to (don't tend to) have time to have a big lunch so I tend to just / just tend to have a sandwich.

Step 4 Ask students to look back at the sentences in A and to think about which ones are true for them, their family or their country.

Step 5 Put students in pairs or threes. Ask them to discuss their and their family's / country's eating habits, using the ideas in A to help them. In a multilingual class, have mixed nationality pairs. Tell students to try to use *tend to / tend not to*. Monitor closely and correct any mistakes in target language.

Step 6 Ask students to write five more sentences about their country, using *tend to / tend not to*. These could be about food, shopping, work, education or character. Put students in pairs and ask them to read their sentences and see whether they agree (in a monolingual class) or are surprised by anything (in a multilingual class).

Alternatively In a multilingual class ask students to write their sentences on sheets of paper. Then circulate these at random and get students to read out each other's sentences. The others should guess who wrote each set of sentences / which country is being described.

pp. 58–59

Next class Make photocopies of **8A** p. 142 and **8B** p. 143.

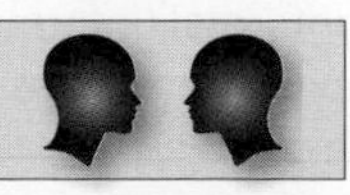

VOCABULARY Restaurants

Aim
To extend the topic and to lead in to the listening.

Step 1 Ask students to look at the pictures and describe what they can see. Ask them what kind of restaurants they like.

Step 2 Put students in pairs / threes. Ask them to discuss whether they think the things in A are positive or negative when applied to restaurants. Ask if they remember *seafood* from the Peruvian dishes *Listening* and *greasy* from describing food *Vocabulary*. Encourage them to help each other with meaning rather than pre-teaching. Check with the whole group and check they understand *packed, portions, huge, rich, trendy, greasy, organic*.

Step 3 Ask students to read the questions in B and think about how they would answer them. Then put them in new pairs to discuss them.

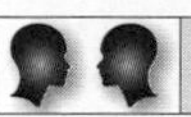

8A see Teacher's notes p. 123.

LISTENING

Aim
To give students practice in listening for specific information.

Step 1 Tell students they are going to hear four conversations. Give them a minute or so to read the questions in A. Check they understand *do up* = redecorate, *swap* = exchange, *threaten* = say you will do something bad. Ask them to listen and note down the answers as they listen. Check in pairs, then check with the whole group.

8.2
Conversation 1
A: Where shall we go, then?
B: How about that bar on the corner?
A: Mmm. The music's a bit loud in there. It's not very good if you want to chat. I'm not sure they do much food either.
B: Oh right. Do you have somewhere else in mind then?
A: Well, if you don't mind walking, I know this really nice café. It has a terrace that looks out over the river.
B: Well, that'd be nice.
A: Yeah, and they do some really nice snacks.
B: Great. So how far is it?
A: Well, it is a twenty-minute walk.
B: That's OK – the walk will give us an appetite!

Conversation 2
C: Have you been to that restaurant in the main street?
D: Yeah, a couple of times.
C: Is it any good?
D: Yeah. The menu's a bit limited. I mean, there aren't really any options if you're vegetarian, but it's good home-style cooking.
C: Right. It's just that I went past and it was almost deserted.
D: I know. I'm surprised they stay in business, to be honest. They should advertise in the paper or something, because the food's nice, and they're very friendly.
C: Well, they might attract a few more people if they redecorated, even if they just re-painted it.
D: That's true. I suppose the restaurant doesn't look very inviting.

Conversation 3
E: How's your fish?
F: It's OK, but it would be better if it didn't have so much sauce on it!
E: There is a lot of it.
F: Yeah, and it's really overpowering. I mean, the sauce is quite spicy so it really overpowers the taste of everything else.
E: Oh dear. Do you want to try some of mine?
F: Go on then. Here, try some of this as well. It's not that bad. Mmm ... that's gorgeous! That steak is so tender! You don't want to swap, do you?
E: Erm, no thanks. I think I'll stick with my one. You can have another bite, though.

Conversation 4
G: When did we ask for the bill?
H: I don't know. At least half an hour ago!
G: I know they're busy, but this is ridiculous. I think we should just go ...
H: What? Without paying? Are you mad?
G: Well, they don't seem to want our money, do they?
H: Don't be ridiculous. I mean, what would happen if they called the police?
G: They wouldn't do that. Anyway, the restaurant doesn't deserve the money. I mean, the food wasn't that great.
H: The asparagus was OK.
G: Yeah, but the portions weren't very generous and the rest of the food was pretty bland. Those vegetables were really overcooked.
H: Yes, but you can't just leave without paying, can you?
G: No, I suppose not!

Answers
1 the music is too loud in the bar on the corner, the restaurant further away has a terrace with a view over the river and good snacks
2 they might attract more customers
3 the sauce on his fish is too spicy / overpowering, the other person's steak is very tender
4 they have been waiting for the bill for ages and the food was not very good

Step 2 Put students in pairs and ask them to try to choose the correct words from the conversations to complete the sentences. Play the recording again for them to check.

Answers

1 a looks out over	b do	c an appetite
2 a limited	b inviting	
3 a overpowers	b tender	
4 a deserve	b generous	

Step 3 Ask students to read the instructions and think about what they will say. Put them in new pairs and ask them to act out the conversations. For conversation 2, tell them to look at the menu on p. 55 for ideas if they like.

VOCABULARY *over-*

Aim
To draw students' attention to the prefix *over-* meaning too much.

Step 1 Ask students what *overcooked* means. Elicit other verbs they can think of beginning with *over.* Ask them to read the vocabulary box or read it out to them.

Step 2 Ask students to complete the sentences with the correct word from the box. Check in pairs then check with the whole group.

Answers

1 overate	5 overestimated
2 overcharged	6 overcooked
3 overdid	7 overreacted
4 overheated	8 overslept

Step 3 In pairs ask students to discuss the situations in exercise A. Do the first example with them e.g. 1 *They went for a meal in a restaurant and ate too much*. Conduct very brief feedback.

NATIVE SPEAKER ENGLISH

Ask students to read the box or read it to them. Check they understand *no wonder* and ask whether it is formal or informal (informal). You could give practice by providing prompts, e.g. I'm not surprised you were late / failed your exam, etc.

GRAMMAR Second conditionals

Aim
To introduce using the second conditional to talk about the unreal present and remote / unlikely future.

Step 1 Write the sentences from the grammar box on the board. Do this while students are doing *Vocabulary*, to save time. Elicit name of tense, form and meaning from students (second conditional – main clause + *if* clause). Main clause = subject + *would / might* + base form. If clause = *if* + subject + past simple or *were* (verb *to be*). Ask students to read the grammar box and complete the rules.

Tip Point out that with the verb to be *was* and *were* are both used. *Were* is still considered more 'standard' and is nearly always used in set expressions, e.g. *If I were you*.

Answers

past	present	would	might

Step 2 Ask students to complete the sentences in exercise B so they are true for them. They could read these out to the class or compare their ideas in pairs.

Step 3 Ask students to complete the sentences in exercise C using the verbs in brackets in the correct form. Do the first example with them. Check in pairs, then check with the whole group in open pairs.

Answers
1 would taste, were (or was)
2 would be, had
3 would explode, ate
4 would help, did
5 would be, told
6 would look, painted, changed.

Step 4 Ask students to think about the items in D and make notes on how they could be improved and why they need to be.

Step 5 Put students in new pairs and ask them to discuss their ideas. They should try to use the second conditional as much as possible. Monitor closely and note down mistakes for a correction slot at the end.

 **8B** see Teacher's notes p. 123.

SPEAKING

Aim
To give fluency practice in the second conditional.

Step 1 Ask students to look at the problems in A. Pre-teach the vocabulary, e.g. *famine* = extreme hunger / lack of food, *obesity* = being seriously overweight, *anorexia* = eating disorder in which people do not want to eat because they want to be thin. Ask students if they have seen or read anything in the news about any of these topics and, if so, what the story was about.

Step 2 Tell students they are going to hear someone speaking about one of the problems in A. They should listen and think about the answers to the questions in exercise B as they listen. Check in pairs, then check with the whole group.

8.3
I think it's a really serious problem nowadays. People are just obsessed with being thin. I know lots of teenage girls who say they are on a diet when they don't really need to lose weight. I blame the media. I recently heard of a reality TV show here in Germany where they were trying to find the next top model. Apparently, one girl was voted off the show because she was too fat. I think she only weighed something like 50 kilos and she was 1 metre 70 tall. That's terrible! No wonder girls get eating disorders! It's difficult to know how to stop this, but maybe they should just ban adverts featuring really thin models – make them completely illegal. If they had bigger, more normal looking people as models, perhaps girls wouldn't worry about their weight so much.

Answers
1 Anorexia
2 A girl who was voted off a top model TV show in Germany because she was too fat
3 Banning adverts with thin models and using more normal-sized models

Step 3 Ask the class the questions in C. Encourage them to use the second conditional in their answers.

Step 4 Ask students to read the suggestions in D and think about whether they agree or disagree. Tell them to think about how to use the second conditional to talk about them. You could do the first example with the whole group as a model.

Step 5 Put students in small groups to discuss the suggestions. Encourage them to use the sentence starters or other second conditionals in their conversations. Monitor closely and note down mistakes in target language. Conduct an error correction slot at the end.

02 REVIEW

LEARNER TRAINING

Aim
To make students more aware of the ways they revise vocabulary and to help them to do this more efficiently.

Step 1 Ask students to look at the comments and check they understand them. Check *alphabetical* and *expression*.

Step 2 Put students in groups of three and ask them to discuss the different ways of revising vocabulary. They should use the questions to help them and perhaps make some notes.

Step 3 Conduct feedback by eliciting and boarding students' ideas or getting students to tell each other across the class. Or, as in Review 1, you could ask students to make posters to put on the walls. For suggested procedure see Review 1, pp. 32–35.

GAME ⟶ CONVERSATION

For aims and suggested procedure, see Review 1, pp. 32–35.

ACT OR DRAW ⟶ QUIZ

For aims and suggested procedure, see Review 1, pp. 32–35.

Answers
1 You might not be accepted because you are unsuitable or not qualified enough – or the course could be full.
2 No, tacky isn't nice. It is generally cheap and in poor taste.
3 You might upgrade your qualifications or your car because you want to improve them.
4 A school in a poor area might be described as rough because there is violence or aggressive behaviour there.
5 The opposite of bright is slow / thick / dim.
6 Postgraduate courses lead to a Master's or PhD. They are second or third degrees.
7 You work in Human Resources: you look after the staff or personnel of a company.
8 You should pay them back.
9 suit: it doesn't look good on you, fit: it is the wrong size
10 It could look or smell disgusting.
11 Because it isn't making a profit, it is making a loss and running up debts; it may not have enough customers.
12 There is not enough space.
13 It might be dangerous or not effective.
14 They force their children to do certain things, particularly to achieve success.
15 sugar / potatoes / rice / pasta / oil / fatty foods

COLLOCATIONS

For aim and suggested procedure, see Review 1, pp. 32–35.

PRONUNCIATION

Aim
To revise consonant sounds.

Step 1 Ask students to listen to the recording and repeat the words, paying attention to the consonant sounds. Play the recording.

R 2.1 Listen and repeat the sounds and the words.

/p/	/t/	/tʃ/	/k/
apply permanent	training tutor	cheat overcharge	accounts contract
/b/ bland diabetic	/d/ discipline avoid	/dʒ/ gorgeous rigid	/g/ rug gig
/f/ afford fake	/s/ civil service juicy	/l/ label lecture	/ʃ/ sugary portion
/v/ venue woven	/z/ overseas raise	/r/ rep research	/w/ warehouse swear

Step 2 Elicit some different ways the sounds are spelt. Ask students which sounds they find most difficult. Get them to repeat the different sounds and concentrate on pushing air out.

Step 3 Put students in pairs and ask them to say the words in C to each other, paying particular attention to the initial consonant clusters. If they find this difficult tell them to try adding a /ə/ sound between the consonant sounds and then speeding up.

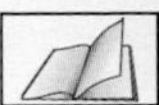 pp. 62–63

Listening

For aims and suggested procedure for the rest of the Review, see Review 1, pp. 32–35. The audio is R2.2.

A Answers

1 chef	3 teacher	5 factory worker
2 model	4 businessman	

B Answers

a 4 b 5 c 2 d 3 e 1

Grammar Talking about rules

Answers
1 can't hand in
2 are supposed to tell me
3 are allowed to use
4 I wouldn't go
5 have to queue / wait in the queue
6 don't have to
7 mustn't
8 Am I allowed / Are we allowed / Are you allowed

Conditionals

Answers

1 c	3 b	5 d	7 a
2 d	4 d	6 d	8 a

Adverbs and prepositions

Answers

1 as	3 off	5 to	7 in	9 round
2 in	4 at	6 under	8 on	10 on

Collocation

Answers

1 scruffy	3 struggling	5 silk
2 deserted	4 rewarding	6 limited

Developing conversations

Answers
1 but, whereas, while; one, phone, type, model
2 kind, type, sort; like
3 must; should, would, can
4 going; hand

Verb – noun collocations

Answers
1 ask for / split the bill
2 cheat in / fail an exam
3 owe / save money
4 ask for / fill in an application form
5 drop / pick up litter
6 skip / have breakfast
7 leave / deserve a tip
8 get into / pay back debt
9 set / break the rules
10 extend / miss the deadline

Forming words

Answers

1 competitive	6 knowledgeable
2 supportive	7 pushy
3 adventurous	8 encouraging
4 practical	9 varied
5 studious	10 risky

Vocabulary

Answers

1 owe	5 without	8 points
2 account(s)	6 sales	9 tend
3 wage	7 homework	10 workload
4 avoid		

09 HOUSES

UNIT OVERVIEW
The main aims of this unit are to enable students to **talk about where people live** and to **describe flats, houses and areas**. The main **grammar** aim is **comparative forms** and **comparing the past with now**. Students also learn how to add **emphasis** and **ask about rules.**

VOCABULARY

Describing where you live

Aim
To introduce / revise and give practice in vocabulary related to houses and flats.

Step 1 Lead in to the topic by asking students what kind of place they live in now and whether they have lived in any other kinds of housing in the past. Check the difference between *house* = a building and *home* = place where you live (could be a flat, apartment, house, cottage, caravan, houseboat, castle, etc.).

Step 2 Draw students' attention to the picture. Elicit a few examples of things they can see. Put them in pairs and ask them to identify the items from the box in the picture. Check with the whole group and model, drill and check concept – especially differences, e.g. *garden, patio, courtyard; terrace, balcony; loft, attic; basement, cellar.* Elicit and mark stress.

Answers
Illustrated: swimming pool, gas central heating, back garden, roof terrace, garage, patio, open fire, balcony, tiled floor, basement.
Not illustrated: courtyard.

Step 3 Put students in pairs / threes and ask them to discuss the questions in B. Ask them also to discuss which of the things they would like to have and why.

Step 4 Ask students to look at the sentences in C and try to guess the meanings of the words in bold from the context. Check in pairs then check with the whole group. Model and drill.

Answers
1 cramped = doesn't have much space
2 bright = has a lot of light
3 conveniently located = within easy reach of shops, transport, etc.
4 a shared flat = a flat where a number of friends (or housemates) live together
5 run-down = old and in a bad condition
6 spacious = having a lot of space (opposite of cramped)
7 affordable = easy to pay the rent / mortgage
8 newly built = of recent construction, modern
9 central = near or in the town centre
10 compact = small but well-designed, neat

Step 5 Put students in pairs and ask them to use the adjectives to describe where they live or where they have lived in the past. Conduct very brief feedback.

LANGUAGE PATTERNS

Aim
To draw students' attention to patterns with *need*, commonly used when talking about housing.

Step 1 Ask students look at the sentences in the box and translate them into their own language, or, if you prefer them not to translate, to notice what the sentences have in common and what patterns they can see.

Answer
Need + noun / noun phrase (+ *to be* + past participle)
Need + gerund

Listening

Aim

To listen for gist and to hear some of the target vocabulary in a natural context.

Step 1 Tell students they are going to hear a conversation about a new flat. Let them quickly read the questions in A and tell them to note down the answers as they listen. Check they understand this use of *place* = house or flat. Play the recording. Check in pairs then check with the whole group.

Alternatively Play the recording once and get students to answer questions 1 and 4, then play it again for them to answer questions 2 and 3.

Answers

1 Their old place was too cramped – they wanted separate rooms for their kids.
2 The front room is huge and the whole place is spacious, much bigger than the old place. It has a huge front room, a big kitchen, wooden floors, huge windows, a balcony and a garden.
3 It's quite run down / needs a lot of work done on it.
4 The old place was more central.

9.1

G = Gavin, L = Lynn

G: Did I tell you I went round to see Nick and Carol the other day?
L: No, you didn't. How are they? I haven't seen them for ages.
G: Oh, they're fine. They said to say 'Hello' to you. You know they've moved recently, don't you?
L: Oh really? No, I didn't, actually. The last time I heard from them they were still in that place near the centre.
G: Oh, OK. Well, yeah, they moved, um I think it was last month. To be honest, they seem much happier now.
L: Oh, that's good. So what's their new place like? Is it nice?
G: Yeah, it is. It's OK. It's quite a lot bigger than their old place. The front room is huge – it's about twice the size of this room – and the whole place is pretty spacious.
L: That must be nice for them, now the kids are growing up.
G: I know. They said the old place was getting a bit cramped for them all. They wanted separate rooms for the kids. They didn't want them sharing forever! That's the main reason they moved out.
L: So what kind of place is it? I mean, is it a house or a flat?
G: Oh, it's a flat. It's on the third floor of an old block. It's a little bit run-down and it does need a bit of work done on it, but they've actually bought it, so they can do what they want to it.
L: Lucky them! All those weekends spend painting and decorating to look forward to!
G: I know! I don't envy them! It has got real potential, though. It's got a great kitchen – it's a similar size to yours, maybe a bit bigger – and it's got these lovely old wooden floors throughout – and huge windows, so they got a lot of sunlight coming in, which is great. Then there's a little balcony where you can sit and eat in the summer, and a shared garden out the back where the kids can play and everything.
L: Oh, it sounds lovely. I must go round and see them sometime soon.
G: Yeah, I'm sure they'd like that. The only problem is, though, it's not as central as their old place was. It's quite a lot further out, so it takes quite a long time to get there.
L: Oh, OK.

Step 2 In pairs ask students to try and complete the sentences in B from memory. Then play the recording again and ask them to check. Check with the whole group.

Answers

1 Did I tell you I went *round to see Nick and Carol the other day?*
2 I haven't seen them *for ages.*
3 They said to say *'Hello' to you.*
4 It's quite a lot *bigger than their old place.*
5 That must be *nice for them.*
6 That's the main reason *they moved out.*
7 I must go *round and see them.*
8 The only problem is, though, it's not *as central as their old place was.*

Step 3 Ask students to look at the questions in C and think about how they would answer them.

Step 4 Put students in groups of four or five and ask them to talk about the questions in C. Encourage them to use the vocabulary from the lesson. Conduct brief feedback.

Pronunciation

Adding emphasis with auxiliaries

Aim

To draw students' attention to the way auxiliary verbs can be used for emphasis and how they would be stressed in this case.

Step 1 Model this sentence ... it *does* need a bit of work done on it, but they've actually bought it ... and ask students what they notice about it.

Answer
The use of the auxiliary *does*. It is stressed to give emphasis. The normal or neutral sentence would be: *Nick and Carol's flat needs a bit of work done on it*. Emphasis is often used in sentences where there is a contrast.

Step 2 Ask students to read the rest of the pronunciation box and check they understand. Illustrate the second point with sentences using *be* or *have*, e.g. It's small but *it is* very light. There's no garden but they *have* got a balcony.

Step 3 Put students in pairs. Ask them to say the sentences in exercise A to each other and underline the word they think would be stressed. Then play the recording for them to check.

9.2
1 I do like Paris. I just don't want to live there.
2 The kitchen's lovely, but it does need a good clean!
3 I did visit their flat once, but it was a long time ago.
4 They did send me their new address but I've lost it.
5 It isn't very central, but it is very affordable.
6 I have been there. I've just forgotten the way.
7 They've got a huge flat, but it is a bit dark inside.
8 It's quite run-down but it has got real potential.

Step 3 Model and drill the sentences.

DEVELOPING CONVERSATIONS
Making comparisons

Aim
To focus on ways of talking about size, in the context of housing; to introduce comparative forms in a covert way before focusing on them in *Grammar*.

Step 1 Ask students to read the examples in the box and check they understand. What are these sentences about? (Size.) Elicit some other examples and write them on the board, e.g. *twice as big as, three times as big as, half the size of*. Model and drill. Draw students attention to weak forms especially *than* and *as*.

Step 2 Ask students to look at exercise A and correct the mistakes. Do the first one with them. Check in pairs, then check with the whole group.

Answers
1 His bedroom's tiny. It's about half *the* size of mine.
2 The kitchen's enormous. It's three times the size of *mine*.
3 The bathroom's OK. It's about *the* same size as yours – maybe a little bigger.
4 They've got a huge garden. It's twice the size of *yours*.
5 They've got a small basement. It's a similar size *to* this room – maybe a little smaller.
6 They've got a lovely front room. It's twice as wide as this room and maybe a little *longer*.

Step 3 Put students in pairs / threes and ask them to talk about the rooms in their home and make comparisons between them.

CONVERSATION PRACTICE

Aim
To give speaking practice, incorporating the vocabulary and comparative forms from the lesson.

Step 1 Ask students to look at the audioscript on pp. 167–168 and try to memorise it as far as possible.

Step 2 In pairs, books closed, ask students to act out similar conversations. They should the swap roles. Monitor closely and note down errors in target language for a correction slot at the end.

Tip If time, ask a few strong pairs to act out their conversations for the class.

pp. 66–67

VOCABULARY Describing changes

Aim
To focus on ways of talking about increase and decrease and to lead in to the reading.

Step 1 Lead in by asking students what is happening to the euro at the moment – is it going up or down compared with the dollar? What reasons are there for such changes?

Step 2 Ask students to read the box and notice the different ways of talking about increase and decrease. Focus on the verbs first and then the adverbs, clarifying differences in meaning. Model and drill a few examples.

Step 3 Ask students to look at the items in A and think about how they have changed in recent months / years. Ask them to look at the explanations in B and think about which ones could go with which item in A (there may be several possibilities) e.g. *Unemployment has risen dramatically – I think it's happened because of problems in the economy.*

Step 4 Put students in pairs / threes. Ask them to discuss the changes in their country and the possible explanations, using expressions of increase and decrease and comparative forms. Conduct feedback with the whole class.

Tip In a multilingual class, both this activity and the group work discussion following *Reading* (exercise D) would work better with mixed nationality pairs / groups.

Reading

Aim
To give students practice in predicting, reading for specific information and responding to a text; to put the topic of housing into an authentic, real world context.

Step 1 Ask students to look at the pictures and the title of the article *Priced out of the market*. How do they think each picture connected to the title? Do not give feedback at this stage

Step 2 Ask students to read the article quickly and find out whether their predictions were correct. When do they think it was written? Why? Tell them to ignore the words / phrases in bold for the moment.

Answers
Picture 1: a block of flats / new build homes – could be social housing in inner cities (Top-down solutions).
Picture 2: shows someone building an extension (And bottom-up ones).
Picture 3: For Sale signs (whole article).
Picture 4: containers in Amsterdam, used as flats (No place like home).

Note
For exercise B it is not important to know when the article was written but to get students to respond to the text and explain their reasons.

Step 3 Ask students to decide which sentences in C are true or false. Then read the article again to check. Check in pairs, then with the whole group. Ask students to correct the false sentences.

Answers
1 F – it is affordable
2 T
3 T
4 T
5 F – demand has increased faster than supply
6 T
7 F – there has been a huge increase in this
8 T

Step 4 Ask students to read the questions in D and think about how they would answer them. Put them in groups of three and ask them to discuss their ideas.

Step 5 Ask students to try to complete the sentences in E with the correct word, without looking at the article. They could check in pairs and then look at the text if they are still unsure. Check with the whole group.

Answers

1 taking	5 gets
2 rises	6 increase
3 protect	7 at
4 investments	8 tackling

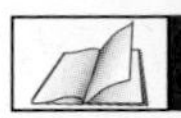
pp. 68–69

Next class Make photocopies of **9A** p. 144 and **9B** p. 145.
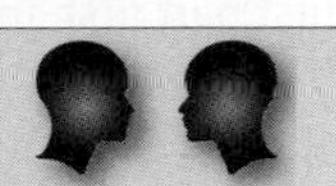

Vocabulary Describing areas

Aim
To further extend the topic and to present the grammar (comparing the past with the present).

Step 1 Lead in to this part of the unit by asking about different areas in the city where you are. How would they describe them?

Step 2 Ask students to look at the words in the box and try to match them with the sentences in A. Do the first example with them. They could do this in pairs, or individually and then check in pairs. Check with the whole group. Drill the words and elicit and mark the stress on the board.

Answers

1 dead	6 posh
2 noisy	7 isolated
3 lively	8 dirty
4 rough	9 convenient
5 green	10 residential

Step 3 Ask students to use a separate sheet of paper and write a list of five areas they know in different towns and cities.

Step 4 Put students in pairs and ask them to swap papers. They should then ask each other about the areas with the question: *What's … like?* They should try and answer using the adjectives from A. Model this with a strong student, then in open pairs, before continuing in closed pairs. Monitor and correct any mistakes in target vocabulary.

Tip In monolingual classes / classes where students might choose the same places for their lists, have a group feedback session to see if they used the same adjectives to describe the same places. Discuss any differences.

9A see Teacher's notes p. 124.

LISTENING

Aim
To lead in to the grammar and give practice in listening for specific information.

Step 1 Tell students they are going to hear two conversations about the areas where the speakers live. Ask them to quickly read the questions and ask them to note down the answers for each conversation as they listen. Play the recording. Check in pairs, then check with the whole group.

Alternatively Divide the listening into two halves. Play the first part first and ask students to write down the answers for Conversation 1. Then play the second half and ask students to write down the answers for Conversation 2. Play both parts again if necessary.

Answers
1 1 Yes
2 convenient for town centre, near the beach, quite cheap, better than it used to be
3 a bit rough and run down, some crime (but less than before)
4 It's been cleaned up and the government has invested money in it to improve facilities.
5 There used to be a lot of problems with drugs.
2 1 Yes
2 very green, residential, not much traffic, good for kids
3 far from centre, noisy from airport
4 much noisier than it was before
5 The airport expanded with the arrival of one of the budget airlines.

9.3
Conversation 1
A: I live near the port.
B: What's it like round there? I've heard it's quite dangerous.
A: I know it has that reputation, and there are still bad things about it but it's better than it was before. There used to be a lot of problems with drugs, but the police have done a lot to clean up the area. There's nowhere near as much crime as there was five years ago. And the government's invested quite a lot of money to improve the local facilities.
B: Oh right. I didn't know.
A: Yeah. I mean, there are still some rough streets that I would probably avoid at night, but everywhere has some crime, doesn't it? I know someone who lives in quite a posh area of the city and he got robbed, so, you're never completely safe anywhere.
B: I guess that's true.
A: And where we live is convenient for the centre of town and it's not far from the beach, and on top of all that it's still quite cheap, so it's good. I like it. It doesn't matter to me that some places are still a bit run down.
Conversation 2
C: I live in an area on the outskirts of town.
D: Oh yeah? What's it like?
C: It's OK. It's just a normal residential area – it's very green, there are plenty of places for the kids to run around and play. I mean, we live on a very small side street, so there's hardly any traffic. The kids just play in the street a lot of the time.
D: Sounds nice.
C: Yeah, on the whole we love it, even though it's not as quiet as it used to be.
D: How come?
C: Well, we're close to the airport. When we moved here the airport was quite small and there were far fewer flights than there are now. Then one of the budget airlines started using the airport and over the past few years it's become bigger and bigger. So it's often quite noisy. You kind of get used to the noise after a while, but it's still quite annoying – especially late at night.
D: I can imagine.
C: Still I can't complain too much. I certainly wouldn't want to move.

GRAMMAR

Comparing the past with now

Aim
To focus on ways of comparing the past and the present and to give practice.

Step 1 Ask students to try to complete the sentences from *Listening*. Then play the recording again, or let them check their answers by looking at the audioscript on p. 168. Check with the whole group. Model and drill.

Answers
1 better, it was
2 nowhere near as, there was
3 not as quiet, it used to be
4 fewer, there are
5 become, bigger

Step 2 Ask students to translate the sentences into their own language.

Alternatively In a multilingual class or if you don't want students to translate, ask questions about form and meaning, e.g. what are these sentences comparing? (Past and present.) Which comparative forms are used? (Adjective + *er* + *than*... *not as* + adjective + *as*, *nowhere near as much* + noun + *as* ... .) Does this mean there is a little less or a lot less? (A lot less.) Which tenses are used for the past? (Simple past / used to.) Point out that if the verb form in the present and past is the same, it is common not to repeat it – 1, 2 and 4. Ask students to look at the grammar reference on p. 148 if they are still unsure.

Step 3 Ask students to complete the sentences in C so that they are true for their town / country / society. Tell them to use the pictures to help them with ideas. Compare their ideas in pairs then check with the whole group.

Step 4 Ask students to look at the question in D and think about how to answer it. Put students in groups of three and ask them to discuss the question. Conduct brief feedback.

9B see Teacher's notes p. 124.

Speaking

Aim
To introduce a new aspect of housing and to lead in to practice in asking about rules.

Step 1 Check students understand *host family*. Ask if anyone has ever stayed with one and what are good characteristics of a host family. Check vocabulary: *half board* = breakfast and dinner (but not lunch) included, *self-catering* = no meals included in the price, *cuisine* = food or the method of preparing meals.

Step 2 Ask students to read the adverts for host families in Berlin and think about which ones they would / would not like to stay with and why. Get them to rate them 1–5 (1 = bad, 5 = great).

Step 3 Put students in pairs and ask them to compare their ideas. Conduct brief feedback as a group.

Developing conversations

Asking about rules

Aim
To focus on ways of making and responding to polite requests.

Step 1 Ask students to read the requests in A and match them with the answers. Check in pairs, then check with the whole group, in open pairs.

Answers
1 d 2 c 3 a 4 f 5 b 6 e

Step 2 Ask students to underline the different ways of making a polite request. Also, ask them to notice the kind of language used in the replies, especially to set limits. Check and drill some of the phrases.

Answers
Would it be OK if I ... + past simple
Would you mind if I ... + past simple
Can I ... + base form
Would it be possible ... + infinitive
Is it OK if I ... + present simple

Step 3 Put students in pairs and ask them to choose one of the host families in *Speaking*. Ask them to discuss and write down six questions they could ask and possible answers. Conduct brief feedback.

Speaking

Aim
To give fluency practice in making and responding to polite requests.

Step 1 Put students in new pairs and ask them to role-play a phone conversation between a student and host family, using some of the ideas they wrote down earlier. They should then swap roles and role-play another conversation. Monitor closely and note down errors in target language for a correction slot at the end.

Optional activity If time, ask a strong student to role-play their questions 'interviewing' several host families. Ask the students watching to take notes on which they think would be the best host family to stay with. They can vote at the end for the best host family and why.

10 GOING OUT

UNIT OVERVIEW
The main aims of this unit are to give students practice in **talking about films, exhibitions and plays** and **describing a night out, giving directions** and **explaining why you don't want to do things**. The main **grammar** aim is **the future in the past**.

VOCABULARY Films, exhibitions and plays

Aim
To extend students' vocabulary about arts events.

Step 1 Lead in to the topic by asking students what they can see in the pictures (main photo – an open-air concert / music festival; bottom photo – an installation / sculpture). Have they been to any good films, plays or exhibitions recently? What were they and what were they like? Check students understand *play* in this context = something you see at the theatre, e.g. *Romeo and Juliet*.

Step 2 Check the idea of *odd one out*. Give examples, e.g. green, red, blue, big. Which is the odd one out and why? (Big – because it isn't a colour.) Ask students to look at A and decide which is the odd one out in each group of words – with a reason. They could do this in pairs or individually and then check in pairs. Check with the whole group and concept check the difficult words. For example, *installation* = a type of exhibition, usually of big pieces or sculptures, sometimes outdoors; *sculpture* = works of art made by carving or shaping wood, metal or clay.

Answers
1 an installation – the others are all types or genres of film.
2 a trailer – the others are all types of painting.
3 the painting – the others are all aspects of film.
4 an audience – the others are all artists or do creative work.
5 a gig – the others are all types of play.
6 sculpture – the others are all aspects of films or plays.

Step 3 Put students in pairs or small groups and ask them to discuss the questions in B. Tell them to try to use the words from A. Conduct brief feedback at the end.

Step 4 Ask students to read the questions in C and find two possible answers that go with them. Do the first example with them. They could do this exercise in pairs or individually and then check in pairs. Check with the whole group.

Answers
1 f 2 e 3 b 4 d 5 a 6 c

Step 5 Drill the questions by asking students, then get them to ask each other in open pairs, giving real answers. Continue in closed pairs. Monitor closely and correct any mistakes in target language.

LISTENING

Aim
To hear some of the target language in context.

Step 1 Tell students they are going to hear a conversation between two friends, Dan and Jason, about plans for the evening. Pre-teach *zombies* = people who are dead but still move around among us. Ask them to listen to the first part and answer the questions in A. Check in pairs, then check with the whole group.

Answers
1 a Brazilian horror film
2 zombies taking over Brasilia
3 9.10 p.m. and 12 midnight
4 the Capitol

10.1
D = Dan, J = Jason
D: Do you fancy going out later?
J: Yeah, maybe. What's on?
D: Well, do you like horror films?
J: Yeah, if I'm in the right mood. Why?
D: Well there's this Brazilian film which is on in town that I'd quite like to see. It's got English subtitles, so it should be OK.
J: Oh yeah? What's it about?
D: Apparently, it's about zombies taking over Brasilia.
J: Oh right. That sounds fun. When's it on?
D: There's a showing at just after 9 and then a late one at 12.

> J: OK. Well, I'm not sure I want to go to the late one. I need to be up quite early tomorrow.
> D: That's OK. The ten past nine showing is good for me.
> J: Where's it on?
> D: The Capitol.
> J: Oh, er, OK. Great.

Step 2 Ask students to listen to the rest of the conversation and mark the cinema on the map. Ask them also what time they arrange to meet. Play the second part.

> **10.2**
> D: Do you know where the cinema is?
> J: I think so. Isn't the Capitol that one near the river?
> D: Er ... no.
> J: Oh right. Well, in that case, no, I'm not sure.
> D: It's in the centre – on Crown Street.
> J: No, I don't know it.
> D: You know Oxford Road, yeah? That's the main street which goes past the railway station.
> J: Yeah, yeah.
> D: Well, if you have your back to the station, you turn right down Oxford Road. You walk about 200 metres and you go past a post office.
> J: OK.
> D: And the next street after that is Crown Street. The cinema's along there, about halfway down.
> J: Oh yeah. I think I know the place now. There's a big sweet shop right opposite, isn't there?
> D: That's the one.
> J: OK. So what time do you want to meet?
> D: Well, the programme starts at 9.10, so shall I just meet you on the steps outside at 9?
> J: Can we make it 8.30? We want to be sure we get tickets.
> D: I doubt it'll be that busy, but I suppose we could get there a bit earlier. We can always get a coffee before the film starts.
> J: Exactly. Maybe whoever gets there first should start queuing, OK?
> D: OK, but I don't think we need to worry. I don't think that many people will want to see a Brazilian zombie movie!
> J: You never know!

Answers

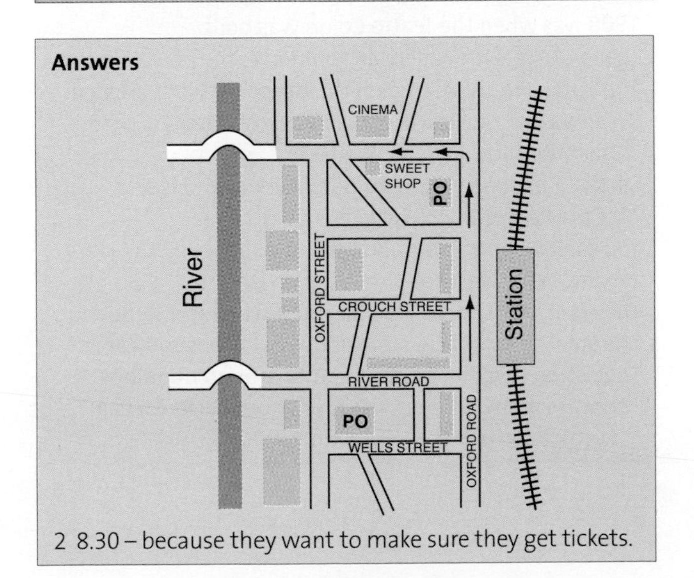

2 8.30 – because they want to make sure they get tickets.

DEVELOPING CONVERSATIONS

Explaining where things are

Aim
To focus on ways of asking for and giving directions.

Step 1 Ask students if they can remember any of the expressions from the recording used to give directions.

Step 2 Ask students to complete the sentences in A with the words from the boxes. Do the first example with them. Check in pairs, then check with the whole group.

Answers

1 halfway	6 back
2 front	7 facing
3 next	8 coming
4 at	9 towards
5 off	10 out

Optional extra For further controlled practice, get students to ask for and give directions to places they all know near the school / college. Encourage them to use the target language as much as possible. Do this in open pairs, then continue in closed pairs.

Step 3 Put students in pairs. Ask them to take turns to draw a map for one of the sentences in A, at random. Their partner should look at the map and identify the sentence.

NATIVE SPEAKER ENGLISH

Ask students to look at the examples in the box and notice the use of *right*. Elicit a few more examples, e.g. Where's the bus stop? *Right outside the school.* Where's the cinema? *Right opposite the library*, etc.

CONVERSATION PRACTICE

Aim
To give further practice of making arrangements.

Step 1 Ask students to look at the instructions for A and prepare what they are going to say. They should take turns to be A and B, so they should prepare both roles.

Step 2 Put students in new pairs and ask them to act out the two conversations. Monitor closely and note down errors in target language for a correction slot at the end / before students swap roles and practise again.

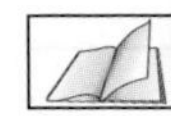
pp. 72–73

VOCABULARY Describing what's on

Aim
To focus on adjectives and adjectival phrases often used to describe arts events.

Step 1 Check students remember the meaning of *What's on*? Lead in by asking students to describe films / plays / exhibitions / concerts they have been to recently. Did they like them or not? What adjectives can they think of to describe them?

Step 2 Ask students to look at the adjectives in the box and decide whether they are positive, negative or could be either. Put them in pairs to discuss their ideas and try to get them to say the words to each other to help with pronunciation. Check with the whole group. Model and drill, elicit and mark the stress on the board. Check concept / collocation by asking questions, e.g. *Could I describe a CD as spectacular*? (Not normally.) *What would I describe as spectacular*? (An installation or exhibition – usually something visual.)

Answers

Spectacular – positive	Weird – both
Touristy – both	Amazing – positive
Terrible – negative	Marvellous – positive
Dreadful – negative	Incredible – positive
Trendy – both	Terrific – positive
Dull – negative	Brilliant – positive

Tip Ask students if they remember how they can use the phrase *be supposed to* and remind them that it's related to rules (Unit 05 p. 39). Elicit one or two examples. Tell them that the phrase *it's supposed to* is used to mean 'people say that' e.g. *The new film at the Capitol is supposed to be really brilliant*.

Step 3 Ask students to read the instructions in B and the examples in the box. Tell them to write six sentences following the model. Monitor as they write and help with ideas / accuracy. In pairs ask students to check each other's sentences and encourage them to correct each other.

Step 4 Elicit some of students' sentences and drill them for pronunciation. Put students in small groups and get them to read their sentences to each other and respond.

READING

Aim
To read for detail and specific information and to extend the topic in an authentic context.

Note Buenos Aires is the capital of Argentina, in South America. It is well known for the tango, a dramatic dance which originated there in the nineteenth century. The photo at the bottom of the webpage on p. 73 depicts the tango.

Step 1 Tell students they are going to read a webpage about what is on in Buenos Aires. Put them in pairs or small groups and ask them to talk about what they know about Buenos Aires. Encourage them to use phrases from B, e.g. *It's supposed to ... There's supposed to be ...* . If anyone has been to Buenos Aires, tell them not to say anything to start with, but to comment at the end on whether other students' ideas are correct.

Step 2 Ask students to look at the photos in the webpage and say what they think they are of (sculpture; an opera house; a wall carving showing the tango). Then get them to read the text quickly and find seven adjectives from *Vocabulary* exercise A with the nouns they describe. Tell them to ignore the words in bold for the moment. Check in pairs, then check with the whole group.

Answers
Spectacular – scenery and lighting in opera
Incredible – dance (the tango)
Trendy – bar
Terrific – cocktails
Weird – décor
Touristy – street
Amazing – street life

Step 3 Ask students to read the text more slowly and try to remember the details. Then put them in pairs and ask them to discuss what they remember about the items in the box, without looking back at the text. When they have done as much as they can, tell them to look at the text again to complete their answers. Check with the whole group.

Answers
1908 was when the Teatro Colon was built.
Luana DeVol is the American soprano in the opera *Electra*.
The 19th century was when the tango was first created.
Broadway-no musical on Broadway (New York) is better than the show at Senor Tango.
Diego Maradona played for Boca Juniors and is one of the best-known footballers of all time.
You can't wear trainers and jeans at Opera Bay, the city's most exclusive disco.
The décor in the bar Mundo Bizarro is weird and wonderful.
The steak at La Chacra steakhouse is the best on earth.
They often don't finish dinner until around midnight.
There are many different kinds of street performers in Avenida Florida.

Step 4 Put students in pairs and ask them to look at the words in bold and try to work out what they mean from the context. Don't conduct feedback, but tell them to go straight on to exercise E when they are ready, as this may help them with any words they are not sure about.

Answers
1 cast = group of actors
2 birthplace = where it began
3 fusion = mix of things
4 authentic = genuine, real
5 catch = see
6 squad = group of players from which team is chosen
7 exclusive = difficult to get in
8 crowd = group of people
9 keen = enthusiastic, dedicated
10 stroll = walk for pleasure

Speaking

Aim
To extend the topic and give fluency practice.

Step 1 Ask students to look at the questions in A and think about how they would answer them.

Step 2 Put students in pairs to discuss the questions. In a multicultural class, make sure pairs are of mixed nationality. Conduct brief feedback at the end.

Developing conversations
Why you do not want to do things

Aim
To give students further speaking practice.

Step 1 Read the information in the box or ask students to read it. Ask them to look at the sentences in A and put them in the correct order.

Step 2 Ask students to listen to the recording to check their answers. Play the recording. You could pause after each example and drill.

10.3
1 It's not really my kind of thing.
2 I don't really feel like it.
3 I'm not really in the mood for that kind of thing.
4 It sounds a bit too trendy for me.
5 It looks a bit too touristy for me.
6 It sounds a bit too weird for me.

Step 3 Model and drill the expressions.

Step 4 Ask students to look at the webpage and think about what they would like to do. Then put them in pairs, A and B. A should invite B to do a number of things, which B should reject, giving reasons. When they agree on something, they should arrange where and when to meet. Then swap roles and repeat the conversation. Monitor closely and note down errors in target language for a correction slot at the end.

pp. 74–75

Next class make photocopies of **10A** p. 146 and **10B** p. 147.
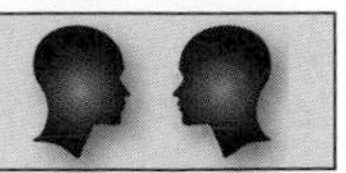

Speaking

Aim
To create a 'need' for the vocabulary and to get students immediately involved.

Step 1 Put students in pairs / threes and ask them to discuss the questions in A. They could use adjectives from *Vocabulary* on p. 72 in the Student's book to answer the question, *How was it*? Conduct very brief feedback.

Vocabulary Describing an event

Aim
To draw attention to ways of describing events.

Step 1 Explain to students that the sentences in 1–8 form pairs with the sentences in a–h and both would be comments made in answer to questions like, *How was the film / club / exhibition*? etc. Do the first one as an example to demonstrate that the pairs of responses don't mean exactly the same thing. 1b (1 may be referring to an exhibition as it uses *it* whereas b may be referring to pictures at an exhibition as it uses *them*). Students should match the pairs of sentences and think about what they might be describing. Check in pairs, then check with the whole group.

Answers
1 b 2 a 3 e 4 c 5 d 6 g 7 h 8 f

Step 2 Put students in pairs / threes and ask them to discuss what each pair of sentences could be describing. Make sure they understand there is more than one possible answer for each pair.

Step 3 Give students a few minutes to look back through exercise A and try to memorise the language. Put students in new pairs. Ask them to 'test' each other by taking turns to ask, *How was the…*? Their partner should close their book and try to answer from memory. After a few examples, they should swap.

Step 4 Ask students in the same pairs to describe films, clubs, etc. using some of the language in A.

They could also talk about places they know or things they have done recently. Encourage them to agree / disagree with each other and give their opinion where possible.

10A see Teacher's notes p. 124.

PRONUNCIATION Intonation and lists

Aim
To draw students' attention to the rise-rise-rise-fall pattern of intonation when giving a list.

Step 1 Model this sentence – *It was fantastic–the music, the people, the food . . . everything.* Make sure your intonation rises on *music, people, food* and falls on *everything*. Ask students why they think this is (this shows the listener that the list is unfinished until the end).

Step 2 Ask students to read the box or read it aloud to them. Then play the recording and get them to repeat after each one, paying particular attention to the intonation.

10.4
1 It was great. The special effects, the soundtrack, everything!
2 It was awful. The music, the venue, everything!
3 It was terrific. The acting, the scenery, everything!

Step 3 Put students in pairs and ask them to practise asking *What was so good / bad about it*? and answering using the sentences in B and the correct intonation. Start off in open pairs, then continue in closed pairs.

Step 4 Ask students what they think each of the sentences in A is describing.

Answers
a film; a party or concert; a play

Alternatively You could do Step 4 immediately after Step 2, or combine it with Step 2.

Step 5 Ask students to think about a great / terrible time they had at the cinema / theatre / a club / on holiday, etc. and what was good / bad about it. Put students in new pairs / threes to ask each other and talk about their experiences using the patterns in exercise B. Monitor closely and correct mistakes in target language, including intonation.

LANGUAGE PATTERNS

Aim
To draw students' attention to the use of superlatives and present perfect with *ever*.

Step 1 Ask students to translate the sentences and compare them to English. What similarities/ differences do they notice? If you prefer not to use translation, ask students to read the examples in the box and look at the patterns? What patterns do they notice? (Superlative + present perfect with *ever*.) Ask them a few checking questions getting them to reply using the form given.

LISTENING

Aim
To listen for gist and specific information and to provide a context for the grammar.

Step 1 Tell students they are going to hear three conversations about what people did the night before. Ask them to listen and decide what kind of event each person went to. Play the recording then check their answers.

Answers
1 film 2 club 3 play

10.5
Conversation 1
A: So how was it?
B: Brilliant – it was much better than I thought it would be.
A: Really. I'd heard it wasn't that good.
B: Well, me too, but I really enjoyed it.
A: So what was so good about it?
B: The story, the acting, everything. It's just really funny and it's quite exciting too. I don't know. Maybe it was because I wasn't expecting very much.
A: I know what you mean. You see so many films these days where there's so much advance publicity – especially from Hollywood. It's all in the papers and everyone's saying 'you must see it'. And then you go and you just think it's a bit overrated. It's nice to have the opposite experience.
Conversation 2
C: Did you have a good night out? How was the gig?
D: Oh, we didn't go in the end.
C: Really? What a shame.
D: No. Hans had promised me he'd pick me up at 7, but of course he was late! He had to finish some work at the office and by the time we got there, there was a massive queue for tickets. So we decided we weren't going to get in, and we went to a club instead.
C: Oh right. So what club did you go to?
D: Radio City.
C: Well, That's supposed to be really good – it's quite trendy, isn't it?
D: That's what they say, but I hated it!
C: Really? What was so bad about it?
D: The people, the music, everything – it's awful. It's one of the worst clubs I've been to.
C: Really?

D: OK maybe I'm exaggerating a bit. I mean, it was OK to begin with, but then it got absolutely packed, so you couldn't really dance properly. And it was boiling hot, so you were sweating like crazy. And then they changed the music later to this heavy techno stuff, which I hate. And the drinks were a rip-off ...
C: Oh dear. Maybe you just went on the wrong night.

Conversation 3

E: I'm a bit tired. I was out late last night.
F: Really? I thought you said you were going to stay in.
E: Yes. I was going to stay in, but I was talking to Clara on the phone last night. She mentioned she'd got a spare ticket for this play in town and I said I'd go with her.
F: Not *A Man for All Seasons*?
E: Yeah that's the one.
F: Oh I've been wanting to see that for ages! It's had some excellent reviews in the papers. How was it?
E: Brilliant! It's one of the best things I've seen in a long time.
F: That's what I'd heard.
E: Yeah. It's so moving. Honestly, I was in tears at the end. And the whole staging – the lighting, the costumes, everything – it's just really well done.
F: I'll have to go.
E: Yeah, you should.

Step 2 Ask students to look at the questions in B and discuss them. You could play the recording again if they need help or play it again for them to check.

Answers
1 no; yes – because her boyfriend Hans was late and there was a long queue for the gig, so they went to a club instead; yes – because her friend had a spare ticket for the theatre
2 yes – good film; no – awful club; yes – brilliant and moving play
3 no; no; yes

GRAMMAR The future in the past

Aim
To introduce taking about the future in the past.

Step 1 Read out the introduction in the box and ask concept questions, e.g. *Did I plan to stay in?* (Yes.) *Did I stay in?* (No.) *Did I like the film?* (Yes.) *Did I expect to like it?* (No.)

Step 2 In pairs ask students to look at the sentences in A and decide what the original plan, promise or prediction was. Look at the example with them Ask them to notice the changes in verb form, e.g. *would – will*.

Answers
2 I'll pick you up at 7.
3 We aren't going to get in.
4 I'm going to stay in.
5 I'll go with you.

Step 3 Ask students to look at the sentences in B and complete them with the correct word in each gap. They could do this in pairs or individually and then check in pairs.

Answers
1 to; would; was 2 were; would 3 would; would

Step 4 You could go through the grammar reference on p. 149 at this point or later, depending on how well students are coping with this grammar point. Ask students to make sentences in the future in the past, using the prompts. Look at the example with them and check they understand. Check in pairs, then check with the whole group.

Answers
2 They were going to have a barbecue but it stated pouring with rain so they had to cook indoors instead.
3 We were going to go to the beach for the day but we missed the train so we ended up going to the park instead.
4 She was going to give me a lift but the car wouldn't start so I got a taxi instead.
5 I was going to walk here but it started pouring with rain so I had to drive.
6 I was going to stay in and study but a friend called so I went out to meet him.

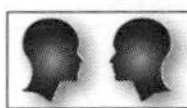
10B see Teacher's notes p. 124.

SPEAKING

Aim
To give practice of the future in the past.

Step 1 Ask students to read the sentences in A and check they understand them, especially the words in bold. They could discuss these in pairs, or, if you have dictionaries, ask them to check any words they are not sure about. Check with the whole group. Model, drill and concept check the words in bold.

Step 2 Ask students to think about how they would answer the questions in A and make a few notes.

Step 3 Put students in groups to discuss the questions. Encourage them to use future in the past forms. Monitor closely and note down errors in target language for a correction slot at the end.

11 THE NATURAL WORLD

UNIT OVERVIEW

The main aims of this unit are to extend students **ability to talk about nature**, especially **wild animals and pets**. They also practise **word formation** and **passive forms**, as well as ***-ing* clauses**. They **listen** to conversations about **unusual experiences with animals** and about **pets** and read newspaper articles about **animals and the environment**.

VOCABULARY Animals

Aim

To extend students vocabulary about wild animals and birds and to lead in to the listening.

Step 1 Lead in by eliciting some names of wild animals, birds and insects. Ask what the photos are of. Concept check the difference between *wild animals* and *domestic animals / pets* by asking for examples of each.

Step 2 Put students in pairs and ask them to look at File 10 on p. 159 and identify the animals, birds and insects in the pictures. Check students understand the difference between *animals, birds, insects, mammals*. Also check *species*. They should then discuss which ones they like and why and which ones they are scared of and why. Check with the whole group and drill for pronunciation. Elicit and mark stress on the board. Check concept by asking what these animals do / where they live, etc.

Answers

1 squirrel
2 lizard
3 bear
4 eagle
5 dolphin
6 cockroach
7 deer (plural deer)
8 whale
9 wolf
10 crow
11 crocodile
12 parrot
13 snake
14 scorpion
15 rat

Step 3 Ask students to close their books and then see how many of the creatures they can remember. Remind them that there are 15 altogether. You could give clues, e.g. *three of them are birds, two are sea creatures,* etc.

Step 4 Check / pre-teach vocabulary in exercise C, e.g. *rock, circling, bushes, crawling*. Ask if anyone remembers *dreadful* = terrible, from Unit 10, Describing what's on.

Step 5 Put students in pairs or threes and ask them to discuss the questions in exercise C. They should think of as many animals as they can for each example.

LISTENING

Aim

To hear the target vocabulary in context and give practice in listening for gist and detail.

Step 1 Tell students they are going to hear three conversations about animals that people have seen. Ask them to listen and answer the questions in A. Give them a moment to read the questions, then play the recording. Pause after each conversation to give students time to note their answers. Check the answers with the whole group.

11.1

Conversation 1

A: You'll never guess what happened last night.

B: Go on. What?

A: Well, I was writing some reports on my computer at home when I suddenly noticed a group of crows looking quite excited. They were all making this dreadful noise, so I went outside to see what was happening.

B: And?

A: Well, the crows were chasing a little parrot up and down the street.

B: A parrot? What was it doing there?

A: I have no idea. I guess it must've escaped from somewhere. Anyway, it was obviously very scared and cold. I felt really sorry for it, so I chased the crows away. I then spent two hours trying to get the parrot off my neighbour's roof.

B: Yeah? So what happened in the end? Did you catch it?

A: Yeah, eventually it came down and I managed to catch it and put it into a box. We've got it at home now!

B: Wow! That's mad. Actually, it reminds me of something I saw a few weeks ago. I was coming home from work on my bicycle when . . .

Conversation 2

C: How was your journey? Was it OK?

D: Yeah, it was fine, but I did see something really strange on the way.

C: Yeah? What was that?
D: Well, at about midnight last night, I was driving along next to a field and the road was quite narrow. In front of me, I suddenly saw this huge snake lying across the road.
C: Ugh! Really?
D: Yeah! I mean, it was obviously dead, but next to it, I could see what I thought was a cat, eating part of the snake. As I got nearer, though, I realised that it was actually the largest, most disgusting rat I have ever seen in my life, staring up at my car. It was so horrible! Actually, I was so shocked, I almost ran it over. I just managed to avoid it and it disappeared into the long grass!
C: Oh, nasty! It actually reminds me of something my brother once told me, about when him and some friends of his were camping in ...

Conversation 3

E: I really thought I was going to die. Honestly, I hope I never see another crocodile in my life!
F: I can imagine. That's awful! It actually reminds me of something that happened to me last year in Indonesia.
E: Oh yeah? What was that?
F: Well, I was there on holiday, and I'd decided to spend a few days trekking through the jungle. On the second day, we were walking along a path through the rainforest when suddenly these huge lizards came running out of the bushes from all sides. They were enormous – much bigger than me! Everyone ran away, leaving me with three of these monster lizards running towards me. I tried to scream, but just couldn't! I really thought they were going to eat me.
E: God! That sounds terrifying! So what happened?
F: Well, luckily, the guides managed to stop the lizards with these big sticks they had, and so I managed to escape.

Answers

1 1 crows, parrot
2 snake, rat
3 lizards

2 1 The crows were chasing a parrot.
2 The snake was lying across the road and the rat was eating it.
3 The lizards were running out of the bushes.

3 1 sorry, sympathetic, concerned
2 disgusted, shocked
3 scared / terrified

Step 2 Ask students to look at the questions in B and try to answer the questions. Play the recording again for them to check. Check in pairs, then check with the whole group.

Answers
a 2 b 1 c 3 d 3 e 2 f 1 g 3 h 1 i 2

SPEAKING

Aim
To personalise the topic and give fluency practice.

Step 1 Ask students to read the questions in A and think about how they would answer them. Pre-teach *trekking*, *jungle*.

Step 2 Put students in pairs or small groups and to talk about the questions. Conduct feedback at the end.

DEVELOPING CONVERSATIONS

Helping to tell stories

Aim
To focus on ways listeners help the speaker to keep going when telling a story.

Step 1 Ask students what way they know / remember of 'helping' a speaker to keep going and elicit *really*? Ask students if they remember any ways in which the listener 'helped' the speaker in the three conversations. You could make a more explicit link here by asking students to read the audioscript on p. 169 and find examples of this. (*Go on, What? And? Yeah?* etc)

Step 2 Ask students to read the box or read it aloud to them. Ask them to look at exercise A and try to put the questions from the box in the correct place in the dialogues. Check in pairs, then play the recording for students to check. Drill the questions with slightly exaggerated intonation.

Answers
1 What?
2 What was that?; Seriously?
3 What was that doing there?
4 So what happened in the end?

11.2

1 A: You'll never guess what happened last night.
B: Go on. What?
A: Well, I was walking home from the bus stop when I suddenly saw a horse, standing there in the street!

2 C: I saw something really strange while we were away.
D: Oh yeah? What was that?
C: We saw this whale stuck on the beach.
D: Seriously? Still alive?
C: Yeah! It was actually quite upsetting! We phoned the police to see if they could organise help.

3 E: I was just about to put my shoes on, when I found a scorpion hiding in one of the shoes!
F: Really? God! What was that doing there?
E: I don't know. I guess it was just looking for somewhere to sleep.
4 G: We spent hours trying to persuade the cat to come down from the tree, but it refused to come.
H: Oh no. That's awful! So what happened in the end?
G: Well, eventually, we gave up. But an hour later it walked into the kitchen, looking for its dinner!

Step 3 Put students in pairs and ask them to read the dialogues. They should take turns being the storyteller and the listener. Monitor closely and correct pronunciation, especially their intonation on the questions.

GRAMMAR *-ing* clauses

Step 1 Read out the box and check students understand. Ask them to read the grammar reference on p. 150 if they seem unsure.

Step 2 Ask students to turn the pairs of sentences in exercise A into one sentence by using an *-ing* clause. Do the first example with them. Check in pairs, then with the whole group. Check *hissing* = the noise a snake makes.

Answers
1 I saw a fox in the street eating an old kebab.
2 I could hear a large animal of some kind moving around in the bushes.
3 As we were walking along I saw an eagle circling right above us.
4 I couldn't sleep because my grandmother's parrot was making a dreadful noise all night.
5 When we were camping I saw a huge lizard lying on a rock in the sun.
6 The bear was lying beneath a tree sleeping.
7 I once saw a wolf disappearing into a forest.
8 I went into the bathroom and there was a snake in the corner hissing at me.

Step 3 Ask students to complete the sentences in B. Ask students to read their sentences aloud to check.

CONVERSATION PRACTICE

Aim
To round off the lesson and give fluency practice.

Step 1 Ask students to read the instructions in A or read them out to them. Give them a few minutes to think about their stories. They can make up a story if necessary.

Step 2 Put students in small groups and ask them to take turns to tell their stories. The other students should try to ask some of the questions from *Developing conversations* to encourage the storyteller. When each one finishes, another should take over by saying *It / That reminds me of something that happened to me* ... etc. Monitor closely and take notes for a correction slot at the end. Conduct brief feedback by asking each group which was the most scary / surprising / funniest, etc. story they heard.

pp. 78–79

Next class make photocopies of **11A** p. 148.
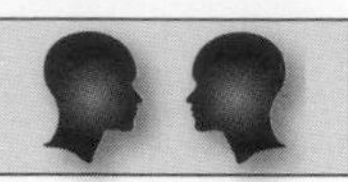

READING

Aim
To give practice in predicting, reading for gist and detail and to provide a context for the grammar.

Step 1 Tell students they are going to read four short articles about animals and the environment. Lead in by asking them if they know any endangered species and why they are endangered. Ask what the endangered animals in the photos are (chimpanzees, *takhi* horses).

Step 2 Put students in pairs and ask them to look at the headlines in A and talk about what each article might be about. Do not conduct feedback on this but help with vocabulary as necessary.

Step 3 Ask students in the same pairs to look at the words and phrases in the box and decide which ones they think go with each of the headlines. Again, do not conduct feedback.

Step 4 Ask students to read the articles quickly and decide which headline goes with which article. Check in pairs, then check with the whole group.

Answers
A Mass extinctions predicted
B Illegal animal trade moves into cyberspace
C Man arrested for smuggling animal skulls
D Back from the point of extinction

Step 5 Ask students to fill in the gaps in each article with the words / phrases from the box in B. Check in pairs then check with the whole group.

Answers
1 destroyed by global warming
2 hunting and trading
3 endangered species
4 organised criminal gangs
5 skeleton
6 tiger skins
7 reintroduced
8 bred

Step 6 Ask students to look at the questions in D and talk about them in pairs / threes. Check with the whole group.

Answers
1 a global warming, destruction of habitats, hunting and trading
  b global warming
2 a to check online trading sites for illegal animal trading
  b because it's relatively safe and makes it possible to reach large numbers of potential buyers easily
3 a they were part of his hobby
  b the police thought he was smuggling them into the country to sell them
4 a because horses have always been very important in the country
  b because some were kept in zoos for breeding and their numbers increased

LANGUAGE PATTERNS

Aim
To draw students attention to the passive constructions using to *be* + the past participle.

Step 1 Ask students to read the examples in the box. Ask them to translate into their own language and notice differences. Alternatively, if you prefer not to use translation, ask students what they notice about the patterns. These are passive constructions using *to be* + the past participle of *know – known*. *Is / are known as* + noun; *is / are known to* + base form; *a lot / a little / not much is known about, very few details are known about ….*

GRAMMAR Passives

Aim
To give practice in forming passives using *to be* + the past participle.

Step 1 Ask students to read the box or read it out to them. Check they understand by asking a few questions, e.g. *How do you form the passive*? (Correct part of *to be* + past participle.) *Why do we use the passive*? (Because we do not know who did the action or because it's not important.) *What could be an example of this*? (Talking about crimes.) If students are still unsure ask them to read the grammar reference on p. 150.

Step 2 Ask students to complete the sentences with the correct passive forms without looking back at the articles. Check in pairs by finding the sentences in the articles, then check with the whole group.

Answers
1 are currently threatened
2 were being offered
3 has been arrested
4 was searched / the skeleton of a dolphin / were found
5 is shown

Step 3 Ask students to read the phrases in exercise B and match each group with one of the past participles in the box. Do the first example with them. Check in pairs, then check with the whole group.

Answers

1 searched	3 taken	5 arrested
2 smuggled	4 released	6 kept

 **11A** see Teacher's notes p. 125.

SPEAKING

Aim
To give fluency practice in the vocabulary and grammar from the reading.

Step 1 Ask students to look at the questions in A and think about how they would answer them. They could make a few notes.

Step 2 Put students in small groups to discuss the questions. Monitor their use of target vocabulary and passives for a correction slot at the end.

 **pp. 80–81**

 **Next class** make photocopies of **11B** p. 149. 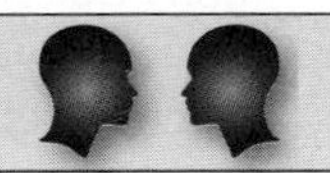

VOCABULARY Keeping pets

Aim
To focus on language related to pets.

Step 1 Lead in by asking students if they have or have ever had a pet or would like to have one. Why / why not?

Step 2 Ask students to look at the words / phrases in the box and complete each group with a similar word / phrase. Do the first example with them. Check in pairs, then with the group. Concept check by asking which words / phrases in the examples apply to which animals.

Answers

1 tank	6 dry food
2 aggressive	7 the litter tray
3 kittens	8 size
4 stroke	9 lick
5 looking after	10 mess

Step 3 Put students in pairs and ask them to look at the pictures. Student A should compare the first two and say which they prefer as a pet and why. Student B can agree / disagree. They should try to use as much of the language from exercise A as they can. They then swap and do the same with the other two pictures.

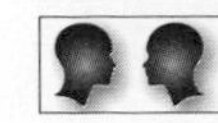 **11B** see Teacher's notes p. 125.

LISTENING

Aim
To hear some of the language in a realistic context.

Step 1 Tell students they are going to hear a conversation about pets. They should listen and mark the statements true or false. Give them a minute or so to read the statements then play the recording. Point out that Al is short for Alastair – a man's name. Ask them to check in pairs then check with the whole group. You could also ask them to correct the false statements.

11.3
S = Suzie, A = Al
S: Oh wow! They're so cute!
A: I know. They're great. They're only three weeks old.
S: What breed are they?
A: Siberian huskies.
S: Really? So what are you going to do with them?
A: Well, I wish I could keep them, but it's too much. They grow so big.
S: Mmm.
A: So I guess we'll just sell them or give them away. You don't want one, do you?
S: Er . . . no! I'm actually more of a cat person.
A: Really? I can't stand cats myself.
S: Why?
A: I just find them annoying. They're only interested in people so they can get food. You know what I mean? Most of the time, they're out of the house. They only come back when they want to be fed.
S: Oh, come on! They're not that bad. They like to be stroked – and it's good anyway, that independence. I mean – don't get me wrong – I do like dogs, but they're very demanding. They always expect you to play with them or take them for walks. And they're always jumping on top of you and licking you. I could do without it.
A: Oh, I like that about them! Dogs are more rewarding – you develop a relationship with a dog.
S: Well, I prefer my relationships to be human!
A: OK, but you know what I mean.
S: I suppose so.
A: So have you got a cat, then?
S: No. We had one when I was younger. In fact, my parents still have him, but it's not fair to have a cat in my flat. Cats need some freedom. And then the litter tray's really smelly!
A: I can imagine. So you don't have any pets?
S: Well, actually, I've got a snake.
A: A snake! You're joking. I'm terrified of snakes.
S: There's no need to be – the one I've got isn't poisonous.
A: OK, but how big is it?
S: About a metre. It's a bit shorter than that table.
A: Well, that's big enough. Where do you keep it?
S: It's in a tank in my bedroom. It doesn't need much looking after. I just give it a mouse every month or two.
A: A mouse? You don't have to catch them, do you?
S: No! I buy them frozen from the pet shop and then I defrost them in the microwave.
A: Oh, what? That's so disgusting!
S: What's so disgusting about it? It's no different to the tinned food you give your dog. It's only meat.
A: I know, but . . . I don't know. So do you ever take it out?
S: Yeah, of course! I've taken it to university a few times to show people. People like to have their photo taken with it around their neck.
A: Not me!
S: It's fun!
A: Forget it.
S: Actually, the last time I took it out at home, it disappeared behind the cooker and wouldn't come out.
A: You're joking! How did you get it out?
S: I had to leave a mouse on the floor to persuade it to come out.
A: Oh man! That's horrible.

Answers
1 F – he'll sell them or give them away
2 T
3 F – her parents still have it (a cat)
4 T
5 F – it eats mice
6 F – he doesn't want to have his picture taken with the snake
7 T

Step 2 Put students in pairs and ask them to try to answer the questions in B from what they remember. Then play the recording again for them to check.

Answers
1 dogs – they grow too big, demanding; cats – only interested in food; snakes – terrifying, disgusting
2 answers will vary
3 it hid behind the cooker – she had to offer it a mouse to persuade it to come out
4 answers will vary

NATIVE SPEAKER ENGLISH

Ask students to read the box or read it out to them. Check they understand by asking a few questions, e.g. *What's a dance / football computer person? What do you call someone who likes films / television / museums?*

Note It's common to use this in the negative, e.g. *I'm not really a ... I'm not much of a ...* . Ask students to give examples of the kind of person they are or aren't.

Pronunciation

Stress and intonation for emphasis

Aim
To focus on the use of stress / intonation on adverbs for emphasis.

Step 1 Read out the box and model the example, exaggerating the stress / intonation, especially on *so*.

Step 2 Ask students to listen to the recording and repeat the sentences after each one, paying particular attention to the stress / intonation.

11.4
1 Oh, they're so cute.
2 He's so lovely
3 He's so annoying.
4 Their dog is just really out of control!
5 It really stinks!
6 It's just incredibly noisy.
7 He even let's the cat walk on the kitchen surfaces!
8 He even lets the dog actually lick his face!

Step 3 In pairs ask students to read the piece about dog owners and underline the adverbs which they think are stressed. Play the recording for them to check.

11.5 / Answers
I don't really like dogs, but I really hate some dog owners. They can be so annoying – the way they talk about their pets like they were actually human beings! They say things like, 'Oh my little baby. You're so beautiful! Yes you are. Yes you are.' It's so stupid. What really annoys me, though, is the way they let their dogs run out of control. They even let their dogs jump on top of you. Then, if the dog bites you, they actually blame you. They say you scared the dog!

Step 4 Students prepare by reading the text quietly by themselves. Monitor and help with pronunciation.

Step 5 Put students in small groups and ask them to take turns reading the text aloud. At the end they should choose the best reader in their group.

Step 6 Ask students to think about the ideas in D. Using the sentence starters ask them to make a few notes.

Step 7 In new pairs students discuss their ideas, paying attention to stress / intonation. Conduct brief feedback.

Vocabulary Forming words

Aim
To give practice in forming nouns from verbs.

Step 1 Lead in by drawing a spidergram on the board with *depend* in the main bubble. Elicit related words and add to the bubble. Check students know part of speech, e.g. *dependent / independent* (adj); *dependence / independence* (noun); *dependently / independently* (adverb).

Step 2 Tell students to complete the sentences in A. Do the first example with them. Check in pairs, then as a group.

Answers
1 freedom
2 destruction
3 extinction
4 warnings
5 threat
6 investigation

Step 3 Ask students to underline collocations which go with the nouns in exercise A and to think of other possibilities.

Answers and examples
To have / enjoy / give someone their freedom
Destruction of their habitats / the rainforest / the planet
In danger of extinction / at risk of extinction / threatened with extinction
Repeated warnings / a health warning / a final warning
A serious threat / an enormous threat /a real threat
Under investigation / a police investigation / a thorough investigation

Speaking

Aim
To draw the unit together and end on a fun note.

Step 1 Ask students to put the sentences in A in the correct order. Ask what the noun is from *poisonous* (poison). Check as a group and drill the questions.

Answers
1 Is it poisonous?
2 What breed is it?
3 Where do you keep it?
4 Can I stroke him?
5 Is it OK if I pick him up?
6 How long have you had it?
7 What do you feed it?
8 How long do they live for?

Step 2 Tell students to think of a pet they have or would like to have. Then, in new pairs, they ask and answer the questions in A. Conduct brief feedback at the end.

12 PEOPLE I KNOW

UNIT OVERVIEW
The main aims of this unit are to extend students' ability to talk about **friends and family**. They practise **describing character** and **using synonyms**, read an article about **personal space** and listen to **one long conversation about family members** and **five short monologues about friends**. The main grammar aims are ***used to*** and ***would*** to talk about **past states / habits** and expressing **past regret** using ***I wish*** + **past perfect**.

SPEAKING

Aim
To lead in to the lesson and revise family relationship vocabulary.

Step 1 Lead in to the topic by briefly brainstorming family relationship words. Check students understand *nephew = your brother or sister's male child, niece = your brother or sister's female child, half-brother / half-sister = a brother or sister who has either the same father / mother as you, but not both, stepmother / stepfather = the woman / man who marries your father / mother after your mother / father dies or your parents divorce, stepbrother / stepsister = the child of your stepmother or stepfather.* etc. and *relative / relation = someone who is part of your family.* Tell students they are going to find about each other's families. Put them in groups of four or five to find out who has the biggest family. They should ask about all the different relatives each student has. Conduct brief feedback with the whole class.

Optional extra If you have a younger class, or if they seem interested, ask students to make a family tree of their families on posters to put up around the class. They could do this for homework.

VOCABULARY Describing character

Aim
To extend students ability to talk about personality using adjectives.

Step 1 Ask students to complete the sentences with a suitable word from the box. They should choose a near-synonym or a word related in meaning to the adjective already there. Do not pre-teach any of the vocabulary but encourage students to guess from context and by a process of elimination. Check in pairs, then check with the whole group. Model, drill and concept check. Elicit and mark the stress on the board. Check other words / phrases, e.g. *affectionate, indulgent, a bit of a dropout.*

Answers

1 bright	7 intense
2 outgoing	8 lazy
3 shy	9 stubborn
4 easy-going	10 generous
5 competitive	11 spoilt
6 naughty	12 chatty

Step 2 Ask students to look at the pictures and describe the people using the adjectives. Use one picture as an example and elicit, model and drill: *he looks* + adjective; *he looks like* + noun; *he looks like he could be* + adjective or noun. Put students in pairs or threes to talk about the pictures. Monitor closely and correct mistakes in their use of the expressions / adjectives, including pronunciation.

LANGUAGE PATTERNS

Aim
To draw students' attention a way of gently describing negative qualities.

Step 1 Ask students to read the box or read it aloud to them. Tell them we use this structure to gently describe negative qualities. Ask them to translate into their own language and notice any differences. Alternatively, if you prefer not to use translation, ask students what patterns they notice and how they are used here. *He / she can be* ... (this is softer than simply using the verb *to be* and is often used after *but*) + adjective; + *such a* + noun; + *so* + adjective. These can be followed by *sometimes* or, more colloquially, by *when he / she wants to be.* Elicit a few examples about students' friends / families or people in the class.

Developing conversations

That's like . . .

Aim

To extend students' ability to talk about character by focusing on a natural response to someone's description of another person and to lead into the listening.

Step 1 Ask students to read the box and check they understand. Then ask them to match a comment from 1–5 with a suitable response from a–e. Check in pairs, then check with the whole group.

Answers

1 e	2 c	3 b	4 d	5 a

Step 2 Put students in pairs and ask them to practise by reading out sentences 1–5, then giving the correct response from a–e, but substituting the people with someone they know so the sentences are true for them.

Listening

Aim

To hear the target vocabulary in a natural context and to give practice in listening for specific information and intensively.

Step 1 Tell students they are going to hear a conversation between two friends, Lewis and Jessica, about Jessica's family. Give them moment to read the questions in A and ask them to note down the answers as they listen. Play the recording. Check in pairs, then check with the whole group.

Answers

1 Because she went out to phone her brother as it was his birthday.
2 They both talk a lot / are very chatty.
3 He's clever and bright but not intense. He's friendly and outgoing.
4 He's lazy and a bit of a dropout and into politics.
5 They used to be close but now they don't really get on and she finds him a bit boring.

12.1

L = Lewis, J = Jessica

L: Where did you disappear to?
J: Sorry, I went out to phone my brother, Noel. It's his birthday today.
L: Oh OK. It's just that you were a long time.
J: I know. I was only going to be five minutes – just wish him 'happy birthday' – but once he starts talking, he doesn't stop!
L: Oh, that's like my mum. She could talk for hours. I sometimes think we could be on the phone and I could go and have a coffee and then come back and she'd still be talking! She wouldn't have noticed I'd gone!
J: Right. I'm not sure he's quite that bad.
L: No? Well, maybe I am exaggerating a bit, but she is very chatty. So do you and your brother get on well?
J: Yeah, really well, but unfortunately I don't see him that much now because he's living in the States.
L: Really! What's he doing there? Is he working?
J: No, he won a scholarship to study Physics.
L: Wow! He must be very clever.
J: Yeah, he's really bright. He was always top of his class – but he's not really intense with it. He's very funny, very outgoing.
L: That's good. So have you got any other brothers or sisters?
J: Yeah, I've got a younger brother – Greg.
L: And what's he like? Do you get on well with him too?
J: OK, I suppose.
L: You don't sound too sure.
J: No. I mean,we used to be quite close. We were both quite sporty – we would go to the beach a lot, we'd play tennis together and that kind of thing – but he's not interested now.
L: Really?
J: No, he's become a bit of a dropout. It's not that he isn't bright – he's just very lazy. He failed most of his exams last year – and then he's really got into politics. He's always going on demonstrations and complaining about me using the car too much and about me wanting to work for big business.
L: Maybe it's just a phase he's going through. How old is he?
J: 17.
L: Well, he might grow out of it.
J: I hope so. He can be quite boring sometimes.
L: Mmm.
J: Anyway, what about you? Have you got any brothers or sisters?
L: Yeah. Actually, there are six of us!

Step 2 Ask students to look at the sentences in exercise B and try to choose the correct answer from memory. Then play the recording again for them to check. Check with the whole group and concept check the difference between the pairs of words.

Answers

1 disappear	5 close
2 exaggerating	6 demonstrations
3 on	7 phase
4 won	8 out of

Step 3 Give students a moment to read the questions in C and think about how they would answer them. They might like to make a few notes. Put them in pairs / threes to discuss the questions.

Step 4 Conduct brief feedback by asking a few pairs to tell the class something interesting they learnt about their partner.

CONVERSATION PRACTICE

Aim
To wrap up the lesson and give personalised fluency practice.

Step 1 Give students a few minutes to look at the instructions in A and think about who they can talk about and what they can say. They could make a few notes if they wish.

Step 2 Put students in small groups to talk about their family members. They should take turns to begin the conversation in one of the suggested ways, with the other students responding by asking questions. Monitor closely and note down errors in target vocabulary for a correction slot at the end.

pp. 84–85

Next class make photocopies of **12A** p. 150 and **12B** p. 151.

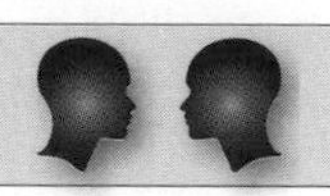

GRAMMAR *Used to* and *would*

Aim
To focus on *used to* + base form to talk about past habits or states and *would* + base form to talk about past states.

Step 1 Lead in by asking students if they can remember what Jessica from *Listening* on p. 83 said about her younger brother and how their relationship had changed. Ask them to look at the sentences in A and try to complete them from memory.

Step 2 Write the sentences on the board with gaps while they do this. Then play the recording for them to check then elicit the answers and fill in the gaps on the board. Check students understand form and meaning by asking concept questions, e.g. What are we talking about here? (Past habits or states.) How is *used to* different from *would* in this context? (*Used to* for both habits and states, *would* only for habits / repeated actions in the past, often used to give details.) Can *used to* replace *would* in these examples? (yes). Can *would* replace *used to*? (No.) Why not? (Because *be close* is a state, not a habit.) Can we use past simple for past habits and states? (Yes, but it is less emphatic.) What is the form after both *would* and *used to*? (Base form.) Ask students to read the box or read it out to them.

Direct them to the grammar reference on p. 151 if they are still unsure.

12.2 / Answers
We used to be quite close. We were both quite sporty – we would go to the beach a lot, we'd play tennis together and that kind of thing – but he's not interested now.

Step 2 Ask students to complete the sentences in B with one word only in each gap. Check in pairs, then check with the whole group. Model and drill some of the answers to focus particularly on the pronunciation of *used to* and the contractions *we'd, I'd*.

Answers

1 1 be
2 was
3 would
4 would
5 got

2 1 to
2 was
3 stayed / camped
4 go
5 went
6 spent

3 1 used
2 go
3 would
4 got

Step 3 Read the instructions and the example in exercise C and check students understand. Ask them to write sentences using the prompts. Check in pairs, then check with the whole group.

Suggested answers
1 My gran used to be / was very religious. She used to / would go to church every Sunday and she always made / would always make us say a prayer before dinner.
2 My grandfather was / used to be very indulgent. He would always buy / always used to buy us sweets and he would / used to let us watch TV all day.
3 When I was a kid we would / used to go to the mountains every summer. We would / used to go walking and we would / used to dive and swim in the river. It was fantastic.
4 I used to play basketball a lot. I would / used to train twice a week. We would / used to have a match every Sunday. We won the league once.
5 We used to sit together at school. We would always / always used to talk to each other. We would / used to pass each other notes and the teacher would / used to tell us off.

Step 4 Ask students to look at the examples in D and choose two of them to talk about. Give them a few minutes to think about what they are going to say and maybe make a few notes. Remind them that they must try and use *used to / would*. Put them in pairs / threes to discuss their notes. Monitor closely and note down any correct and incorrect use of in target language for a correction slot at the end.

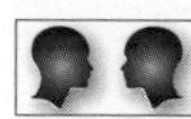

12A see Teacher's notes p. 125.

LISTENING

Aim
To extend the topic and give practice in listening for specific information and detail.

Step 1 Tell students they are going to hear five people talking about how they met the same person, Nicolas. Lead in by putting students in small groups and asking them to tell each other how they met their closest friend, girlfriend / boyfriend or partner.

Step 2 Give students a minute or so to read the statements a–f. They should number them as they listen according to which speaker matches each statement. One statement is not necessary. Check students understand *fall out* = to have an argument with someone. Play the recording. Check in pairs, then check with the whole group.

Answers
a 3 b 1 c ✗ d 5 e 2 f 4

12.3
1 Doug
I met him while doing a summer job in England. We were both working in this café – he was in the kitchens and I was a waiter. Our boss was a bit of an idiot. He was really strict – he was always shouting at us and was just horrible. Anyway, we used to go out after work and we'd sit and complain about our boss. We'd talk about the things we wished we'd said to him. Nicolas was always very funny about it.
2 Sandra
We were going out for a while. I met him when we were studying in Rome on an Erasmus programme. It was a great few months. We tried to keep the relationship going after he went back to Belgium, but it's difficult maintaining a long-distance relationship. We couldn't afford to visit each other very often and in the end, we split up. We've remained friends – which I suppose is important – but I sometimes wish we'd stayed together. Yeah, I wish we hadn't split up.
3 Shane
I met him while I was backpacking. We were staying in a hostel and we had to share a room. We got talking and found we had a lot in common. We ended up spending a couple of weeks sightseeing until I went back to Australia. We kept in touch via email after that and two years ago I moved to Britain. Since then, I've been over to Belgium to see him a couple of times.
4 Brigitta
We met at university. We didn't have much to do with each other at first. We're a bit different – I'm quite quiet and, as you know, he's very outgoing. It's not that we didn't get on at all. We'd see each other in class and in the library and we'd chat a bit. Over time, though, our chats got longer, and then just before we left university, he asked me out on a date. We've been seeing each other for about two years now. It's a shame it took so long for us to get together, really!
5 Franck
I met him through a friend, Jef, who he was sharing a flat with. We all used to go out quite a lot. so I'd talk to Nicolas and got to know him very well. At some point. I had an argument with Jef. It was about something stupid, but we basically stopped talking to each other. We're both very stubborn and I didn't want to be first to apologise, but of course, neither did he! I regret that, really. Anyway, to cut a long story short, I haven't seen Jef for years, but I'm still friends with Nicolas.

Step 3 Put students in pairs and ask them to discuss the questions in C. You can play the recording again if they need help. You could also help them by putting some questions on the board for them to answer (from memory if possible or when listening again). For example, *What nationality is he? What places has he been to? What's he like? Where has he worked?*

Answers
He has worked in a café. He is Belgian. He has been to England and Rome, where he was on an Erasmus programme. He used to have a girlfriend called Sandra and he now has a girlfriend called Brigitta, who he met at university and who he's been with for two years, though he's known her for longer. He once shared a flat with Jef.
He's outgoing, adventurous, bright, funny, likes travelling, and has a lot of friends. He's loyal to them.

VOCABULARY Synonyms

Aim
To focus on phrases or chunks connected with keeping in contact and give practice.

Step 1 Ask students to read the examples from *Listening* and elicit what they have in common (all to do with carrying on or continuing relationships). Tell students they are going to look at common collocations used about continuing relationships. Ask them to look at the groups of words / phrases and decide which verb from A goes with each group. Point out the questions: *Which two words share the most collocations? Which verb does not share any collocations with the other three?*

Answers
1 stay
2 keep
3 remain
4 maintain
Stay and *keep* share the most collocations. The odd one out is *maintain*.

Step 2 Give students a few moments to look at the questions and think about how they would answer them. Put them in pairs / threes to discuss the questions. Conduct brief feedback.

GRAMMAR Expressing regrets (*wish*)

Aim
To focus on *I wish* + past perfect to express past regret and give practice.

Step 1 Write up the sentences in A from *Listening* on the board while students are talking in groups. When they have finished, draw their attention to the sentences and elicit what form they notice in each one (*I wish / we wish(ed)* + past perfect). Highlight the form by underlining or boxing in a different colour. Concept check by asking: *Are they talking about the present or the past*? (Past.) *Did they stay together / split up / say things to him*? (No.) *How do they feel now*? (Sorry / regretful.) Model and drill the first two sentences, then elicit more examples, both positive and negative from students own lives. If they can't think of anything, give oral prompts, e.g. *I didn't go to university, I crashed my dad's car, I got married when I was 17, I didn't stay with my first boyfriend.*

Direct them to the grammar reference on p. 151 if they still seem unsure.

Step 2 Ask students to look at the questions in A and check they can answer them.

Answers
I wish it hadn't taken so long to get together. / I wish we'd got together sooner.
I wish I hadn't wanted to be the first to apologise. / I wish I hadn't been so stubborn.

Step 3 Ask students to think of possible situations in which people might say the sentences in B. They should think of as many situations as they can. Check their ideas. Exploit this further by asking students to read out their situations in random order and getting another student to reply with the correct *I wish* sentence.

Step 4 Ask students to listen to the recording and repeat after each example, paying particular attention to stress and linkage (elision and catenation).

12.4
1 I wish I'd known him.
2 I wish I'd met him.
3 I wish I'd never asked.
4 I wish they'd told me earlier.
5 I wish I'd tried harder at school.
6 I really wish we hadn't moved house.
7 Honestly, I wish I hadn't said anything.
8 I wish I hadn't gone to the meeting.
9 I sometimes wish they'd given me a different name.
10 I think she sometimes wishes she'd studied something else.

Step 5 Ask students to read the instructions in D. They should write three sentences about their past regrets.

Step 6 Put students in pairs and ask them to tell each other about their past regrets. They should develop conversations by asking each other questions, e.g *Why do you wish you hadn't...? Have you always wished you'd...?* Demonstrate this with a strong student, continue in open pairs then in closed pairs. Monitor closely and take notes for a correction slot at the end.

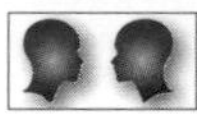
12B see Teacher's notes p. 125.

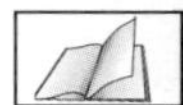
pp. 86–87

READING

Aim
To extend the topic and give practice in reading for specific information, responding to text and guessing meaning from context.

Step 1 Lead in to the topic by asking students how they feel about keeping in touch with friends via the Internet – what are some advantages and disadvantages? What do they know about social networking sites? Which are the best? Do they belong to one, why? (These could be left to the end.)

Step 2 You could ask students to skim the text very quickly and say what each paragraph is about, before going on to exercise A.

Answers
1 the writer uses the Internet but thinks it has a number of drawbacks
2 he hates social networking sites
3 he doesn't understand why people want to contact old school friends
4 he likes talking to people / prefers face-to-face contact

Step 3 Ask students to read the article a bit more slowly and choose the best answer to the questions in A. They should underline where they found the answer in the text. Check in pairs, then check with the whole group.

Answers
1 b (... there are also lots of things about it that worry me ... – paragraph two)
2 a (If one more person ... I'll scream! – paragraph three)
3 b (people only want you to join these sites to make them look even more popular – paragraph three)
4 a (I worry ... in the future. – paragraph four)
5 b (People drift apart because ... worth staying in touch! – paragraph five)
6 b (I don't need to go ... when to go out. – paragraph six)

Step 4 Ask students to read the text again and put a tick where they agree with something, a cross where they disagree and a question mark where they do not understand or are not sure. Then put them in pairs / threes to discuss their responses.

Step 5 Tell students they are going to guess the meanings of some of the words / phrases in the text from the context. The sentences in C are there to help them. Ask them to complete each sentence with one of the words / phrases from the box. They should look back at the way the word / phrase is used in the text and try to work out its meaning from the surrounding context.

Answers

1 endlessly	5 drift apart
2 distant friend	6 track down
3 paranoid	7 ego trip
4 come across	8 struggle with

Alternatively You could reverse the order of B and C to discourage students from asking about vocabulary earlier and if you prefer to end this section of the lesson with speaking practice. This would be especially advisable if you have a weaker class.

Native speaker English

Step 1 Ask students to read the examples in the box and check if they have any questions. Alternatively, read out the box to them, exaggerating the stress and intonation. Concept check by asking, *What's another way of saying if you ask me*? (In my opinion, if you want my opinion, If you want to know what I think.) *Is it formal or informal*? (Informal.)

Step 2 Ask for brief opinions on a few things, e.g. social networking sites, to practise straightforward responses – *If you ask me ... it's / they're terrible / rubbish / a great idea*, etc.

Speaking

Aim
To exploit the text further by looking at some common expressions for the phases in a friendship and to give fluency practice.

Step 1 Ask students to look at the stages in a friendship and put them in the correct order. Check in pairs, then check with the whole group.

Answers

1 g	6 a
2 h	7 f
3 c	8 b
4 i	9 d
5 e	10 j

Step 2 Ask students to look at the questions in B and think about how they would answer them. They could make a few notes if they prefer.

Tip Encourage weaker students to look back through the unit to find as many useful vocabulary words and phrases as they can to help them and ask them to make notes on what they want to say before they start.

Step 3 Put them in pairs or small groups to discuss the questions. Conduct brief feedback.

03 REVIEW

LEARNER TRAINING

Aim
To get students thinking about pronunciation and focus on some ways of improving it.

Step 1 Ask students to read the comments and check they understand *accent* and *phonetic script*.

Step 2 Put students in groups of three and ask them to discuss the comments, using the questions to help them. They could make some notes as they talk.

Step 3 Conduct feedback by asking students to share their ideas across the class or elicit their ideas and board them. Or, as in the previous Reviews, you could ask students to make posters to put on the walls.

GAME ⟶ CONVERSATION PRACTICE

For aims and suggested procedure, see Review 1, pp. 32–35.

ACT OR DRAW ⟶ QUIZ

For aims and suggested procedure, see Review 1, pp. 32–35.

Answers
1 spacious or big / large
2 Prices, the birth rate, pay, the temperature can all drop dramatically.
3 Crime and violence happen in rough areas; buildings are run down; the streets are dirty.
4 A play could be a tragedy, a comedy, a history play, a family drama, a mystery, etc.
5 Yes, terrific is good.
6 You feel uncomfortable, as if you don't belong, perhaps in a new class or at a party where you don't know anyone.
7 keeping a promise.
8 birds, especially eagles, vultures or other birds of prey.
9 tigers, Mongolian horses, some fish, e.g. cod, bees.
10 because they are looking for something or someone.
11 People exaggerate about their talents or achievements or sometimes about their injuries or accidents.
12 Naughty kids might disobey or cheek their parents, scribble / draw on walls, break a window, etc.
13 People grow out of clothes, shoes, childhood hobbies, habits.
14 Two friends might fall out because they disagree about something or one gossips about the other or lets the other down.
15 You could track someone down by calling them on their mobile phone or looking them up on social networking sites, e.g. facebook.

COLLOCATIONS

For aims and procedure, see Review 1, pp. 32–35.

PRONUNCIATION

Aim
To revise diphthong sounds and give practice.
For procedure, see Review 1, pp. 32–35.

R 3.1 Listen and repeat the sounds and the words.

/ɪə/	/eə/	/ʊə/	/eɪ/
weird	spare	rural	safe ....
/aɪ/ tiger	/ɔɪ/ destroy	/əʊ/ crow	/aʊ/ power ....

SPEAKING

Aim
To give students practice in describing pictures and to give fluency practice.

Step 1 Put students in pairs and ask them to look at the pictures and tell each other what they think is happening and what the people are saying.

Step 2 Tell students they are going to act out the two conversations. They should decide which role each is going to take and spend a few minutes preparing. They could look back at Unit 9, p. 69 and Unit 12, p. 84 for ideas if they need to. When they are ready, they should act out the conversations. Monitor and take notes for a brief correction slot at the end. Alternatively, a few pairs could act out their conversations in front of the class.

Step 3 Round off by asking the whole group the questions in C.

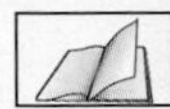 **pp. 90–91**

Listening

For aims and suggested procedure for the rest of the Review, see Review 1, pp. 32–35. The audio is R 3.2.

A Answers

a 2 b - c 3 d 1 e 4

B Answers

a 3 b 1 c 4 d e 2

Grammar Comparing the past with now

Answers

1 as good as
2 as quiet as
3 bigger, bigger
4 more expensive
5 worse
6 less polluted
7 as touristy as
8 as noisy

Expressing regrets

Answers

1 I wish I had known / met my grandfather.
2 I wish I hadn't told her how I felt.
3 I sometimes wish I had studied harder when I was at school.
4 I wish I had asked her out for a drink.
5 I wish we had had time to visit you when we were in Milan.

Prepositions

Answers

1 over
2 at
3 on
4 on
5 across
6 in
7 on
8 to
9 to
10 to

Language patterns

Answers

1 It still needs discussing / to be discussed more at the next meeting.
2 The whole place needs a good clean.
3 It's one of the worst films I've ever seen in my life.
4 It's the nicest thing anybody's ever done for me.
5 Suzhou is sometimes known as the Venice of the East.
6 She's nice, but she can be quite intense sometimes.
7 You can be such an idiot sometimes.

Passives

Answers

1 Police fear that drugs and guns are still being smuggled across the border.
2 I'm afraid my flight has been delayed, so don't wait for me. Go home and I'll get a taxi to the hotel.
3 I just worry that all sorts of private details could be posted online.
4 The mosque was built in the twelfth century.
5 I had a horrible feeling I was being followed, so I started to run.
6 Some of the most beautiful parts of the country are slowly being destroyed by global warming.

Developing conversations

Answers

1 size
2 possible
3 mind
4 long
5 front
6 mood
7 alive

Collocations

Answers

1 f 2 g 3 h 4 a 5 b 6 c 7 d 8 e

Forming words

Answers

1 extension
2 investment
3 shortage
4 extinction
5 habitat
6 independence

Vocabulary

Answers

1 distance
2 terrace
3 decorating
4 potential
5 portraits
6 sculptures
7 exhibition
8 Gallery
9 pleasantly
10 venue
11 rounded
12 competitive
13 chatty
14 determined
15 stubborn

13 TRAVEL

UNIT OVERVIEW
The main aims of this unit are to extend students ability to talk about **travel**, including **transport, travel problems** and **whose fault problems**. They **read** an article about **immigration** and **listen** to two conversations about **journeys** and a number of short exchanges about **travel problems**. The main **grammar** aims are **third conditional** and ***should have*** for criticism of past actions. They also practise **phrasal verbs** and **strong adjectives.**

SPEAKING

Aim
To lead in and introduce some vocabulary related to travel.

Step 1 Lead in by asking students if they enjoy travel, what are some of the best places they've been to, etc.

Step 2 Put students in pairs and ask them to discuss what the words in bold mean. Check in pairs, then check with the whole group.

Answers
1 a short excursion for the day
2 travel for business purposes
3 day out shopping / with your school or class / hunting (chasing animals)
4 without much luggage
5 on a long journey – or series of journeys – possibly in a number of countries
6 a single trip

Tip *Travel* is usually used as a verb. As a noun it is usually singular and uncountable, *I love travel. A journey* can be either long – *my journey to the far East*; or short – *his journey to work every day. A trip* is usually a short journey with a particular purpose, *a day trip, a business trip.*

Step 3 Put students in small groups and ask them to ask and answer the questions. Conduct brief feedback.

VOCABULARY

Ways of travelling and travel problems

Aim
To extend students ability to talk about transport.

Step 1 Ask students to put the words / phrases in the box in A in the correct column and try to add two more words / phrases to each column. Check in pairs then add two more words / phrases to each column. Check with the whole group and drill for pronunciation.

Answers
By train – carriage, line, platform
By ferry – crossing, deck, harbour
By car – bend, tyre, traffic lights
By plane – take-off, check-in desk, security
Note crossing could also belong to train (level crossing) or car (pedestrian crossing).
Other possible words:
By train – railway, station, compartment
By ferry – boat, port, foot passenger
By car – traffic jam, motorway, crossroads
By plane – passport control, crew, customs

Step 2 Ask students to complete the sentences in C with a suitable word / phrase from the box in A. Check in pairs, then check with the whole group.

Answers

1 platform	5 crossing
2 deck	6 line
3 tyre	7 security
4 take-off	8 bend

Step 3 Ask students to look at the pictures and think about the advantages and disadvantages of each type of transport using the vocabulary from A and other words and phrases that they know. Then put them in pairs to discuss them.

LISTENING

Aim
To extend the topic and to listen for gist and detail.

Step 1 Tell students they are going to hear two conversations about journeys. They should think about the answers to the questions as they listen.

Answers
1 plane /car
2 1 They nearly missed the flight because of long queues at check-in and security.

2 It was very bumpy (turbulent) as they went through a storm.
3 It was dark and the roads were slippery, she took a wrong turning and got lost, she almost had an accident.

13.1

Conversation 1

M = Maria, B = Belinda, A = Andre

M: Thanks for picking us up. It's really kind of you.
B: That's OK. It's no problem. So how was your journey?
M: Oh, quite stressful, actually. It's a relief to finally be here.
B: Oh no! What happened? You weren't delayed or anything, were you?
M: No, no. It wasn't that, thank God, but everything else that could go wrong, did! To begin with, we almost missed the flight – because Andre didn't want to spend too long hanging around at the airport.
A: I've already said I'm sorry!
M: He said we'd be OK if we got there an hour and a half before take-off, but there was a huge queue at the check-in desk – and then another one going through security, so in the end we only just caught the flight.
B: Oh, it's horrible when that happens, isn't it?
M: Yeah – and then the flight was dreadful as well. As we were coming over France, we hit a big storm and it was really bumpy. Honestly, at one point, I thought we were going to crash.
B: That sounds terrifying.
M: It was! I don't want to go through that again, I can tell you!
B: I'm sure. What do you want to do now? Do you want to go to the office, or do you want to check in at the hotel first?

Conversation 2

L = Lara, K = Karen

L: Hi. There you are! I was starting to worry.
K: Yeah, sorry I'm so late. I had a bit of a nightmare getting here.
L: Oh really? How come?
K: Well, to begin with, it was still dark when we set off.
L: Really. What time did you leave?
K: Six. And then it immediately started to pour down, so the roads were really slippery.
L: Oh I hate driving in the rain – especially in the dark.
K: So do I. That's probably why I took a wrong turning. I got completely lost and ended up going round in circles for ages. I couldn't work out where I was or where I was going! Then, when I finally got back onto the right road, I almost had an accident.
L: Seriously? What happened?
K: Oh, it wasn't anything bad. It was just this stupid guy in a big expensive car who drove straight across me. I had to brake to avoid hitting him. I wasn't hurt or anything, but I did have to stop and park the car for a few minutes to calm down.
L: Oh, you poor thing. That's awful – but that's male drivers for you!

Step 2 Put students in pairs and ask them to look at the adjectives in the box in B and try to remember what they referred to. Point out that they are in the same order that they heard them and that the first three refer to Conversation 1 and the last four to Conversation 2. Then play the recording again for them to check.

Answers
huge – queue
bumpy – flight
terrifying – experience / flight
slippery – roads
wrong – turning
stupid – male driver
hurt – the speaker (wasn't hurt)

Step 3 Let students read the questions in C and think about how they would answer them. Then put them in pairs / threes and ask them to discuss the questions.

LANGUAGE PATTERNS

Aim

To draw students' attention to the use of *end up*.

Step 1 Ask students to read the box or read it aloud to them. Ask them to translate into their own language and notice any differences. Alternatively, if you prefer not to use translation, ask students to read the box and tell you what patterns they notice (*end up* + verb in *-ing* form, *end up* + preposition, *end up* + adjective). Check they understand what this means = this is what happens in the end / after a series of events.

VOCABULARY Phrasal verbs

Aim

To focus on a set of phrasal verbs commonly used when talking about travel.

Step 1 Lead in by checking students know what a phrasal verb is (verb + particle [adverb or preposition] or verb + two particles) and elicit some examples from their knowledge in general. Ask them to read the box.

Step 2 Ask students to try to replace the words in italics with a phrasal verb from the text in the correct form. Check in pairs. If they still need help, tell them to check with the audioscript on p. 171. Check with the whole group.

Answers

1 hanging around	5 pour down
2 go through	6 work out
3 check-in	7 got back
4 set off	8 calm down

Step 3 Ask students to complete the sentences in B with the correct particle. Check in pairs, then check with the whole group.

Answers

1 set *off*	5 calm *down*
2 checked *in*	6 went *through*
3 hang *around*	7 work *out*
4 get *back / in*	8 pour *down*

Step 4 Ask students to write a sentence of their own to illustrate each of the phrasal verbs. Check in pairs.

Conversation practice

Aim
To round off the lesson and give fluency practice.

Step 1 Ask students to think about terrible journeys they have had – or someone they know has had.

Step 2 Put students in pairs and ask them to take turns asking and talking about their terrible journeys. They should try to use vocabulary / phrasal verbs from the lesson. The listener should encourage the speaker by asking questions. Ask students if they remember ways of doing this (see Unit 11). They could look at the audioscript for *Listening* on p. 171 to find ways of encouraging the speaker, e.g. *What happened? Really? Seriously?* Monitor closely and note down errors in target vocabulary for a correction slot at the end.

pp. 94–95

Speaking

Aim
To lead in to the reading and focus on key vocabulary.

Step 1 Lead in by asking students about emigration and immigration, What is the difference? Why do people emigrate? What problems do immigrants have?

Step 2 Ask students to look at the questions in A and try to work out what the words in bold mean. Then put them in pairs to discuss the questions.

Answers
stamp = place a mark in your passport to say you entered the country
visa = the document that shows you can legally enter a country
restrictions on immigration = letting fewer people not originally from the country move there
bureaucracy = administration system operated by a large number of officials
emigrate = leave your own country to live in another
refugee = people who are forced to leave their country because of war, political / religious beliefs

Reading

Aim
To extend the topic and to give practice in predicting, reading for specific information and guessing meaning from context.

Step 1 Ask students to read part 1 of the article on immigration then work in pairs to answer the questions.

Answers
1 It's more difficult than it used to be.
2 People will always look for a better life abroad and richer countries will always welcome them to do the jobs they don't want to do. Immigrants often build walls / fences which are designed to keep other immigrants out.
3 the needs of rich countries; poverty, curiosity, love, weather, land – or escaping war, famine or persecution

Step 2 Put students in pairs / threes and ask them to look at the pictures and discuss the questions. Do not conduct feedback on this but tell them to read part 2 to check.

Answers
1 Vietnam
2 because they were a rich, anti-communist family
3 sickness, claustrophobia, storms, pirates, getting caught
4 The captain took them to Malaysia and Mai-Ho eventually got a visa to Australia.

Step 3 Ask students to look at the words in italics in D and try to guess what they mean. They should look back at how they are used in part 2 (point out that they are in the same order here as in the text). Check in pairs, then check with the whole group.

Answers
1 to put money into something in the hope of making more money (Mai-Ho's family invested all their money in a boat)
2 took away / removed (their boat was confiscated)
3 gave them something to make them behave in a certain way (Mai-Ho bribed government officials to get the boat back)
4 treating people differently because of their sex / race / sexuality / age / disability, etc. (many immigrants suffer racial discrimination)
5 started / established (Mai-Ho set up two successful businesses)
6 received the most votes / chosen (Mai-Ho was elected mayor of her town)
7 because of / as a result of (individual refugees and host nations develop thanks to immigration)

Step 4 Put students in threes / small groups to discuss the questions in E. In a multilingual class aim for mixed nationality groups. Conduct brief feedback.

GRAMMAR Third conditionals

Aim
To introduce the third conditionals to talk about imagined / unreal situations in the past.

Step 1 Ask students to complete the examples from the article in the box, then check with the whole group. What tense do we use in the *if* clause? (Past perfect.) What verb form is in the main clause? (*Would* [*not / never*] + *have* + past participle.) Model and drill for pronunciation, paying particular attention to weak forms and contractions. Ask students to complete the box and check with the grammar reference on p. 152 if they are still unsure. Check with the whole group.

Answers
been, never, have, had

Answers
past, would, participle

Step 2 Ask students to look at the sentences in B and match a sentence beginning with a suitable ending. Check in pairs, then check with the whole group.

Answers
1 d 2 e 3 b 4 a 5 f 6 c

Step 3 Ask students to write their own endings to the sentence beginnings in B. Then work in pairs, swap papers and correct each other's sentences.

Optional activity Refer students back to *Reading* exercise E and ask them to discuss what would / would not have happened if the people they talked about hadn't moved countries.

pp. 96–97

Next class Make photocopies of **13A** p. 152 and **13B** p. 153.

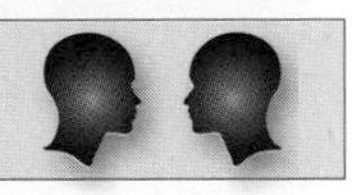

VOCABULARY Strong adjectives

Aim
To focus on strong adjectives, e.g. *terrified, furious.*

Step 1 Lead in by writing some adjectives on the board e.g. *hot, cold, wet, frightened*. Ask students if they know how to make these stronger.

Step 2 Read out the box to students, then ask them if they know a strong adjective for *good* (*fantastic*) and do a quick drill and focus on the intonation in preparation for later, *Was it good?* It was absolutely fantastic!

Step 3 Ask students to match the questions 1–6 in A with a suitable response from a–f and the comments 7–12 with a suitable response from g–l. Check in pairs, then play the recording for them to check. Elicit answers from the whole group.

13.2

1 A: What was the weather like in Greece? Was it hot?
B: Yeah, it was boiling – over 40 degrees most days.
2 A: What was the weather like in Finland? Was it cold?
B: Yeah, it was freezing – around minus 10 most days.
3 A: What was Istanbul like? It's quite a big city, isn't it?
B: Yeah, it's huge. The population's around 12 million.
4 A: What was the food like in Italy? Was it good?
B: Great, really delicious. They really know how to eat.
5 A: So what was your trip like? Was it good?
B: Yeah, it was fantastic! We had a great time.
6 A: How was the journey back? Did you get wet in that storm?
B: We got absolutely soaked! I didn't have an umbrella or anything.
7 A: You must be very angry about them losing your luggage.
B: I am. I'm absolutely furious.
8 A: You must be tired after such a long journey.
B: Yeah, I am. I'm exhausted. I'm ready for bed.
9 A: You must be hungry after such a long journey.
B: I am. I'm starving. Have you got anything to eat?
10 A: It's supposed to be quite a dirty city, isn't it?
B: Yeah, it was really filthy! I couldn't believe it.
11 A: It's supposed to be quite crowded, isn't it?
B: Yeah, it was. It was absolutely packed when we went!
12 A: Tabriz is supposed to be quite an interesting city.
B: Yeah. It's fascinating. It dates back over a thousand years.

Answers

1 d	3 e	5 c	7 k	9 l	11 i
2 f	4 a	6 b	8 h	10 g	12 j

Step 3 Put students in pairs and ask them to say the strong adjectives to each other and mark where they think the main stress is. Play the recording again for them to check. Elicit and mark the stress on the board. Point out also that the intonation on the strong adjective is also quite emphatic. Demonstrate by getting a student to ask you one of the questions and exaggerating the stress / intonation on the strong adjectives. Continue with a few more examples in open pairs.

Step 4 Ask students to close their books and test them e.g. *Which adjective means very dirty? What about very crowded?* Then ask students to test each other. Student A reads out sentences 1–6 from exercise A, Student B should try to remember the answer. Then swap for 7–12. Monitor and correct their use of the target vocabulary.

Step 5 Ask students to make a list of places – cities or countries – they've been to. Tell them to work in pairs and ask each other about the places, e.g. *What was Prague like?* It was really fascinating. Demonstrate in open pairs, then continue in closed pairs.

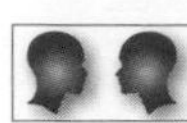

13A see Teacher's notes p. 126.

LISTENING

Aim

To hear the target vocabulary in context and introduce the grammar (*should / should not* + *have* + past participle).

Step 1 Tell students they are going to hear four conversations about travel experiences. They should listen to the conversations one at a time and note down which strong adjectives the speakers use and what each one is describing. Check in pairs, then as a group.

Answers

1 freezing – the weather in Peru; amazing – time
2 filthy – hotel room; horrible – situation
3 boiling (hot) – the weather in Greece; horrible – being sunburnt
4 tiny – the space in the hand baggage / luggage; ridiculous – having to pay an excess; huge – the queue at the desk

13.3

Conversation 1

A: What was the weather like in Peru? Was it hot?
B: No, it wasn't, actually. We arrived at night, and it was freezing. Then, during the day it was still chilly and cloudy.
A: Oh dear.
B: I wish I'd taken some warmer clothes – I only had T-shirts and one thin jacket.
A: Oh no!
B: It was stupid – I should've thought more carefully about what to pack. I knew we'd be in the mountains and could've checked the forecast.
A: I guess, but South America – you assume it'll be hot.
B: Exactly! It's silly, really! Anyway, we still had an amazing time!

Conversation 2

C: Hello, mum. It's me. Alan.
D: Oh hello. I was worried. Did you arrive safely?
C: Yeah, sorry, we got here late – that's why I didn't phone.
D: Oh right. So, is everything OK? Are you both well?
C: Yeah, fine, except for the cockroaches in the hotel.
D: Cockroaches!
C: Yeah. We stayed in this little place last night and the room was filthy.
D: That's horrible!
C: We were silly. We should've looked around more, but because we got here so late, we just chose the first cheap place we came across.
D: Oh Alan!
C: Don't worry – we'll check the place out better next time.
D: I hope so.

Conversation 3

E: How was Greece? Nice and hot?
F: Yeah, it was. It was boiling!
E: Lucky you! I bet that was nice.
F: It was, but I did get sunburnt on the first day.
E: Oh no!
F: It was really hot and I was sunbathing and just fell asleep. The next day, my skin went purple! It was horrible.
E: Oh, you poor thing!
F: Oh it was my own fault. I shouldn't have stayed in the sun for so long, especially with my skin! I should've at least put on some sun cream!

Conversation 4

G: Hello, Sir. You're flying to Prague.
H: That's right.
G: Is that your only bag to check in?
H: Yes.
G: I'm afraid there's an excess baggage charge of €200 to pay.
H: What? But there are three of us! The baggage allowance is 15 kilos each.
G: I'm sorry sir, but the rules are very clear: the maximum for any one bag is 15 kilos. You can transfer some weight to your hand baggage, if you like.
H: How can we fit 15 kilos in there – it's tiny!
G: Well, in that case you need to pay the excess.
H: That's ridiculous.
G: I'm sorry, but it really isn't my fault. The ticket conditions are very clear. I'm afraid you have to go back to the desk over there and pay the excess.
H: But the queue's huge!
I: I told you we should've brought another suitcase.
H: I just thought it would be easier with one.
I: €200! That's such a rip off!

Step 2 Ask students to look at the sentences in B and try to complete them from memory. They should think about why each person made the mistake. Play the recording again for them to check.

Answers

1 thought more carefully – thought South America would be hot

2 looked around more – it was late
3 stayed in the sun; put on some sun cream – fell asleep in the sun
4 brought another suitcase – had to pay extra for excess weight

Native speaker English

Ask students to read the box or read it out to them. Check they understand by eliciting a few more examples. Is this formal or informal? (Informal.)

Grammar *Should have*

Aim
To introduce *should have* + past participle to talk about past mistakes.

Step 1 Write examples 2 and 3 from *Listening* exercise B on the board. Highlight form and meaning and drill for pronunciation, especially weak forms.
We should've looked around more. (Subject + *should* + *have* + past participle.)
Did they look around much? (No.) Was this wise? (No.) How do they feel now? (Stupid.)
Read the box out to students. If they still seem unsure direct them to the grammar reference on p. 152.

Step 2 Remind students of third conditional by using the situations from *Listening*, e.g. *I should've thought more carefully about what to pack.* Why? *Because if… (if I'd thought more carefully about it, I wouldn't have got so cold).* Elicit further examples from the other situations and drill for pronunciation.

Step 3 Put students in pairs and ask to look at the sentences in A and think about what happened in each case. Then they should use a third conditional to explain what would've been a better idea and why. Do the first example with them.

Suggested answers
1 They had a terrible crossing and were late for something, e.g. a wedding – if we'd gone by plane we wouldn't have missed the wedding.
2 I got terribly hot – if I'd worn something lighter, I wouldn't have got so hot.
3 He crashed into a tree – if he hadn't been driving so fast, he wouldn't have crashed.
(Note the use of continuous tense with *drive* to show the action went on for some time.)
4 We broke our new washing machine – if we'd read the instructions more carefully, we wouldn't have broken the washing machine.
5 We couldn't get in to the concert – if we'd booked the tickets in advance, we would've got into the concert.
6 We missed the party because we already had another arrangement – if they'd told us about it sooner, we wouldn't have missed it.
7 He set fire to the house – if they hadn't left him on his own, he wouldn't have set fire to the house.
8 Someone stole my bag – if I hadn't left it there, they wouldn't have stolen it.

Optional activity Revise *I wish* from Unit 12 to incorporate into the next activity. Elicit examples from the situations in A, e.g. 1 *I wish we'd gone by plane*, 2 *I wish I'd worn something lighter.*

Developing conversations

Blaming people

Aim
To extend and put the grammar into a realistic context.

Step 1 Look back at some of the sentences in *Grammar* exercise A, especially the ones involving another person (3, 4, 6). Ask what people are doing when they say this (criticising past actions). Elicit other ways of doing this – *it's your / his / her fault; you're / he's / she's to blame for + -ing* form; *I blame him for + -ing* form). When we are criticising ourselves we use *it's my fault / I blame myself for + -ing* form. Read out the box or ask students to read it.

Step 2 Ask students to read the sentences in A and complete them with a suitable word in each gap. Check in pairs, then check with the whole group.

Answers

1 blame, should	4 fault, should
2 my, taken, have	5 myself, had
3 yours, been	6 have, fault

Speaking

Aim
To draw the unit together and give freer practice.

Step 1 Ask students to read the situations in A. Then put them in pairs to discuss them. They should try to use the target language and to incorporate *I wish* + past perfect where appropriate. Encourage them to use *should have* or third conditionals.

Step 2 Put students in new pairs. They should choose one of the situations in A and prepare to role-play a conversation. Give them a few minutes to decide their roles and think about what they are going to say. They should then act out the conversations. Monitor closely and note down errors in target language for a correction slot at the end. Repeat the activity with the other situations or get stronger pairs to act out the conversation in front of the class.

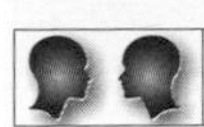 **13B** see Teacher's notes p. 126.

14 TECHNOLOGY

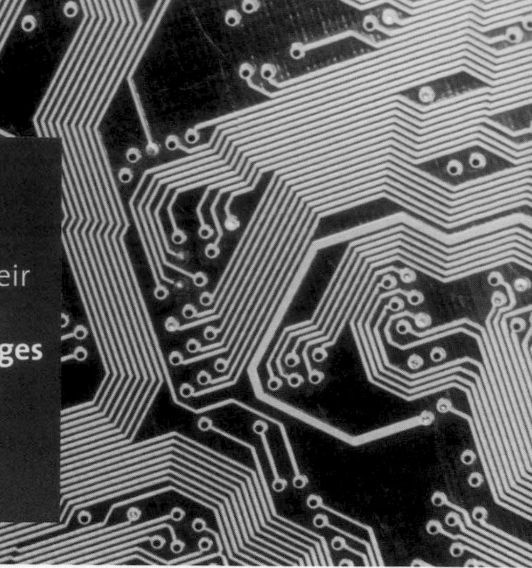

UNIT OVERVIEW
In this unit students extend their ability to talk about **technology**, particularly **computers** and **computer problems, programs and gadgets**. They also extend their vocabulary about **different kinds of markets**. They practise **responding to advice** and discuss **things that affect the environment**. They **read** an article about **changes in technology** and **listen** to a **telephone conversation** about **computer problems** and to **conversations** about **gadgets and technology**. The main grammar aim is ***-ing*** **forms and *to*-infinitives.**

SPEAKING

Aim
To lead in and get students immediately involved through personalisation.

Step 1 Lead in by asking students what inventions have most changed our lives in the last 50 years. Put them in pairs / threes and ask them to discuss the questions in A. Students who don't have their own computer could talk about a family computer or one they use at work / college. Conduct brief feedback.

VOCABULARY Computers

Aim
To extend vocabulary for the parts of a computer.

Step 1 Draw students' attention to the picture. Elicit some examples of the names of the parts. Ask students to label the other parts, using the words in the box in A (tell them that one arrow has two labels). Check in pairs, then as a group. Model and drill for pronunciation.

Answers

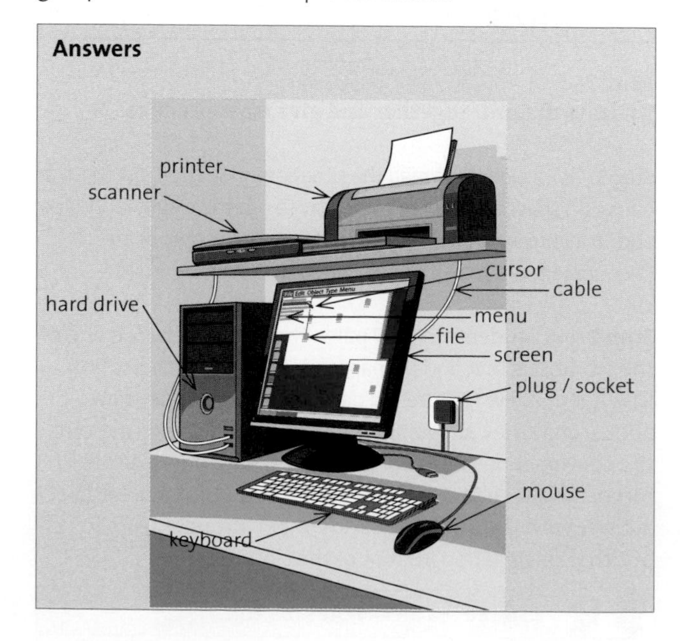

Step 2 Ask students to complete the sentences in B with one of the nouns from A. Do the first example with them. Check in pairs, then check with the whole group.

Answers

1 scanner
2 socket
3 menu
4 cursor
5 plug
6 hard drive
7 file
8 screen
9 cable
10 printer
11 keyboard
12 mouse

Step 3 Ask students to underline the words that collocate with the nouns they wrote in A. Then ask them to translate into their own language.

Alternatively In a multilingual class, or if you don't want students to translate, ask them to check in a monolingual dictionary.

Answers
scan (something) in
plug (something into) a socket
drop-down menu
move the cursor over the image
a three-pin plug
external hard-drive
delete a (really important) file
the screen (kept) freezing
tripped over a cable
the printer ran out of ink
spill (something) all over the keyboard
right click on the mouse

Step 4 Ask students to look at the questions in D and think about how they would answer them. Then put them in pairs / threes to discuss their experiences. Conduct brief feedback.

PRONUNCIATION Abbreviations

Aim
To raise students' awareness of common abbreviations and how to pronounce them.

Step 1 Lead in by writing a few well-known abbreviations on the board, e.g. USA, UK, AIDS. Elicit what they are (abbreviations) and why we use them. Read out what is in the box or ask students to read it. Check they understand.

Step 2 Put students in pairs and ask them to look at the abbreviations in A and discuss what they are. Check with the whole group.

Answers
IT = information technology
USB = universal serial bus
PC = personal computer
URL = uniform resource locator
RTF = rich text format
PDF = portable document format
DVD = digital video / versatile disc
FAQs = frequently asked questions
ASAP = as soon as possible
GPS = global positioning system
JPEG = joint photographic experts group
WiFi = Wireless fidelity
RAM = random access memory
CD-ROM = compact disc-read only memory
AIDS = acquired immune deficiency syndrome

Step 3 Play the recording and ask students to repeat after each one. Make sure they notice that AIDS and RAM are said as words.

14.1
IT
USB
PC
URL
RTP
PDF
DVD
FAQs
ASAP
GPS
JPEG
WiFi
RAM
CD-ROM
AIDS

LISTENING

Aim
To hear the target vocabulary in a realistic context.

Step 1 Tell students they are going to hear Ella and Jirka talking. Give them a time to read the questions in A and ask them to note down the answers as they listen. Play the recording. Check in pairs, then as a group.

14.2
J = Jirka, E = Ella
J: Hello. Jirka Kaspar. IT.
E: Oh hello, Jirka. This is Ella. From Marketing.
J: Hi. What can I do for you?
E: Well, I've actually got a fairly major problem. My computer crashed yesterday and when I turned it on again today I seem to have lost all my really important files.
J: OK. Well, firstly – don't panic! I'm sure everything will be in there somewhere. What makes you think you've lost them?
E: Well, the folders I keep all my files in have just disappeared from the screen.
J: OK. Have you made back-up copies at all? Haven't you copied them onto an external hard drive or onto online storage or anything?
E: I was worried you might ask me that! It's stupid of me, but I haven't, no. I just kept all my files on the computer.
J: Ah! OK. Well, in future, you might want to think about backing the files up more! Anyway, you say it crashed yesterday.
E: Yes, but it'd been strange all week. The screen kept freezing and I kept having to re-start it all the time.
J: Right. And was it slow?
E: Yes, very.
J: That might be because the memory was full.
E: Oh, OK. And then I turned it on today and everything had gone. I'll be in such trouble if I can't find things again!
J: Have you done a search for them?
E: Kind of, yes. I've tried searching for specific files, but nothing comes up.
J: And have you tried re-booting it at all?
E: Um . . . what does that mean?
J: Turning it off and then turning it on again.
E: Oh, OK. I need these things in plain English, you see! But yes, I have – and it didn't make any difference.
J: Right. Well, in that case, Ella, I think the best thing to do is just leave it as it is. Don't touch it or do anything else to it and I'll come down to you as soon as I have a minute and have a proper look at it. I can't promise anything, but I'll see what I can do.
E: Oh, that's great, Jirka. Thank you so much for that. I really appreciate it.
J: That's OK. It's why I'm here.

Answers
1 Her computer crashed yesterday and she seems to have lost all her important files.
2 The screen kept freezing and she kept having to re-start the computer.
3 Jirka suggests doing a search for the files and re-booting the computer (turning it off and on again).
4 She says she's tried it.
5 She says she should leave it and she will come and have a look at it.

LANGUAGE PATTERNS

Aim
To draw students' attention to some patterns used in questions and negative statements.

Step 1 Ask students to read the examples in the box and check they understand. Ask them to translate into their own language and notice any differences. Alternatively, if you prefer not to use translation, ask students to look at the sentences in the box and tell you what patterns they notice (*at all* used at the end of a question or negative clause / sentence to give emphasis; *hardly* used in an affirmative sentence to mean *almost not* – can be combined with *at all*).

SPEAKING

Aim
To exploit the listening with further discussion about the topic and to give fluency practice.

Step 1 Ask students to look at the questions in A and think about how they would answer them.

Step 2 Put students in pairs or small groups and ask them to discuss the questions in A. Encourage them to use *hardly* and *at all*. Conduct brief feedback.

DEVELOPING CONVERSATIONS

Responding to advice

Aim
To give practice in giving and responding to advice.

Step 1 Read the box and check that students understand the pattern of asking and answering. Ask them to translate into their languages and compare this to English. What similarities / differences do they notice? Ask them to discuss this in pairs, then as a class.

Alternatively If you prefer not to use translation, ask students to briefly practise having the conversation in pairs, then go on to Step 2.

Step 2 Put students in new pairs if possible. Ask them to read thought statements 1–5 and to take turns giving and responding to advice. Monitor and note down errors for a correction slot at the end.

CONVERSATION PRACTICE

Aim
To draw together the lesson and give fluency practice.

Step 1 Put students in pairs. Ask them to make a list of possible computer problems. They should use the ideas in the lesson to help them. Ask them to check with another pair and add to their lists.

Step 2 Put students in new pairs if possible. Ask them to choose a problem and a role (person with a problem or a help desk worker). They are going to have a telephone conversation about the problem. They should take a few minutes to think about what they are going to say and maybe make a few notes (individually). When they are ready they should act out the conversation. Then swap and repeat. Monitor and note down errors for a correction slot at the end. You could also ask a few pairs to act out one of their conversations in front of the group.

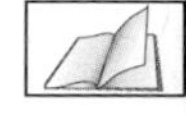

pp. 100–101

Next class Make photocopies of **14A** p. 154.

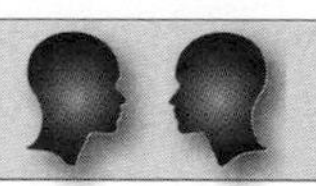

READING

Aim
To give practice in predicting, reading for gist and specific information and guessing meaning from context.

Step 1 Lead in by asking students how many mobile phones they have had and why they've changed them.

Step 2 Ask students to look at the pictures and tell them that each one illustrates the article they are going to read in some way. Put them in pairs / threes and ask them to discuss what they think the article is about and how the items are connected. Do not conduct feedback.

Step 3 Ask students to read the article quickly (ignore the words / phrases in bold) to find out if their predictions were accurate. Put them in pairs and ask them to discuss what they remember about each of the items in the pictures. Conduct brief feedback.

Answer
The pictures show canals, floppy discs, videotapes and the Sinclair C5 – an electric car. They were all very common at one time (apart from the Sinclair C5) but largely fell out of use when they were replaced by something more modern. The videotapes are VHS format, the format which was adopted in preference to Betamax. In a way the C5 was ahead of its time as electric or battery run cars are now being developed again.

Step 4 Ask students to read the article again and decide if the statements in C are true or false. They should underline the part of the text which gave them the answer. Check in pairs, then check with the whole group.

Answers
1 F – . . . the date on them clearly said 'October 1998'!
2 T – . . . they were an essential part of the industrial revolution . . . a network of canals was developed to transport goods . . .
3 T – . . . they have enjoyed a revival as a holiday destination . . .
4 F – . . . many believed it was inferior . . .
5 F – The victory was short-lived . . .
6 T – Intended to be a green alternative . . .
7 F . . . with vehicles that could go over that speed [24 kph] you had to have a driving licence . . .
8 T – That hot new piece of technology you queued all day to buy could well be out of date before too long . . .

Step 5 Ask students to look at the questions in D and give them a few moments to think about how they would answer them. Put them in pairs / small groups to discuss the questions. Conduct brief feedback.

Native speaker English

Read out the last sentence of the text and ask them what they think *hot* means in this context (exciting, new and interesting). Read out the box and check they understand. You may also like to check students understand *she's really hot* = sexually attractive (informal) and compare with *cool* = fashionable, attractive (informal) – see *Vocabulary* on p. 102 in the Student's book.

Step 1 Put students in pairs and ask them to look at the words in bold and try to guess what they mean. They should look at the surrounding words to help them. Check with the whole group.

Answers
reveals = shows
non-starters = things which don't become a success
fallen out of use = stopped being used
bitter = hard-fought, acrimonious
market share = proportion of people buying / using this product / service as opposed to a similar one
vehicle = form of transport which is driven
creator = person who creates or invents something
thus = in this way

Vocabulary Talking about markets

Aim
To focus on different meanings of the word *market* and common collocations.

Step 1 Ask students to look at the sentences in A and check they understand all the words / phrases in italics. Also check they understand *beauty salon* and *package holiday.* Check they understand *market* in this context = the number of businesses being opened or products / services being sold.

Step 2 Ask students to choose the alternative in A which best describes the situation in their country at the moment. Ask them to compare their ideas in pairs (different nationality pairs in a multilingual class). Conduct brief feedback.

Step 3 Put students in new pairs if possible and ask them to look at the examples in B and decide which phrases in A best describe the state of these markets in their countries. Check they understand *black market* = illegal trade in goods. They should use the phrases from A and some of their own ideas to develop conversations.

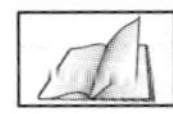
pp. 102–103

Next class Make photocopies of **14B** p. 155.
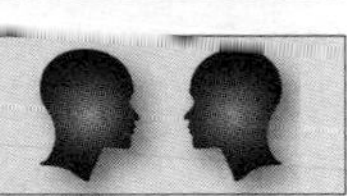

Vocabulary
Technology programs and gadgets

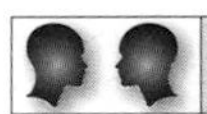
14A see Teacher's notes p. 126.

Aim
To extend the topic and introduce more words / phrases commonly used in the context of technology.

Step 1 Ask students to look at the sentences in A and complete each one with one of the pairs of words from the box. Check they understand *gadgets* = small machines or devices that do useful jobs. Check in pairs then check with the whole group.

Answers

1 upgrade + powerful	7 set + switches
2 100 GB + store	8 warns + dangerous
3 screen + picture	9 allows + formats
4 save + efficient	10 lighter + carry
5 saves + automatically	11 use + straightforward
6 design + cool	12 runs + greener

Step 2 Put students in pairs and ask them to discuss what they think is being described in each sentence in A. Check with the whole group.

Suggested answers
1 computer or mobile phone
2 computer
3 monitor / TV
4 light bulbs, solar panels
5 dishwasher
6 mobile phone, ipod, MP3 player
7 washing machine, egg cooker, satellite TV
8 virus protection software
9 computer
10 laptop or notebook
11 mobile phone, digital camera, GPS
12 house, shower

SPEAKING

Aim
To give fluency practice and extend the topic.

Step 1 Ask students to look at the questions in A and think about how they would answer them. Check they understand *technophobe* = someone who hates or is afraid of technology. Elicit other words with phobia, e.g. claustrophobia = fear of small spaces. *What does phobia mean?* (Fear.) *What is a phobe?* (Someone who is afraid of something.)

Step 2 Put students in pairs / small groups and ask them to discuss the questions. Conduct brief feedback.

LISTENING

Aim
To hear some of the vocabulary in context and give practice in listening for gist and specific information.

Step 1 Tell students they are going to hear three conversations. They should listen and try to identify the item in each case and decide whether the speakers think they are good or bad. Play the recording, pausing between conversations if you think it necessary. Check answers with the whole group.

14.3

1 A: Are those solar panels on your house?
B: Yeah. The whole place runs off them.
A: Very green.
B: Lots of people have them in Germany. Look – you see them on those houses there as well.
A: Oh yeah! You don't see them much in Britain.
B: That's because you don't have any sun!
A: Very funny. Germany's not exactly the sunniest place in the world either! I mean, how much electricity do they produce? Isn't it very expensive?
B: I can't remember exactly how much they were to install – a few thousand euros – but they reckon you can get back the money you invested within ten years.
A: Really? But my electricity bill isn't that much.
B: No, no. It's not like that. You actually end up saving on electricity because you sell it back to the company for three or four times more than the normal price.
A: So it's subsidised by the government?
B: Kind of. And the price is guaranteed for twenty years.
A: Wow! But you still need the cash to install the panels.
B: Sure.

2 C: I got completely lost in the one-way system. I was going round in circles for ages. Then I must've taken the wrong turning and I ended up on the motorway going out of town!
D: Haven't you got a GPS?
C: No. I did consider getting one at one point, but I decided it wasn't worth it. I just don't drive that much.
D: They're not that expensive. They've come down in price a lot, you know. And they're very straightforward, very easy to use.
C: Right, but even so, I think I can do without one.
D: But think of the time you'd save.
C: Well, today maybe. But don't you worry about all those satellites tracking you all the time?
D: Now you're just being paranoid.

3 E: What's this?
F: That? It's for making boiled eggs.
E: You're joking! What's wrong with just putting them in some water?
F: I don't know ... you forget to check the time when you put it on, and then you don't know how long it's been cooking, if it's hard or soft ...
E: Well ...
F: But with this, you just set the timer and then it switches itself off when the egg's ready. You just stick the egg in there, press the button and you're done! And you don't have to bother with water or pans or washing-up or anything.
E: Come on! It's not that much trouble. You only normally have to rinse the pan quickly in some water.
F: And dry it and put it back in the cupboard.
E: Man, you're so lazy!
F: No, it's like a toaster. And using this is more energy-efficient than boiling eggs in water. And the egg never cracks. If you want to have the perfect boiled egg ...
E: I don't know. It just seems a waste of money to me. They should invent something really useful like a self-cleaning floor, so you don't have to mop or vacuum.

Answers
1 solar panels, GPS, egg boiler
2 solar panels – both think they're good; GPS – one speaker thinks it's good, the other doesn't; egg boiler – one speaker thinks it's good, the other thinks it's a waste of money

Step 2 Ask students to look at the questions in B and try to answer them from memory. Play the recording again if they need more help. Check in pairs, then check with the whole group.

Answers
1 a Because solar panels save people a lot of money / the government subsidises them.
  b No, you still need the cash to install the panels.
2 a Because the woman got lost.
  b He thinks they are a waste of money and enable people to keep track of you by satellite.
3 a It makes a perfect boiled egg and it's energy-efficient.
  b A self-cleaning floor, because there's no need to mop or vacuum.

Step 3 Ask students to look at the questions in C and think about how they would answer them. Then put them in pairs / small groups to discuss the questions. Conduct brief feedback.

GRAMMAR *-ing* forms and *to*-infinitives

Aim
To focus on constructions with either *-ing* form (gerund) or *to*-infinitives.

Step 1 Lead in by asking students what *-ing* forms and infinitives are. Elicit some examples of when we use each.

Tip This is a difficult area for students because there appears to be no logical reason for using either a gerund / *-ing* form or an infinitive in certain constructions. They are similar in that they can both be 'verbal nouns', but many languages do not have a gerund equivalent so students would often be inclined to use an infinitive rather than a gerund. Some languages have an equivalent to an *-ing* form, but this is only used as part of a tense. Students can also get confused about when they need to use *to* and when not (e.g. after modal verbs, *make* and *let*). In this lesson the contrast is between *-ing* form and *to*-infinitive only. Direct them to the grammar reference on p. 153 if they still seem unsure.

Step 2 Ask students to look at the sentences 1–5 in exercise A from *Listening*. Ask them to underline the *-ing* form or infinitive in each sentence and notice what comes before it. Then ask them to match each sentence with one of the rules from a–e.

Answers
1 a 2 d 3 b 4 e 5 c

Step 3 Put students in pairs (mixed nationality in a multilingual class) and ask them to discuss the questions in B. Conduct brief feedback.

Step 4 Ask students to look at the sentences in C and decide whether they are correct or not. They should correct the incorrect sentences. Check in pairs then check with the whole group.

Answers
1 keeps crashing (*-ing* form after *keep*)
2 OK (infinitive of purpose)
3 Making (*-ing* form as subject)
4 seeing (*-ing* form after a preposition)
5 OK
6 damaging (*-ing* form after preposition)
7 not driving (*-ing* form after *get used to*)
8 OK (infinitive after *agree*)

Step 5 Ask students to complete the sentences with either a *to*-infinitive or a *-ing* form, so that they are true for them. Put them in pairs to talk about their examples. Get them to try to develop conversations by asking *why? where?* etc. Conduct brief feedback.

Answers
Many possible answers but check students have used correct forms before putting them in pairs.

1 *-ing* form	5 *-ing* form
2 infinitive / for + *-ing* form	6 *-ing* form, *-ing* form
3 *-ing* form	7 *-ing* form
4 infinitive	8 infinitive

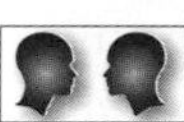 **14B** see Teacher's notes p. 126.

SPEAKING

Aim
To give freer practice and to extend the topic.

Step 1 Ask students to read the instructions in A. Use the first example to elicit some ideas. Encourage them to use constructions with either a *-ing* form or a *to*-infinitive. Ask them to look at the other examples and think about what they might say. Check any vocabulary they are not sure about.

Step 2 Put students in small groups and ask them to discuss each of the topics. Monitor closely and note down any mistakes for a correction slot at the end.

Step 3 Ask students to write four or five sentences about things they have heard are good / bad for the environment, using *supposed to*. Check that they remember this use of *supposed to* from Unit 10. Then put them back in their groups to talk about their ideas and decide whether they agree or not.

Step 4 Ask students to look at the questions in C and discuss in pairs. Conduct brief feedback.

15 INJURIES AND ILLNESS

UNIT OVERVIEW

In this unit students talk about **injuries and illness** and about **causes and results**. They also focus on **forming words** and practise **talking to the doctor** and **telling stories about accidents**. They **read** an article about **facts and myths** related to **medicine** and **listen** to two conversations between **doctor and patient** and a conversation about a **holiday accident**. The main **grammar** aims are **reported speech** and **reporting verbs**.

SPEAKING

Aim

To lead in to the topic and get students immediately involved through personalisation.

Step 1 Draw students' attention to the questions in A. Check they understand *symptom* = sign of an illness. Put them in pairs to discuss the questions. Conduct brief feedback.

VOCABULARY Injuries and illness

Aim

To extend students vocabulary about injury and illness and to lead in to *Listening*.

Step 1 Ask students to look at the sentences in A and try to guess what the words in bold mean by looking at the whole sentence. Check in pairs then check with the whole group. Model and drill and elicit and mark the stress on the board.

Alternatively If you don't want students to translate, or in a multilingual class, you could take in monolingual dictionaries and ask them to check anything they are not sure about in the dictionary. The easiest way for you to get the meanings across is to mime or give a 'scenario', i.e. a situation where this injury or illness would typically result.

Answers

1 coughing = forcing air from throat with harsh noise
2 sneezing = blowing breath through nose with a noise
3 stomach ache = pain in the stomach
4 sprained = damage by twisting
5 stiff = hard to move, rigid
6 swollen = bigger than normal
7 a dizzy = feeling you are losing your balance and about to fall
7 b high blood pressure = when the force with which blood is pumped round the body is dangerously high
8 a rash = red marks on skin
8 b itchy = causing you to want to scratch
9 migraines = very severe headaches, including dizziness, etc.
10 bump = small swelling

Words in italics
1 flu = influenza, a virus like a very bad cold, with temperature, aches and pains
2 allergy = when your body has an extreme reaction to certain foods, chemicals, etc.
3 arthritis = illness which causes pain in the joints, especially in the elderly
4 cut = an injury caused by a knife or scissors

Step 2 Put students in pairs and ask them to talk about injuries and illnesses they have had in the last five years or that they have never had, using the vocabulary from A.

Step 3 Ask students to look at the pictures. Elicit, model and drill the items, *bandage, elasticated support, painkillers*, (e.g. aspirin, paracetamol), *thermometer, cream, medicine.* Put students in pairs and ask them to discuss when these things might be used. They should try to use the language from A as much as possible.

Answers

A Bandage – for cuts, burns, sprains (remind students about plaster for a broken leg / arm – refer them to Unit 4 p. 28 if they don't remember)
B Elasticated support – for sprained ankles
C Painkillers – for headache / migraine or a stiff neck or the flu / a cold
D Thermometer – for taking your temperature, when you have flu
E Cream – for an allergy or insect bites or rash
F Medicine – for a cough or stomach ache

Step 4 Ask students to look at what the patient or doctor says in sentences 1–8 in D and match each one with the response from a–h. Check in pairs, then check with the whole group.

Answers
1 c 2 h 3 f 4 a 5 b 6 g 7 e 8 d

Step 5 Give students a few minutes to try to memorise the comments in D. Then put them in pairs to test each other. Student B should close their book and try to give the correct response as Student A reads out sentences 1–4. They could then swap for questions 5–8.

LANGUAGE PATTERNS

Aim
To draw students' attention to informal ways to ask / persuade someone to do something for you using *get*.

Step 1 Ask students to translate the sentences into their own language and tell you what similarities / differences they notice. Alternatively, if you prefer them not to use translation, ask students to look at the box and say what patterns they notice (*get someone to do something* in various tenses = ask / persuade – informal).

LISTENING

Aim
To give practice in predicting and listening for specific information and detail.

Step 1 Tell students they are going to hear two conversations between a doctor and a patient. Ask them to look at the questions the doctor and patient ask in each conversation and try to decide what the problem is in each case. Check any vocabulary they are not sure about. Then play the recording for them to check. Check with the whole group.

Answers
1 Swollen ankle (sprained or broken)
2 Stomach virus – vomiting and high temperature

15.1
Conversation 1
A: Hello. Mr Gomez?
B: Yes?
A: I'm sorry. Have you been waiting long?
B: About two hours.
A: I'm sorry, we're quite busy today. You've done something to your ankle?
B: Yes.
A: Mmm, it's quite swollen. Does this hurt?
B: Yeah, it's very painful.
A: Can you put any weight on it at all?
B: No, no. It hurts too much.
A: Mmm. And how did you do it?
B: I was just coming out of the hotel and I slipped on the stair and my ankle . . . It just . . .
A: You just fell over on it. Nasty. Well, I think we should have it X-rayed. It might just be badly sprained, but it could be broken. You'll have to wait again, I'm afraid, but I'll give you something for the pain in the meantime.
B: Right. How long will I have to wait for the X-ray?
A: Hopefully, it won't be more than half an hour. Are you on any medication?
B: Er, I take something for my asthma.
A: That's fine. Any allergies?
B: No.
A: You've never had any adverse reactions to any drugs – paracetamol or anything?
B: No, never.
A: OK fine. Well, I'll get the nurse to give you some painkillers and then have you sent down for the X-ray.
Conversation 2
C: Hello
D: Hello
E: Hello. Take a seat. What seems to be the problem?
C: It's my boyfriend. He's been up all night throwing up, he's hardly slept, he had a high temperature – 39 – he was sweating.
E: And how long have you been like this?
C: Sorry, he doesn't speak much English. He first said he felt a bit sick yesterday afternoon and then he threw up about 7 and he hasn't really stopped since.
E: Oh dear. Any diarrhoea?
C: No, none actually.
E: And has he been able to drink anything?
C: No, that's the problem. When he drinks water, he's sick again.
E: Right, well let's have a look. Can you just take off your jumper and sit up here? Open your mouth and stick your tongue out. Lovely. And now take a deep breath. Again – breathe in . . . and out. Just lie down. I'm just going to press. Does this hurt at all? And here?
D: Mmm. It's OK.
E: Maybe a bit uncomfortable – but no pain.
D: Yes . . . no pain.
E: OK, you can put your jumper back on. I think it's a viral gastroenteritis, so there's no need for antibiotics. I'll give him an injection to stop the vomiting and then he just needs to rest and take lots of fluids. Can you explain for me?

Step 2 Ask students to look at the first set of questions and elicit possible answers. Then play the recording again, pausing after each answer for students to write it down. Check in pairs then check with the whole group.

Answers

Conversation 1

Yeah, it's very painful.
No, no. It hurts too much.
I was just coming out of the hotel ...
Half an hour.
Er, I take something for my asthma.
No.
No, never.

Conversation 2

It's my boyfriend ...
since yesterday afternoon
No, none actually.
No.
Mmm it's OK.

Step 3 Put students in pairs, A and B. Ask them to choose a role – doctor or patient – and read their part in Conversation 1 in the audioscript on p. 173 and try to remember as much as they can. Then ask them to role-play each conversation. They should use the questions as a guide but not look at the audioscript. They should swap roles for Conversation 2 and repeat the procedure. Monitor and note down any mistakes they make in target language for a correction slot at the end.

DEVELOPING CONVERSATIONS

Short questions with *any*

Aim

To draw students' attention to the use of *any* to start a question, especially a follow-up question.

Step 1 Ask students to read the box and check they understand. Then ask them to re-write the sentences in A using *any*. Make sure they realise they must sometimes change a clause to a noun. Elicit a few examples of the transformations before they start. Check in pairs, then check with the whole group.

Answers

1 Any other symptoms?
2 (On) any medication?
3 Any itchiness?
4 Any dizziness?
5 Any stiffness?
6 Any vomiting?
7 Any questions?
8 Any pain?

CONVERSATION PRACTICE

Aim

To give freer practice of the language used when visiting the doctor.

Step 1 Put students in pairs and tell them they are going to role-play a conversation between doctor and patient. They should choose a medical problem and decide who is taking which role. If they prefer, they can make up a medical complaint. They should then spend some time individually preparing what they are going to say. When they are ready, they should role-play the conversation. Then swap roles and repeat with a different problem. Monitor and take notes for a correction slot at the end. Ask a few pairs to act out their conversations in front of the class.

 **pp. 106–107**

READING Myth or fact?

Aim

To give practice in predicting, reading for gist and specific information.

Step 1 Tell students they are going to read an article from a medical website called *Fact or myth*? Check they understand *myth* = a commonly held belief which is not true. Put students in pairs and ask them to look at the statements in A. They should decide whether they are true or not. Do not conduct feedback on this.

Step 2 Ask students to read the text quickly (ignoring the words in bold) and check whether the statements in A are true or not. Check in pairs then check with the whole group.

Answers

1 Myth – viruses cause colds
2 Myth – antibiotics can't cure viruses
3 Myth – there is no link between diet and acne
4 Myth – no types are caused by this
5 Myth – cholesterol is natural and essential for life
6 Myth – it passes through you
7 True – it's addictive

Step 3 Ask students to try to remember what the article said about the questions in C. Check in pairs, then look at the text again to check / find the exact words used. They could underline the actual words in each case.

Answers
1 'wrap up warm' / 'dry your hair or you'll get a cold'
2 wash your hands regularly when there's a bug going around.
3 if you develop a throat or ear infection
4 go to bed and drink lots of fluids
5 washing too much
6 smoking, stress and high blood pressure
7 it stays in your stomach forever or blocks your insides
8 they may suffer withdrawal symptoms, e.g. headaches, irritability and restlessness

Native speaker English

Ask students to read the box and check they understand it. Elicit some examples, e.g. *stomach bug, flu bug* but not throat bug or chest bug (*throat infection / chest infection*). Check they understand the difference between *virus / bug* and *infection*. Ask them what we mean by computer bug or virus. Ask if they remember *anti-virus software* from Unit 14 on technology.

Vocabulary Forming words

Aim
To draw students' attention to word families related to medicine and raise their awareness about how different parts of speech are formed.

Step 1 Ask students to look at the words in the box and find words from the same family in the text. Start by eliciting a few examples of word families. Point out that the words (reading across from left to right) are in the same order as in the text. Check in pairs, then check with the whole group.

Answers
viruses (n pl) viral (adj)
infection (n)
incurable (adj)
medical (adj)
fatty (adj)
naturally (advb)
addictive (adj)
irritability (n)

Step 2 Ask students to correct the sentences in B by changing the form of one of the words. Check in pairs, then check with the whole group.

Answers

1 infectious	5 fatty
2 medical	6 irritable
3 curable	7 naturally
4 addictive	8 virus

Speaking

Aim
To give students an opportunity to respond to the text.

Step 1 Ask students to look at the questions in A and think about how they would answer them. You could also ask them if there are any other similar myths in their countries, especially in a multilingual class. Put them in pairs or small groups to discuss the questions. Conduct brief feedback.

Vocabulary Explaining causes and results

Aim
To focus on different ways of talking about causes and results.

Step 1 Ask students to look back at the text and focus on the words in bold. Ask them to notice the patterns which follow them (*cause something to happen, make something* + base form / + comparative adjective, *lead to* + noun / *caused by* + verb *-ing, mean* + clause, *lead to* + noun, *link to* + noun). Then ask them to look at the sentences in A and complete them with one of the words in each gap. They may need to change the form slightly.

Answers

1 means	3 linked	5 makes
2 lead	4 made	6 caused

Step 2 Ask students to look at the problems in the box in exercise C and prepare to talk about the causes and results, using the language from B. Check they understand *asthma, malaria, HIV* (human immunodeficiency virus – AIDS in Unit 14), *diabetes, insomnia*. Do one or two examples with the whole group to start them off then put them in pairs to continue. Monitor closely and note down errors in target language for a correction slot at the end.

Step 3 Ask the whole group the questions in exercise D.

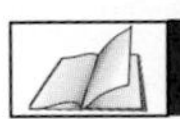
pp. 108–109

Next class Make photocopies of **15A** p. 156 and **15B** p. 157.
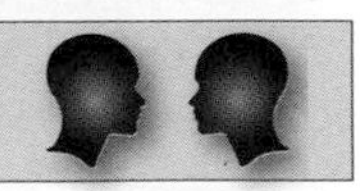

Vocabulary Accidents and problems

Aim
To extend the topic and to give practice.

Step 1 Lead in by asking students to look at the pictures and tell you what is happening in each one. Don't pre-teach the vocabulary at this point – just use the pictures to lead in and find out what students know.

Step 2 Ask students to look at the sentences in A and choose the correct word to complete them. Check in pairs then check with the whole group. Model and drill the words and elicit and mark the stress on the board. Look at the alternatives in sentences 2 and 9; 4 and 10 and elicit the difference in the way each pair of words is used. Then check the difference between the pairs of words and elicit other situations in which you might suffer these injuries.

Answers

1 burned	6 poisoning
2 tripped over	7 sunburn
3 fell off	8 fainted
4 bit	9 slipped
5 crashed into	10 stung

Step 3 Put students in pairs. Ask them to look at the pictures again and to each choose one. They should imagine they are the person in their picture and prepare to describe what happened. Give them a few minutes to prepare then ask them to tell each other their stories. They could then repeat with the other two pictures.

Step 4 Ask students to re-tell any particularly good stories they told or heard to the rest of the class.

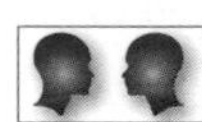 **15A** see Teacher's notes p. 127.

Listening

Aim
To introduce the grammar (reported speech) and give practice in listening for specific information.

Step 1 Tell students they are going to hear a conversation between Anna and her colleague, Dan, about an accident he and his friend James had on holiday. Give students a few moments to look at them in A and to answer them as they listen. Play the recording.

15.2
A = Anna, D = Dan

A: How was your holiday? You went mountain biking in Austria, didn't you?
D: That's right. It was great, except for James's accident.
A: God! Why? What happened?
D: Well, we'd been cycling in the mountains round Kaunertal, and we were going back to the hotel down this steep road. James went round this tight bend too fast and he went off the road into some bushes and fell off. It was horrible.
A: It sounds it! Was he badly hurt?
D: Well, we thought so. He kept saying he was OK, but you could see that his knee was really swollen. He also had quite a few cuts and bruises and was bleeding quite a bit. The problem was, though, we were still miles from the next village.
A: So what happened? How did you get him to a hospital?
D: Well, luckily, we were actually on a road and a car came past a minute or two later. It stopped and the woman driving offered to take James to the nearest hospital. He kept saying he'd be OK, but she insisted on taking him and in the end we persuaded him to go – just to be safe. We got him into the car – and she took my mobile number and she promised to call me once there was more news.
A: Wow! That was nice.
D: I know. It was really kind of her. Anyway, we then cycled back to our hotel and waited to hear from them.
A: And did they call?
D: Yeah, they did! After a couple of hours, they rang and told me they'd given James an X-ray and there was nothing broken. They said he needed to stay there a bit longer, though, as he was waiting to have a few stitches in the cuts.
A: Oh, poor guy!
D: Yeah, I know. In the end, he spent the rest of the holiday hanging around the hotel. He was desperate to go out with us, but the doctors told him not to cycle for a week and rest the knee. It spoilt his holiday really.
A: I bet!
D: And on top of all that, I spoke to him yesterday and he said he's going to have to buy a new bike now because of the accident. He's found out the bike frame's broken.
A: Ouch! That actually reminds me of something that happened to some friends of mine when they went camping in Croatia.

Answers
1 It was a mountain biking holiday in Austria.
2 James went round a tight bend and crashed into some bushes and fell off his bike.
3 Yes. His knee was swollen and he had a few cuts and bruises and was bleeding a lot.
4 A woman stopped and took him in her car.
5 They told him nothing was broken but he had to wait to have some stitches. (And he couldn't cycle for a week.)

Step 2 Ask students to look at the sentences in B and try to put them in the order in which they happened in the story. Then play the recording again for them to check.

Answers
f, c, a, h, e, d, b, g

Step 3 Ask students to look at the questions in C and think about them for a few moments. Then put them in pairs to discuss them.

GRAMMAR Reported speech

Aim
To consolidate students' knowledge of reported speech (statements only).

Tip One of the most common student mistakes is *He said me ...* – often because there is only one verb for *say* and *tell* in students' own language. Make sure you focus on this by writing sentences with either *say* or *tell* on the board and eliciting the difference. Drill by transforming each sentence to the other verb, e.g. *He said it was lovely* (told) becomes *He told me it was lovely*.

Step 1 Lead in by asking students the difference between direct and reported speech. Illustrate with an example e.g. *Today is Wednesday. What did I say? = You said today was Wednesday*. Point out that you could also say *You said today is Wednesday* – because it still is. Compare *Martin Luther King said he had a dream* – because Luther King is dead. Read out the box then ask students to do exercise A. They should look at the sentences from *Listening* and decide what verb forms are used in each case and what the people actually said. Direct students to the grammar reference on p. 154 if you still think they need help. Check in pairs, then check with the whole group.

Answers
1 he would be – I'll be OK
2 they had given (past perfect) We have given ... there was nothing broken (past simple) there is nothing broken
3 past simple, past continuous – He needs to stay in a bit longer, though, as he's waiting ...
4 be going to (no change because this is still the case) – I'm going to ...

Step 2 Ask students to complete the sentences in B using the correct verb form. Check in pairs, then check with the whole group. Ask students which ones need not change because they are still true (2 – needs, 4 – is).

Answers
1 had, gave
2 ate, needed
3 would have, was
4 would not hurt, was
5 had done (would do / was doing), could
6 had done, had caused

Step 3 Put students in pairs and ask them to practise asking each other *What did the doctor say*? Tell them to answer with one of the sentences from B. They could then continue with their own examples, in reported speech.

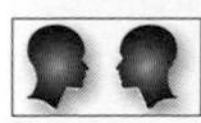 **15B** see Teacher's notes p. 127.

GRAMMAR Reporting verbs

Aim
To extend the topic of reported speech and introduce some alternatives to *say* and *tell*.

Step 1 Elicit some examples of reporting verbs (other verbs used to introduce reported speech apart from *say* and *tell*) either from *Listening* or from their general knowledge. Ask students to look at the audioscript on pp. 173–174 and notice the way the verbs given are used. Elicit the examples and highlight the form on the board.

Answers
- *The woman driving offered to take James ...* offer + *to*-infinitive (**not** offer + object + *to*-infinitive)
- *She insisted on taking him...* insist + *on* + *-ing* form
- *We persuaded him to go ...* persuade + object + *to*-infinitive
- *She promised to call me ...* promise + *to*-infinitive (**not** promise + object + *to*-infinitive)
- *The doctors told him not to cycle...* tell + object (+ *not*) + *to*-infinitive (**not** tell + object + *don't* + bare infinitive)

Optional activity You could give controlled practice of some of these by providing oral prompts in direct speech and eliciting responses, using the reporting verbs, e.g. *come on, you can do it – she persuaded me to do it, don't open the window – you told me not to open the window.*

Step 2 Ask students to look at the questions in B and think about how they would answer them. Put them in pairs to tell each other. Monitor closely and correct any mistakes in target language.

SPEAKING

Aim
To round off the lesson and give fluency practice.

Step 1 Ask students to read the instructions in A or read them out to them. Give them a few minutes to think of a scenario and prepare what they are going to say. If they can't think of a real scenario, they could invent one.

Step 2 Put students in pairs / small groups to tell each other their stories. Encourage them to use reported speech and ask them to try to develop conversations by asking 'interested' questions as they listen. Monitor and note down errors in reported speech for a correction slot at the end. You could also ask students to re-tell any particularly good stories to the rest of the class.

Optional activity Ask students to write one of the stories they told or heard, either in class or for homework.

16 NEWS AND EVENTS

UNIT OVERVIEW
In this unit students extend their ability to talk about the **news, newspapers** and **celebrities**. They **read** an article about **seeking fame and fortune.** They **listen** to five conversations about **stories in the news** and three conversations about **famous historical figures**. They also practise **responding to news** and **defining relative clauses**, the main **grammar** aim.

VOCABULARY Newspapers

Aim
To extend students' knowledge of different sections of a newspaper and to get them immediately involved through personalisation.

Step 1 Lead in by asking students which newspapers they read or have read in their own language / in English. Do they read newspapers online? How does this change things?

Step 2 Ask students to look at the newspaper sections in A and tick the ones they usually read. Check they understand *reviews, gossip pages, horoscopes.* Ask if there are any other sections not mentioned which they read (e.g. weather, listings, arts pages, obituaries).

Step 3 Put students in pairs to discuss their ideas from A. Conduct brief feedback.

Step 4 Put students in pairs and ask them to discuss the meanings of the words / phrases in bold and which section of the newspaper they refer to. Check with the whole group.

Answers
1 marks out of ten = score given / how it was rated – a film / book / play / album – review pages.
2 exchange rate = how much you get for your money in another country's currency – business pages
3 premiere = opening of a film or play – gossip pages
4 the score = the result – sports pages
5 ceasefire = agreement to stop fighting – international news /national news
6 star sign = astrological sign, depending on month of your birth, e.g. Capricorn – horoscopes

LISTENING

Aim
To extend the topic of newspapers and lead in to practice of responding to news; to listen for specific information and language.

Step 1 Tell students they are going to listen to five conversations about news stories. Explain that there are two words / phrases from each conversation in A but they are in the wrong order. Ask students to look at the words / phrases in A and try to match the pairs of words (one from the left-hand column with one from the right-hand column). They should then decide what kind of story each pair of words might come from. Do not conduct feedback on this.

Step 2 Ask students to listen to the recording and check their answers. Check with the whole group.

Answers
Conversation 1 – get divorced, have an affair – gossip pages
Conversation 2 – close down, made redundant – business news
Conversation 3 – stab, victim - national news
Conversation 4 – pass away, funeral – arts pages, obituaries
Conversation 5 – sign, midfielder – sports pages

16.1
1 A: Did you see that thing in the paper about Shaynee Wilson?
B: No. What was that?
A: Well, you remember she got married last September, right?
B: Yeah, I think so. It's hard to keep up.
A: Well, she's just got divorced! Apparently, she found out that her husband was having an affair with another Hollywood actress.
B: God, that didn't last long, did it? So did he get much of her money?

2 C: Did you see that thing on TV about the mobile phone factory closing down?
D: No. What was that?
C: Oh, one of the biggest factories in the country is closing down, which means about five thousand people will be made redundant.
D: That's bad news, isn't it?
C: Yeah. It must mean the economy is starting to slow down.
D: What's the employment situation like in that area? Do you think people will be able to find new jobs?

3 E: Did you see that thing on TV about the murder last night?
F: Yeah. It was shocking, wasn't it? Stabbed fifteen times and left to die in the street.
E: I know. The victim was only 16 as well. And apparently they think his attackers might've been even younger.
F: Oh, it's depressing, isn't it? Do you know if they've arrested anyone for it yet?

4 G: Did you see in the paper that Sven Larstrom passed away? His funeral is next Saturday.
H: No, I didn't. Who is he? I don't think I've heard of him.
G: Sven Larstrom. He was a really great Swedish director. He made some of my favourite films. Haven't you ever seen *Oranges in August*?
H: No, never.
G: Or *Anna and Maja and Jens*?
H: No. Sorry. So how did he die?

5 I: Hey. Did you see that we've finally signed Geraldinho?
J: No, I missed that. Who is he again?
I: Oh, he's a Brazilian midfielder. He's supposed to be great.
J: Yeah? How much did you have to pay for him?
I: Thirty-three million euros! It's a new club record.
J: Yeah? That's a lot for a player I've never heard of! Has he played for the national team yet?

Step 3 Put students in pairs and ask them to try to remember the sentences each of the words / phrases in A came from. Ask them to write down as much as they can, but tell them not to worry if it isn't word-for-word. Play the recording again for them to check. They could either read the audioscript on p. 174 as they listen or read it at the end for a final check.

Answers
See underlined sentences above in audioscript 16.1.

Step 4 Put students in pairs and ask them to practise reading out the conversations in the audioscript on p. 174. They should try to extend these by adding their own ideas.

Language patterns

Aim
To draw students' attention to some common patterns often used in the context of news.

Step 1 Ask students to look at the sentences in the box and translate them into their own language. What similarities / differences do they notice? Alternatively, if you prefer not to use translation, ask students to read the sentences in the box and tell you what patterns they notice. (*Did you read / hear about* ... + object + *-ing* form; *get* + past participle as a passive form, *Did you see that thing on TV / in the papers about* ... ?)

Developing conversations

Apparently

Aim
To present a common way to introduce a news story and to give practice.

Step 1 Write the two sentences from the box on the board. To save time you could do this while students are practising the conversations in *Listening* exercise D. Ask students what they think *apparently* means here. Read out the box, or ask students to read it.

Step 2 Read out some of the examples of question tags with falling intonation from the audioscript. Ask students what these are and why we use them (question tags, to keep the conversation going). Ask whether the intonation rises or falls and why (falls – because it's not really a question / we expect agreement).

Step 3 Ask students to look at the sentences in A and complete them with their own ideas. Check in open pairs by asking students to read out the questions and getting another student to answer with their own sentences. Correct where necessary.

Step 4 Put students in pairs and ask them to tell each other about stories they have read / heard about recently, using *apparently*. Conduct brief feedback.

PRONUNCIATION Responding to news

Aim
To give further practice of question tags with falling intonation when responding to news.

Step 1 Ask students to read the box, or read it aloud to them.

Step 2 Ask students to listen to the sentences and repeat after the recording. Make sure they get the falling intonation right. Model and drill if necessary. You could also try back-chaining, i.e. start with the question tag, exaggerating the falling intonation, then add the 'stem' when modelling and drilling.

16.2
1 I know. It was dreadful, wasn't it?
2 Yeah. It was incredible, wasn't it?
3 I know. It was funny, wasn't it?
4 Yeah. It was a lot of money, wasn't it?
5 Yeah. It was a disaster, wasn't it?
6 I know. It's crazy, isn't it?
7 I know. It's ridiculous, isn't it?
8 Oh, it's depressing, isn't it?
9 I know. It's looking bad, isn't it?
10 Yeah. It's becoming a major problem, isn't it?

Step 3 Put students in pairs and ask them to take turns reading out the sentences in B and answering with a suitable response, including a question tag. Monitor closely and correct mistakes in target language.

CONVERSATION PRACTICE

Aim
To give authentic speaking practice and draw the lesson together.

Step 1 Ask students to think of news stories they have heard or read about recently. They should introduce their stories by asking a suitable question from *Language patterns*. Give them a few minutes to prepare.

Step 2 Put students in groups and ask them to tell each other about their stories and respond, using as much language from the lesson as they can. Monitor closely and note down errors in target language for a correction slot at the end.

pp. 112–113

Next class Make photocopies of **16A** p. 158 and **16B** p. 159.

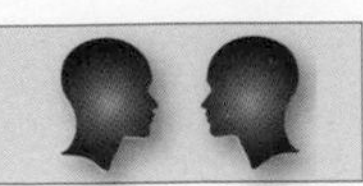

SPEAKING

Aim
To extend the topic and introduce ways of talking about well-known historical figures.

Step 1 Ask students to look at the expressions in A and prepare to use them to talk about the pictures on p. 112. Use one of the pictures as an example and elicit different possible responses from students using the expressions or others that they know, e.g. *I'm certain that's ... That's definitely ... I've got absolutely no idea ....* Then put students in groups to discuss the rest of the pictures.

Answers
1 Kemal Ataturk
2 Sergey Bubka
3 Martin Luther King
4 Marie Curie

VOCABULARY Explaining who people are

Aim
To introduce words for people's professions and phrases for explaining more about them.

Step 1 Ask students to complete the sentences in A with one of the words from the box. Put them in pairs to check their answers. Ask them to discuss the meanings of the phrases in italics, and translate these into their own language. Alternatively, if you don't want them to translate, or in a multilingual class, you could take in monolingual dictionaries and ask them to check anything they are not sure about. Check with the whole group and model and drill the profession words. Elicit and mark the stress on the board.

Answers
1 scientist
2 activist
3 dictator
4 founder
5 athlete
6 mathematician
7 doctor
8 artist

Step 2 Ask students to make a list of five or six famous people. They should take turns to ask and answer about the people on their lists, using the language in italics from exercise A.

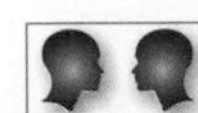
16A see Teacher's notes p. 127.

Listening

Aim

To hear some of the target language in context and give practice in listening for gist and specific information.

Step 1 Tell students they are going to hear three conversations about four famous people. Ask them to keep their books closed at this point. They should listen and number the people in the order they are mentioned. Write these on the board: a cyclist, a military leader, an artist, a writer. Play the recording. Check the answers (1 Garibaldi, 2 Comenius, 3 Eddy Merckx, 4 Magritte). Ask students to open their books and match the names in exercise A question 1 with the what they did (military leader-Garibaldi, writer-Comenius, cyclist-Eddy Merckx (pictured), artist-Magritte.

Note One of Magritte's famous works is pictured. Language: French. Translation: *This is not a pipe*.)

Answers

1 They are looking at a statue of Garibaldi. In conversation 2, the second speaker has just been to Germany on a Comenius project. In conversation 3, the second speaker is going to Brussels to go to the Eddy Merckx metro station. The other speaker suggests going to the Magritte museum, also in Brussels.

2 Garibaldi was an Italian military leader who helped to unify Italy in the nineteenth century. He also fought in South America.
Comenius was a seventeenth century Czech writer who wrote about education, regarded by some as the father of modern education.
Eddy Merckx was a cyclist from Belgium.
Magritte was a Belgian painter who painted surrealist paintings and has a museum dedicated to his work in Brussels.

3 Garibaldi, Italy; Comenius, Czech Republic; Eddy Merckz, Belgium; Magritte, Belgium

4 Garibaldi also fought in South America.
Comenius wrote in seventeenth century but was before him time arguing for equal education for both sexes.
Eddy Merckz has a metro station named after him, which is full of cycling memorabilia, including the bike on which he set a cycling record.
Magritte did the pictures of office workers raining down from the sky.

16.3

Conversation 1

A: Who's the statue of?
B: That's Garibaldi.
A: Garibaldi?
B: You've never heard of him?
A: No, I don't think so. Who was he?
B: He was a military leader in the nineteenth century who helped unify Italy. He's like a national hero. He fought in South America as well. He was part of some liberation struggles in Brazil and Uruguay. I think his first wife was even Brazilian. I'm surprised you haven't heard of him.
A: Well, I'm not really interested in history.

Conversation 2

C: You've been away, haven't you?
D: Yeah, I went to Germany as part of a Comenius project.
C: Comenius project?
D: Yeah, it's a European Union scheme which provides grants to teachers so they can go on courses or set up partnerships with other schools abroad.
C: Sounds interesting. I've never heard of it. Why Comenius then? What does that mean?
D: He was a Czech writer who wrote about education. Apparently, he's seen as the father of modern education.
C: Oh yeah? I've never heard of him.
D: To be honest, neither had I before I went on this course. He sounds incredible, though. He wrote in the seventeenth century, but even then he was arguing for education for both boys and girls, and he was against just learning by heart. You know, he wanted to teach kids by doing things and encourage them to think for themselves. He was really ahead of his time.

Conversation 3

E: So what are you going to do while you're in Brussels?
F: Work mainly, but I'm hoping to go to the Eddy Merckx metro station while I'm there.
E: Really? Why do you want to go there?
F: It's where they have Eddy Merckx's bike, which he used to set the hour record.
E: What? What are you talking about?
F: Eddy Merckx. He's like the greatest cyclist of all time! They named the metro station after him and it has all kinds of memorabilia there.
E: Oh right.
F: You've never heard of him?
E: Er ... no. And you're not planning to go anywhere else like the Magritte Museum.
F: Magritte?
E: The surrealist painter. He was the guy who did like pictures of office workers raining down from the sky.
F: It doesn't sound familiar.
E: *Ceci n'est pas une pipe*?
F: Sorry, you've lost me.
E: You must know it! It's one of his paintings. I'm sure you'd recognise it if you saw it. It's really famous.
F: Yeah, well, so's Eddy Merckx, but *you* didn't know *him*!

Step 2 Ask students to look at the questions in A and try to answer them from memory. Play the recording again for them to check.

Step 3 Check students understand *named after* and *memorabilia* (see Eddie Merckx above). Ask them to look at the questions in B and spend a few moments thinking about them.

Step 4 Put students in pairs or threes to discuss the questions in B. Conduct brief feedback.

GRAMMAR Defining relative clauses

Aim
To consolidate and extend students' knowledge of defining relative clauses.

Step 1 Ask students to look at the audioscript on p. 174 and underline examples of defining relative clauses and say what each one refers to, e.g. *Who helped unify Italy*? (Garibaldi.) *What does this refer to?* (A military leader in the nineteenth century.)

Answers
See underlined examples in the audioscript 16.3

Step 2 Ask students to read the Grammar box or read it out to them. Ask them if they have any questions. Elicit some examples by giving prompts e.g. *He's the actor* ... (who won an Oscar, whose daughter is a rock star). *That's the house...* (where I was born).

Alternatively You could write some examples on the board and elicit from students which is the relative pronoun and what it refers to in each case.

Direct them to the grammar reference on p. 155 if they still seem unsure.

Step 3 Ask students to read the sentences in A and cross out the word / words which are not correct. Check in pairs, then check with the whole group.

Answers (words which are not possible)

1 which	5 who, that
2 who	6 who
3 who, when	7 when, that
4 where	8 who, which

SPEAKING

Aim
To give freer practice of defining relative clauses and draw the lesson together.

Step 1 Put students in pairs and tell them they are going to role-play a conversation about the town / country where they live at the moment. Student A should imagine they are a visitor and ask about buildings, monuments and famous places in the town / country. Student B should explain, using relative clauses (you might give them a few moments before they start to think about what they are going to say). When they finish, they could swap roles. Monitor closely and note down errors in target language for a correction slot at the end.

Step 2 Ask students to work on their own and list the people who they think are the four greatest living people in their country and the four greatest historical figures.

Step 3 Put students in pairs. Ask them to compare their lists and justify their choices using relative clauses and try to reach an agreement. If their partner doesn't know the people they have chosen, they should explain their choices to each other, using relative clauses. Monitor for use of target language and conduct a feedback / correction slot at the end.

Step 4 If time, try to reach a class consensus on the lists (or a number of these in a multilingual class).

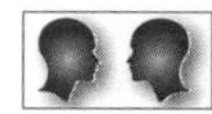
16A see Teacher's notes p. 127.

pp. 114–115

READING

Aim
To extend the topic and give practice in predicting, reading for specific information, gist and detail and to raise students' awareness of collocations.

Step 1 Lead in to the topic by asking students why they think so many people want to be famous. You could use *Big Brother* as an example. Then ask them to read the short introductory text in A and work in pairs to answer the questions.

Step 2 Ask students to read the headings in the article and find the answers to the last question in A (the six ways to become rich and famous). Did students come up with the same six? If they came up with other ways to become rich and famous, do they think theirs are better than the ones in the text? Why / Why not?

Answers
The paragraph headings: Date someone who's already famous; Go on a reality TV show; Inherit a Fortune; Set up a blog or set up a website; Become a hero; Don't give up!

Step 3 Ask students to answer the questions in B. You could do this with the whole group

Answers
a *World Idol / Pop Idol* – section 2
b retired people – section 6
c leaving £10 million – section 3
d removing bomb – section 5
e forwarding emails between friends until millions of people have seen it – section 4
f catching the eye of a famous person – section 1

Step 4 Ask students to read the article in detail and find out why the things or people in C are mentioned. Put them in pairs to check / discuss their ideas.

Answers
- the gossip magazines – people who date someone famous will soon be featured
- an advertising company – might become interested if you feature in a gossip magazine
- *The Guinness Book of Records* – over 12 million people visited Mahir Cagri's website and he had an entry in the *GBR*
- Kurt Nilsen – became a star in Norway after he sang well-known songs and appeared on World Idol
- Paris Hilton – became famous because her parents are incredibly rich
- Kim Sing / Bee Lian Man – Chinese restaurant owners who were left £10 million in someone's will (Golda Bechal's)
- Golda Bechal – left £10 million in her will (see above)
- Mahir Cagri – Turkish teacher (see above)
- karaoke – the standard on TV reality shows is often no better than this
- Kuldeep Singh – bus driver in India who removed a bomb from the bus he was driving
- The Zimmers – British pensioners who formed a band and had a documentary film made about them
- The Who – wrote *My Generation*, the Zimmers' hit single

Step 5 Ask students to look at the questions in D and complete the sentences with one of the words in the box in the correct form. They should look back at the text to help them. Check in pairs, then check with the whole group.

Answers
1 option
2 footsteps
3 barrier
4 control
5 will
6 saved
7 forward
8 caught
9 repay
10 came into

Step 6 Ask students to underline the collocations that go with the words / phrases in D. Check with the whole group.

Answers
1 that option isn't available
2 to follow in his footsteps
3 is no barrier to a successful …
4 just got out of control
5 left me a house in her will
6 saved my life
7 forward the email
8 caught my eye
9 repay your kindness
10 came into a lot of money

Step 7 Ask students to look at the collocations in D and choose three that refer to their own lives. Put them in pairs and ask them to tell each other about their examples.

Native speaker English

Ask students to read the box or read it out to them. Check they understand *easier said than done* = this may be a good idea, but it's very hard to put into practice. Ask them for a few more examples of things that are *easier said than done*.

Speaking

Aim
To give fluency practice about the topic of fame and fortune and to round off the unit.

Step 1 Ask students to read the questions in A and think about how they would answer them. They could make a few notes to help them.

Step 2 Put them in pairs / small groups to discuss the questions. Conduct brief feedback.

04 REVIEW

LEARNER TRAINING

Aim
To make students more aware of the ways they learn English outside class and to help them expand on these.

Step 1 Ask students to read the comments and check they understand them. Check *audio books* and *language exchange*.

Step 2 Put students in groups of three and ask them to discuss the comments, using the questions to help them. For the second question, they could make a list of possible ways to continue their studies after the course.

Step 3 Conduct feedback by asking students to share their ideas across the class or elicit their ideas and board them. Alternatively, as in previous Reviews, you could get them to make posters with their recommendations and put these on the wall.

GAME ⟶ CONVERSATION PRACTICE

For aims and suggested procedure, see Review 1, pp. 32–35.

ACT OR DRAW ⟶ QUIZ

For aims and suggested procedure, see Review 1, pp. 32–35.

Answers

1 a business trip, a day trip, a short or long trip, a hunting or fishing or shopping trip.
2 when they go to another country or start a business.
3 people insult or attack you or you get paid less than others.
4 You might get distracted in class / if you hear a noise.
5 No, a saturated market is not good – it means there is more supply than demand.
6 A book, film, TV series or pop group could enjoy a revival.
7 A government can subsidise housing, sports or cultural events, education.
8 You can run out of food, water, petrol, drugs.
9 Having the flu is worse – it includes aches and pains and a temperature.
10 You could sprain your wrist by turning it over suddenly or by using a keyboard too much.
11 You should use cream or stop doing what is causing it (often an allergy of some kind) or see a doctor.
12 Drugs, chocolate, coffee, alcohol, cigarettes can be addictive.
13 Two countries at war might agree to a ceasefire.
14 Capricorn, Aquarius, Pisces, Aires, Taurus, Gemini, Cancer, Leo, Virgo, Libra, Scorpio, Sagittarius.
15 company goes out of business, to save the firm money, because they do not do the work properly.

COLLOCATIONS

For aims and suggested procedure, see Review 1, pp. 32–35.

PRONUNCIATION

Aim
To revise phonetic symbols

Step 1 Ask students to look at the phonetic script and write the words.

Step 2 Play the recording (R 4.1) for them to check. Elicit and write the words on the board to check the spelling. Check students remember the meanings.

Answers

1 harbour
2 refugee
3 exhausted
4 cursor
5 inferior
6 automatically
7 diarrhoea
8 diabetes
9 horoscopes
10 dreadful

SPEAKING

Aim
To develop students' fluency and to revise vocabulary for talking about animals.

Step 1 Ask students to look at the pictures and think about what they could say about each in relation to the role of animals in our lives.

Step 2 Put students in pairs or small groups and get them to discuss the different pictures. Conduct brief feedback at the end.

 pp. 118–119

Listening

For aims and suggested procedure for the rest of the Review, see Review 1, pp. 32–35. The audio is R4.2.

A Answers

1 pilot 3 computer programmer 5 businessman

B Answers

a 2 (doctor)
b 5 (businessman – was made redundant as engineer)
c 1 (pilot)
d 4 (engineer)
e 3 (computer programmer)

Grammar conditionals

Answers

1 been 3 have 5 had
2 wouldn't 4 hadn't 6 would

Expressing regrets

Answers

1 should've told
2 shouldn't have said
3 shouldn't have posted
4 should've booked
5 shouldn't have eaten
6 should've been working

-ing forms and *to*-infinitives

Answers

1 smoking 2 to move 3 to listen 4 to hearing 5 to cut 6 working 7 cheating 8 to find

Defining relative clauses

Answers

1 He's someone whose music was ahead of its time.
2 Yalta is where they held a big meeting after the war.
3 She was a nurse who set up her own hospital.
4 She was an activist campaigning / who campaigned for women's rights.
5 The story was written around 500BC, during the time when Persia and Greece were at war.
6 We started living together – and that's when I realised how different we were!
7 That's the house where my mum used to live. / That's the house my mum used to live in.

Reporting verbs

Answers

1 persuade
2 warned
3 recommended
4 offered
5 insists on
6 has threatened
7 denies
8 apologise

Forming words

Answers

1 elected
2 allergy
3 incurable
4 creator
5 connection
6 poisoning
7 environmentally
8 bravery
9 infectious
10 generosity

Collocations

Answers

1 d 2 j 3 e 4 h 5 a 6 c 7 i 8 g 9 b 10 f

Vocabulary

Answers

1 missed
2 platform
3 delayed
4 line
5 hanging
6 security
7 strong
8 decline
9 upgrade
10 energy
11 straightforward
12 dizzy
13 migraines
14 under
15 pressure

AN INTRODUCTION TO WRITING IN *OUTCOMES*

In this section we will look at two broad reasons for writing in a foreign language: to practise and play and for the real world. We explain what we mean by them and how they may differ in teaching, tasks and feedback.

Practise and play

The first reason for writing as a foreign language is simply to practise new language, experiment and learn more English. Writing may have significant benefits for students learning English. In contrast to speaking, students have time to plan what they want to say; they can look words up in a dictionary, they can check and re-write grammar, they may be more able to notice how English works. That might then give benefits in terms of their overall competence in English.

Writing for the purpose of practice and play does not depend on any particular genre or standard organisation in writing; it could be short sentences, paragraphs, dialogues, etc; it could be about anything the student wants or it could be a theme the teacher chooses; it could be random connections of sentences – true or imagined. Some grammar and vocabulary tasks in the Student's book are of this nature, with students having to complete sentences using their own ideas. Below are some more tasks. The idea is to focus on revising language but it doesn't have to be so.

- Write a diary about your day trying to include new words or structures that you've learnt.
- Write five to ten lines of English every day about anything you like.
- Write every day / week about a story in the news you saw or read about.
- Write a poem or story using a new word you've learnt.
- Write a conversation based on one you had with someone during the class.
- Write an imagined conversation with someone you know based on a topic you've studied.
- Write an imagined conversation that takes place in a particular place.

As these kinds of writing tasks are unconnected to any particular genre, they require no 'teaching' or preparation and can be set at any time. In terms of feedback, you may want to simply write a personal response to what the student wrote such as *This really made me laugh* or *That's interesting*. Alternatively, you could engage in a dialogue with the student by asking them genuine questions, which they answer in writing. You may want to correct aspects of the key structure or words which they practised or use common errors from different students as a way to re-teach language in class. However, we feel correction should be kept to a minimum with these kinds of texts. The aim is not assessment, it is to encourage students; to engage with them and get them to play with language.

For the real world

The second broad reason is that students need to write a specific kind of text for an assessment or for a 'real life' task such as sending an email. Such texts are generic in some way. They often have specific vocabulary (including large chunks or expressions) or grammar connected with them. They also have rules about the way they are presented, how they are paragraphed and ordered and other aspects of discourse. The problem for foreign learners of English is that these rules of discourse might be different to their languages. Unlike speaking, where listeners might accept errors because they can see other things to interpret the message, with writing, a reader may misunderstand a message or even be offended when the rules or conventions of a genre are broken. For this reason, students need careful preparation for writing such texts and feedback should be more thorough.

The writing units in the Student book aim to provide this careful preparation. They are based on genres commonly tested in international exams such as PET, FCE and IELTS, or on functional writing tasks we may perform at work or when studying in an English-speaking context.

WHAT'S IN *OUTCOMES* WRITING UNITS?

Each double page spread teaches a different style of writing. You can follow them in any order or do them after every two units in the main Student's book. In the units there is:

Speaking The units aim to be interactive. Speaking activities provide a warmer, relate to the topic, discuss the text types or may part of planning for writing.

Writing The writing sections present model texts. While there may be some basic comprehension questions around these, the main focus is noticing useful language for the genre and how the texts are organised.

Key words This section focuses on words / expressions which link sentences and clauses and give texts coherence. They follow a similar pattern to grammar exercises, with a short explanation or guided questions and a controlled practice.

Vocabulary and grammar There are often short grammar or vocabulary sections if there is a close relation to the text type. Note there's *no* link to the grammar reference or Vocabulary builder.

Practice This is a task for students to write a similar kind of text to the one they looked at in **Writing** and try to incorporate some of the other language they have learnt in the unit. This section can be set as homework or be done in class. Doing the practice in class can be interactive, particularly if using a 'process writing' approach.

Process writing
Process writing approaches focus on the fact that good writers often go through several stages to produce a good piece of writing. They may:

- brainstorm ideas
- write a plan
- write a draft
- discuss their draft with someone
- write a second draft
- put it through a spell-checker
- have corrections made by someone
- write the final draft

Obviously, we don't always go through these stages when we write, but in the case of our students, having different stages and allowing for more than one draft gives more opportunity for teaching and learning. In fact, brainstorming and planning stages are often included in **Practice** or at some other stage of the lesson. However there is no reason why any of the stages above shouldn't be done in pairs in class. Another way you might want to incorporate a process approach is to give the **Practice** task for homework *before* they do the actual writing lesson. They then re-write their essay in the light of what they learn.

Marking and feedback
There are a number of options to teachers to mark and give feedback on students' writing.

Using symbols You can mark essays using symbols above the inappropriate word or grammar. Here are some examples:

t = wrong tense
wf = wrong word form (e.g. noun not adjective)
col = wrong collocation (e.g. the noun is the right meaning but doesn't go with the verb)
voc = you have the wrong word (it makes no sense here)
prep = you need a different preposition
pl = plural is wrong or should be plural
sp = wrong spelling
wo = the word order is wrong
art = the article is wrong or absent

The idea of doing this is to make students notice their errors and try to find answers. You could do this as a pair activity in class. It may help them to become more aware of their common errors and edit their own work more carefully. The difficulty is that mistakes don't fit neatly into categories and students may still get the language wrong. You should mark the text again.

Re-formulation You may simply want to cross out and re-write things which are 'wrong' in the text. This may have the advantage of teaching students the correct language (though note they may still be unclear *why* it was wrong). It may also be time-consuming for you and demoralising for students if they see lots of crossing out.

In this case – and indeed with all cases of teacher feedback – you need to strike a balance. At intermediate, you may want to ignore some things which are understandable but not necessarily how we would say things: priority should be given to clarity.

Content and structure When you mark the texts you could ignore 'grammar' and individual vocabulary mistakes and focus only on whether the writing answers the question and is organised well. You simply write comments on the writing or at the end. This is often quicker for you, the teacher – and it's probably easier to deal with these issues separately from language.

Marking this way trains students to appreciate the importance of these aspects of writing over basic 'accuracy'. Readers in fact will often ignore mistakes if the overall structure of the text is clear and the content is relevant, logical and / or interesting.

However, students will want to know if their writing is correct unless you clearly warn students beforehand that you'll only deal with content and structure.

Peer correction Students can also give feedback. Get them to read each other's writing and evaluate the texts and / or suggest changes. To do this they really need a 'mark scheme'; this could be a list of statements they tick or adapt such as:

I enjoyed this.
I wanted to know more about.
I didn't understand the bit about.
You used some words / grammar I didn't know how to use.

Another way is to give them marking criteria from an established source such as UCLES PET exam. Check they're not too difficult for your students.

The advantage of peer correction is that it's interactive and based on genuine readers' responses. It's also easy on the teacher! However, it is not so good for dealing with language, apart from general statements, as students may not trust each other's judgement – often with good reason! But it is a useful stage and may save you time by reducing mistakes or inconsistencies before you come to mark the texts.

Writing and portfolios
Whichever way you choose to correct the students' texts, we suggest you get students to re-write them. This would guarantee that the students focus on their errors and produce an improved text which they could then keep in a portfolio. Portfolios of work are recommended by the CEF and can provide evidence of students' progress and level.

WRITING LESSONS

UNIT AIMS

There are eight writing units in total. The aims of these units are to give additional writing practice and to introduce students to the kind of texts they might need or want to write. They focus on developing fluent, coherent writing. It is suggested that you use these units towards the end of every two units of the Student's book as extra material, especially when you feel your students would benefit from the change of focus that writing activities provide. It is also recommended that you follow the steps suggested in the Student's book, although of course other variations are possible. You could either set the final writing task (*Practice*) in class and get students to mark / correct each other's work, or you could set it as a test or for homework.

01 INTRODUCING YOURSELF

VOCABULARY Free-time activities

A Answers

1 karaoke
2 trekking
3 waterskiing
4 kick-boxing
5 aerobics
6 gardening

WRITING Introducing yourself

B Answers

1 on
2 to
3 which
4 who
5 really
6 quite
7 also
8 as well
9 about
10 in

KEY WORDS FOR WRITING

Too, also, as well, as well as

A Answers

As well, too at the end of the sentence; *also* placed between subject and verb (but after the verb *to be*).

B Answers

1 ... having fun too.
2 ... I also do photography...
3 ... staying in and reading as well.
4 ... I'm also into ...
5 ... I go running a lot as well.
6 ... I'm also doing ...

Tip Make sure students understand they should use a noun or gerund after *as well as* and that you can use *also* or *too* in the same sentence, but you would not repeat *as well.*

C Answers

1 As well as being really into computers, I like going out and having fun (too).
2 As well as liking reading and writing, I (also) do photography.
3 As well as going to the theatre quite a lot, I like staying in and reading (as well).
4 As well as (loving) gardening, I'm (also) into yoga.
5 As well as doing a lot of kick-boxing, I (also) go running a lot.
6 As well as studying Art History, I'm (also) doing a French course at the moment.

GRAMMAR Common questions

A Answers

1 What do you usually do in your free time?
2 What kind of music are you into?
3 Who is your favourite band?
4 What was the last film you saw?
5 Do you have a favourite writer?
6 What was the last book you read?
7 Do you like sport?
8 Have you got a favourite team?

02 SHORT EMAILS

WRITING Explaining why you are writing

Tip *A quick one* is very informal and would probably not be used with sentences c or d, which are more formal than the others.

Note We wouldn't use *a short one…* .

A Answers
a any combination of first three columns (except *a short one*) to remind …
b … to say I'm sorry …
c … to say thank you …
d … to let you know …
e … to ask …
f …to tell …
g … to say congratulations …

C Answers
1 Just a quick email / note / short note to ask if you could do me a big favour.
2 Just a quick email / note / short note to say I'm sorry I missed you when you were in Berlin.
3 Just a quick one / email / note / short note to say congratulations.

GRAMMAR Leaving out words

A Answers
1 and *I* really need
2 and *I'll* ask; or *I need to* know about
3 and *I* am
4 or *have you* lost

B Answers
1 We left Sydney on Friday night and arrived in Hong Kong on Saturday morning.
2 I really want to send some of the photos to my mum and burn some of the other photos onto a CD.
3 Don't worry about missing class tomorrow or taking time off if you need to.
4 Don't feel you have to wear a suit to the party tonight or bring a present.
5 I am going to Prague tomorrow and Bratislava on Friday, so I won't be at the meeting on Thursday afternoon or at work for the rest of the week.
6 I thought the story was great and the acting was really good but I didn't really like the ending or some of the songs.

VOCABULARY Ending emails

A Suggested answers
1 Kind regards, Yours faithfully, Yours sincerely, Yours
2 Many thanks, All the best,
3 Love, Lots of love, Cheers for now

03 STORIES

WRITING A story

A Answers
Connection: they are all part of the same story about a parachute jump.
Order: c, a, d, b.

GRAMMAR Narrative tenses

B Answers

1 said / had said	5 screamed
2 seemed	6 was really flying
3 was beating	7 opened
4 was thinking	8 landed

KEY WORDS FOR WRITING

Just about to, just as

A Answers
1 c 2 a 3 e 4 d 5 f 6 b

C Answers
1 We were just about to leave when they gave us a table.
2 I was just about to give up and go home when I saw him walking towards me.
3 I was just about to go to bed when the doorbell rang.
4 Just as we were walking towards our car, a police car drove up and stopped right in front of us.
5 Just as we were starting to think the holiday would be a disaster, the sun came out.

VOCABULARY Ways of doing things

A Answers

1 whisper	3 stare	5 shout	7 grab
2 creep	4 slam	6 rush	

C Answers

1 rushed	3 stared	5 shouting	7 whisper
2 slammed	4 grabbed	6 crept	

04 MAKING REQUESTS

GRAMMAR Requests

A Answers
1 b 2 d 3 c 4 a

B Answers
I was wondering if ...?
1 *could* = modal verb
2 *give* = infinitive without *to-*
3 *could* = modal verb
4 *pay* = infinitive without *to-*

WRITING

B Answers

	a	b	c
1	made	think	soon
2	say	chance	like / love
3	busy	favour	be
4	let	wondering	All

KEYWORDS FOR WRITING *as*

A Suggested answers – many variations possible
1 Do you think you could send me another copy of the invoice as I've lost the first one? Many thanks in advance.
2 I was wondering if you could give me a lift as my car's in the garage. I'd be really grateful.
3 Is there any way I could stay at your place for a few days as I've got builders working in my flat and it's a real mess? I'd be really grateful.
4 Could you do me a favour and extend the deadline for my essay as I've been ill for three days? I'd be incredibly grateful.
5 Do you think you could complete the work by Thursday as I'm seeing the director then? Thanks.

VOCABULARY *as ... as* expressions

A Answers
1 as soon as possible
2 as far as I know
3 as quickly as you can
4 as soon as you hear
5 as soon as you arrive
6 as far as the hotel is concerned

B Answers
a as soon as you hear
b as quickly as you can
c as soon as you arrive
d As far as the hotel is concerned
e as soon as possible
f As far as I know

05 SUGGESTING CHANGES

VOCABULARY *Programme*

A Answers
1 last-minute
2 swap
3 full
4 exciting
5 include

KEYWORDS FOR WRITING
However, although and *but*

A Answers
1 Although, but; Although
2 However

B Answers
1 Although
2 However
3 but / although
4 Although
5 however

C Answers
1 ... is a nice idea, but it ...
2 ... like rock music, some of ...
3 ... look great. However, I think ...

06 REPORTS

WRITING

B Answers
... this is rarely used ... / ... more could be done ... / ... so it could be used ... The passive is used because it is more formal and impersonal and the person / people doing the action is / are unclear or unimportant.

C Answers
... the council could provide ... / ... more could be done ... / why not show ...? / ... the council should consider...

VOCABULARY Describing facilities

A Answers
1 small / limited
2 hang
3 courts
4 runs
5 rarely
6 wider
7 done
8 subsidise
9 consider

KEYWORDS FOR WRITING

Referring to things

A Answers
1 f   2 d   3 b   4 c   5 a   6 e

B Answers
Many different possibilities.

07 FOR AND AGAINST

WRITING

D Answers
1 Personally
2 Firstly
3 Secondly
4 thirdly
5 However
6 obviously
7 Otherwise
8 In conclusion

E Answers
1 first paragraph – increase in number of cars, running out of oil
2 end of first paragraph – Personally, I do not believe ...
3 second paragraph – get directly from A to B, comfortable, car industry is a large employer
4 third paragraph – unable to move around in our cities, increase in road deaths, environmental damage
5 whole text
6 second, third and fourth paragraphs – they allow one, people feel comfortable ...
7 whole text – I do not believe, It is time, etc.

GRAMMAR Describing trends

A Answers
1 has improved – over the last few years; are driving – everyday
2 is getting – at the moment,
has recently increased – recently
3 is getting – these days
has stopped – today
4 has increased – in recent years
are now becoming – now
5 have been – over the last few years
it has become ; are now calling – now

KEYWORDS *As such*

A Answers
1 c   2 d   3 a   4 e   5b

08 A REVIEW

VOCABULARY Describing films

A Answers
1 funny
2 moving
3 scary
4 entertaining
5 uplifting
6 gripping

B Answers
1 chosen
2 acted
3 written
4 filmed
5 directed

WRITING

B Answers
1 present simple (including passive), present continuous
2 no = the review doesn't want to give away all the film's secrets
3 at the end of the review

KEYWORDS FOR WRITING

While and *during*

A Answers
1 during
2 while
3 While
4 During
5 during
6 While

GRAMMAR

Adding information after the noun

B Answers
1 This is a moving love story about a disabled woman.
2 This is a comedy action film starring Akshay Kumar.
3 The film is directed by Lasse Hallstrom, who also directed *The Cider House Rules*.
4 The film is set in a small town, during the mayoral election.
5 The main character is a brilliant but lonely doctor, (a part) superbly played by Jennifer Jenkins.
6 The documentary follows the lives of four couples who have recently emigrated to Australia.

1A English outside of the classroom

Aim

To encourage students to improve their English outside of the classroom.

Before class

Make one copy of the questionnaire for each student.

In class

A Introduce the idea by asking students to give you a few ideas of how they can do this, e.g. watch films in English.

B Explain that they are going to do questionnaire on the topic. Tell them to read and discuss in pairs.

C Handout the questionnaires. When ready, tell them to ask their partner the questions. While students are talking, write these on the board.

I do this. = 3 points

I don't do this and I'm not interested in it. = 0 points

I don't do this but I'd like to try it. = 1 point

D After five minutes stop them. Tell them to work out their partner's score and talk about their results.

E Then ask them to write down two or more new ideas for improving their English outside of the classroom.

F Discuss their ideas. You could get them to write a promise list, i.e. three things they promise to try in the next week.

1B Pair stories

Aim

To revise narrative tenses.

Before class

Make enough copies of each of the stories for half the class.

In class

A Give half the class story A and the other half story B. Ask them individually to read their stories and put the verbs in the correct tense – either past simple, past continuous or past perfect.

B Put them in same story pairs to check their answers.

C In AB pairs ask them to tell each other their stories, from memory if possible, using all three narrative tenses. Ask them to find similarities and differences between the stories.

D Feedback by asking As to re-tell story B and vice versa.

Answers

Story A 1 was giving, 2 was going, 3 noticed, 4 was laughing, 5 had not / hadn't given, 6 was, 7 were enjoying, 8 finished, 9 clapped, 10 pointed, 11 looked, 12 realised, 13 had forgotten.

Story B 1 was going, 2 noticed, 3 were moving, 4 finished, 5 clapped, 6 asked, 7 was, 8 told, 9 were not / weren't, 10 were visiting, 11 had given.

2A Mime the sentence

Aim

To revise *-ing* and *-ed* adjectives.

Before class

Make one copy for each student.

In class

A Divide the class into AB pairs. Explain that students are going to be given a set of sentences and in pairs they should mime their sentences to each other and their partner should guess what happened.

B Give out one set of sentences to student A and the other set to student B. Ask them to mime their sentences.

C The winning pair are the ones that correctly guess all their sentences first.

2B Make a bid game!

Aim

To revise present simple and present continuous.

Before class

Make enough for one copy between two.

In class

A Explain to students that they are going to play a game where they make bids on which sentence is correct.

B Model before you start, e.g.

a How sweet – they hold hands!

b How sweet – they're holding hands! Which one is correct? (B) Why? (Because the action is happening now.)

C Put students into pairs. Tell them they have 500 euros to bid on their sentences. Give each pair a sheet of sentences and their money. If you can find fake money to use it adds to the fun.

D When they are ready, hold an auction.

E Once all the sentences are sold, take a vote on who thinks the sentences are correct and why. Check answers. The winners are the pair with the most money.

Answers

1 Both possible. Present simple suggests a habit or permanent state. Present continuous suggests a temporary arrangement.

2a not possible – *like* is a stative verb and doesn't usually occur in the continuous form. 2b is correct: it expresses an opinion.

3a not possible; use present continuous for definite future arrangements.

4a not possible; see 2a above. 4b is correct.

5a not correct. 5b is correct – use present simple with adverbs of frequency to talk about habitual actions.

3A Vocabulary race

Aim
To revise vocabulary related to holidays.

Before class
Copy a set for each group of three / four students.

In class
A Divide the class into groups of three / four. Give each group a set of cards and ask them to place them in a pile face down. They should take turns to take a card and look at the word / phrase without showing it to the other students. They should define the word / phrase, but not say it and the others should guess. Students who guess correctly should keep the card. The one with the most cards at the end is the winner.
B You could conduct this as a race i.e. the first group to finish is also the winner.
C Check meaning and pronunciation as a class.

3B Snakes and ladders – the future

Aim
To revise future forms.

Before class
Make one copy of the game for every two / three students. You also need enough dice for each group. If you don't have dice, use slips of paper with numbers 1–6 in an envelope for students to pick.

In class
A Explain to students that they are going to play a game of snakes and ladders. They need a different counter each – a coin, ring, paper clip etc.
B They should take turns to throw the dice and move that number of squares from the START square. If they land on a ladder they go up, on a snake they go down. If they land on a blank square, they stay there until their next turn. If they land on a square with a sentence they should decide if the sentence is correct or not. If it's not correct they should correct it. Their partner(s) should decide if they are right.
C You should monitor and help if they don't agree. If they're right, they move forward two squares. If not, they move back two squares. The students all take turns throwing the die and working through the board until one student reaches the FINISH square. The first player to reach FINISH wins.

Answers
2 I'm thinking of going to Japan next summer.
4 correct
6 I went to see the doctor yesterday.
7 correct
9 It will probably rain later.
11 correct
13 correct
15 Have you got to work on Saturday? / Are you working on Saturday?
17 correct
18 correct
19 The school got a new swimming pool last year.

4A Frequency and duration

Aim
To revise expressions of frequency and duration.

Before class
Make one copy of the sentences for each student.

In class
A Ask students to look at the sentences and form a question for each one. They should write the questions in the spaces. Do the first example with them.
B Put them in pairs to check their answers (i.e. they should check their questions are correct, but sometimes there is more than one possible answer).
C Put them in new pairs to ask each other the questions. They should note down their partner's answers.
D Conduct brief feedback with the whole group at the end.

Answers
1 How long have you been living in your present home?
2 When did you go to primary school?
3 Do you ever (often) miss / skip breakfast?
4 Have you ever stolen anything?
5 How often do you have problems sleeping?
6 How long have you been learning English?

4B Vocabulary – mix and match

Aim
To revise vocabulary related to leisure and music.

Before class
Make enough copies for every pair of students.

In class
A Explain to students that they are going to make as many correct collocations as they can, by taking a verb from A and a noun / noun phrase from B.
B Put them in pairs and tell them to write down all the correct collocations they can find. Make this a race with a time limit (five minutes).
C When the time is up, ask pairs to swap papers to check their answers.
D Check with the whole group. The pair with the most correct answers are the winners.

Possible answers
go – home, shopping, swimming, clubbing
play – tennis, music, jazz, heavy metal, the guitar, pop music
go for – a walk, a meal, a bike ride, a coffee
go to – the supermarket, a football match, the cinema, a restaurant, a concert
listen to – the radio, music, jazz, CDs, heavy metal, pop music

5A What's my job?

Aim

To revise vocabulary of jobs and practise question forms.

Before class

Make enough copies of set A for half the class and enough copies of set B for the other half.

In class

A Explain to the class that they are going to play a guessing game about jobs. They are going to guess their partner's jobs by asking yes / no questions. Demonstrate with the whole class e.g. writer. *Are you responsible for other people?* (No.) *Do you do a lot of paperwork?* (Yes.) Make sure students understand they can only answer *yes* or *no*.

B Put students in AB pairs and give out the sets of jobs according to their letter. Ask them to check they understand all the jobs and ask you quietly if they don't. Students should take turns to ask questions to find out their partner's jobs.

C You could tell them to score e.g. 20 points for guessing after 5 questions, 10 points for guessing after 10 questions, etc. You can then stop the game at any time and the winner is the student with the most points.

5B Rules matching

Aim

To revise grammatical structures for talking about rules.

Before class

Make enough copies of the sets of sentences for each group of four students. Cut them up into separate sentence strips. If possible, laminate them or stick them on card to make them stronger. Put each set in a paper clip or envelope.

In class

A Explain to the class that they are going to play a game of pelmanism. They lay the cards face down and take turns to turn two over and find matching pairs. If a student finds a matching pair they keep it and have another go. They finish when all the pairs of sentences are collected and the player with the most pairs wins.

B Put students in groups of four. Give out the sets of sentences and ask them to shuffle them and spread them face down on the table. They take turns to find matching pairs. Monitor and check they are playing correctly.

Answers

1g 2e 3a 4h 5f 6b 7c 8d

6A Spot the difference

Aim

To revise vocabulary related to clothes and accessories.

Before class

Make enough copies of picture A for half the class and enough of picture B for the other half.

In class

A Explain to the class that they are going to do a spot-the-differences activity. They must find ten differences between their and their partner's picture without looking at each other's picture. They should ask *yes / no* questions about the other picture to find the differences and write them down.

B Divide the class into AB pairs. Give out the pictures according to the letters. Ask them to sit back to back to make sure they cannot see their partner's pictures. They should take turns to ask *yes / no* questions about the other picture. When they discover a difference they should both write it down in note form.

C Quickly check with the whole group at the end. Ask them to give complete sentences to describe the differences.

6B Must

Aim

To revise three uses of *must*:

1 *Must* shows we believe something is probably true.
2 We can use *You must* to strongly recommend things.
3 *I must* = we feel something is very important for us to do. *I mustn't* = it's important for us not to do something

Before class

Make enough copies of A and B cartoons so that every pair of students has one A or B.

In class

A Put students into pairs. Each pair is an 'A' or a 'B'. Explain that they are going to look at a picture and that they have to write down as many sentences as they can about the cartoons using the modal verb, *must*. Remind them of the three uses of *must*. Model by asking them what someone might say if they looked at a picture of their class, e.g *I must study English. They must be* (the nationality of the student).

B Tell them they are going to compete against the other pairs: 'A's against 'B's. First, they have to write as many sentences as they can about picture A or B. Then they swap pictures and have to write as many sentences as they can about the second picture. Tell them they only have two minutes to write about each picture. After the game they swap pictures and score the other pair's sentences: 2 points for a sentence with *mustn't*; 1 point for an idea that the other pair doesn't have; -1 point for a grammatical mistake.

C Handout the pictures face down and tell them not to look until you say 'Go'. After two minutes shout, 'Stop! Change pictures!!' When time is up again, shout, 'Stop!'

D Put students into groups of four and get them to mark each others' sentences and then discuss the results.

7A Wordsearch

Aim
To revise vocabulary related to education.

Before class
Make enough copies of the wordseach for each student.

In class
A Explain to the students that they are going to do a wordsearch. They should look at the grid and find as many words about education as they can. Words go either across, down, diagonally or backwards.
B Students do this in pairs. You could also do it as a race i.e. the first pair to finish wins.
C Check with the whole class at the end and check meanings and pronunciation.

Answers

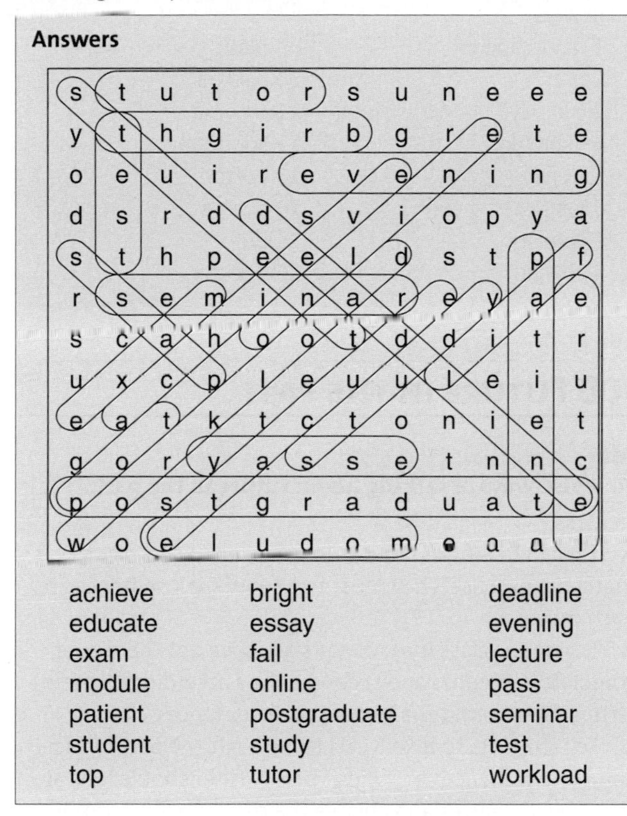

7B Conditionals matching

Aim
To revise first conditionals.

Before class
Make enough copies of set A for half the class and enough copies of set B for the other half.

In class
A Explain to the class that they are going to do a dictation / matching exercise. They must not show their sentences to each other.
B Divide the class into AB pairs and give out the sets according to their letters.
C Tell students to take turns to read out the part of their complete sentences in italics. Their partner should look at their second halves and choose the correct one to complete the sentence. They should read it out to their partner to check it is correct. If it is not correct, they should suggest another possibility. They should write the first answers in the correct space.
D Model how the exercise works with a student.
E Check answers quickly. If there's time, ask students who says / said each sentence, a teacher or a student.

Answers

A a4	b8	c1	d5	e2	f6	g3	h7
B a4	b2	c3	d7	e6	f8	g5	h1

8A Cooking vocabulary

Aim
To revise vocabulary related to food and cooking.

Before class
Make enough copies for each student to have one.

In class
A Tell students that they have anagrams of food words. They should work on their own to unscramble them.
B Check in pairs. Together, they should then write the words in the correct column, depending on whether they are ways of cooking or describing food.
C Check meanings and pronunciation with the class.

Answers
Ways of cooking *Grill, roast, stir-fry, boil, deep-fry, mash, slice, grate*
Words to describe foods *Tasty, bland, greasy, fattening, healthy, filling, rich*

8B What would you do if...?

Aim
To revise the second conditionals.

Before class
Photocopy and cut up a set of situations for each small group of students.

In class
A Put students into groups of three or four. Put one set of cut-up situations face down between each group and tell them they are going to play a guessing game. Explain that each strip of paper has an imaginary situation that happens in a restaurant on it. Students take it in turns to pick up a piece of paper then give clues about what the situation is, but their clues shouldn't be too easy.
B Model the activity with this situation – *If you were served snake, what would you do?*
Give them clues and correct the grammar if it's wrong.
Examples: *I'd ask the waiter if it was alive or dead.*
If it was alive, I would let it slide off my plate.
C Tell one student in each group to start. When someone has correctly guessed the situation they have a turn. The game continues until all the situations have been talked about.

9A Guess my word – housing and areas

Aim

To revise vocabulary related to housing / areas.

Before class

Make enough copies of set A for half the class and enough of set B for the other half.

In class

A Divide the class into AB pairs. Tell students they are to take turns describing their words / phrases to each other. They should define the word / phrase or give clues, but not say it.

B Give out the sets according to their letters. Give students time to check they know the meanings and to ask you quietly if they are not sure.

C You could conduct this as a race i.e. the first pair to finish are the winners.

D Check meanings and pronunciation with the whole class at the end.

9B Now and then

Aim

To revise language to talk about differences between the past and the present.

Before class

Copy enough sets of both pictures for each student, or for one between two.

In class

A Put students in pairs and explain that they are going to compare a picture of Woodside now and Woodside as it was in 1970.

B Give out the pictures. Elicit some differences. Write these language structures on the board and remind them to use them: *there used to be / didn't used to be, it's not as ... as it was, it's more ... than it was, the number of ... has increased / risen, decreased / fallen.*

C They should work together and write ten true sentences about the changes in Woodside.

D Check with the whole class at the end.

10A Vocabulary race

Aim

To revise vocabulary related to leisure activities

Before class

Make enough copies for each student to have one, or you could do one copy between two.

In class

A Put students in pairs and tell them they are going to complete the words about leisure activities, from the definitions and initial letter. The first pair to finish win.

B Check meaning and pronunciation with the whole class at the end.

Answers

1 landscape	9 plot
2 gig	10 packed
3 tragedy	11 moving
4 exhibition	12 soundtrack
5 trendy	13 horror
6 weird	14 audience
7 touristy	15 dull
8 sold out	16 director

10B Future in the past

Aim

To revise ways of talking about future in the past.

In class

A Explain to the class that they are going to do a dictation / matching exercise. They must not show their sentences to each other.

B Divide the class into AB pairs and give out the sets of complete sentences and second halves according to their letters. Give them time to read their sentences.

C Tell students to take turns to read out the part of their complete sentences in italics. Their partner should look at their second halves and choose the correct one to complete the sentence. They should read it out to their partner to check it is correct. If it is not correct, they should suggest another possibility. They should write the first half of the sentence in the correct space.

D Check with the whole group at the end. Get students to suggest a 'scenario' for each sentence.

Answers

A	a 4	b 1	c 2	d 3
B	a 1	b 3	c 4	d 2

11A Passives

Aim
To revise passive forms.

Before class
Make enough copies of the sets of sentences for each student or one set between two.

In class
A Explain to students that they are going to look at some sentences. Some are correct and some are not. Ask them to work together and tick the ones they think are correct and correct the ones they think are wrong.
B Put students in pairs or groups of three and hand out one set of sentences per student or per group.
C Check with the whole class at the end.

Answers
1 The drugs were smuggled into the country.
2 Correct
3 The man was arrested as he tried to leave the country.
4 The prisoner is being released tomorrow.
5 These pills should not be taken by children.
6 Correct
7 They've never been involved in anything like that.
8 Correct

11B What animal am I?

Aim
To revise names of animals.

Before class
Make enough copies so that you can give a complete set to each small group.

In class
A Cut out the animal words and put them into an envelope. Explain to the class that in groups they are going to have turns to pick a card out of the envelope with the name of an animal on it. They must not show the card to their group. They must mime the animal on the card and the others should guess. Whoever gets it right gets 1 point.
B Put the class into small groups to play and remind them that all the animals are included in the unit.
C Give them a time limit (e.g. five minutes or once everyone has had a turn). The winner is the person with the most points.
D Quickly check pronunciation as a class at the end.

12A When I was a kid

Aim
To revise ways of talking about past habits and states via the topic of childhood.

Before class
Make one copy for each student.

In class
A Explain to students that they are going to interview each other about their childhood.
B First, put students in pairs and ask them to put the questions in the correct order.
C Check the sentences are correct with the whole group.
D In new pairs and ask students to interview each other using the questions and they note their partners' answers.
E Ask students to tell the group one interesting thing they learnt about their partner.

Answers
1 What used to be your favourite game in the playground when you were a child?
2 Did your parents use to let you stay up late sometimes? What was the latest you ever stayed up?
3 What food would you refuse to eat when you were a kid?
4 What did you always use to fight about with your brothers and sisters?
5 What cuddly toy would you always go to bed with when you were little?
6 Who used to be your favourite teacher when you were 12?

12B I wish...

Aim
To revise *wish* + past perfect.

Before class
Make enough copies for each student to have one.

In class
A Ask students to read the instructions. They have to fill in the bubbles and then their partner will guess which bubble goes with which word / phrase. Tell them not to fill the bubbles in in the same order as the instructions. They should write single words or phrases rather than sentences *e.g.* Write something you wish you'd done when you were younger.
more football
B When they have finished, put students in pairs. They should try to guess which bubble goes with which instruction by asking complete questions e.g. *Is playing more football something you wish you'd done when you were younger?* (Yes.)
C Conduct brief feedback by asking about things they heard which they found surprising, strange, etc.

13A Guess my word – travel, travel problems and strong adjectives

Aim

To revise vocabulary related to travel and strong adjectives.

Before class

Make enough copies of set A for half the class and of set B for the other half.

In class

A Explain to the class that they are going to work in pairs to guess each other's words. They are to take turns describing their words / phrases to each other. They may give clues but not say the word / phrase.

B Give out set A to half the class and set B to the other half. Ask students to think about how to explain their words.

C Put students in AB pairs to guess each other's words.

D Check meanings and pronunciation as a class.

13B Snakes and ladders – should've / third conditionals

Aim

To revise should've / third conditional in a fun way.

Before class

Make one copy of the game for every three / four students. You also need enough dice for each group. If you don't have dice, you can use slips of paper with numbers 1–6 in an envelope for students to pick.

In class

A Explain to students that they are going to play a game of snakes and ladders. They need a different counter each – a coin, ring, paper clip, etc.

B They should take turns to throw the dice and move that number of squares from the START square. If they land on a ladder, they go up, on a snake they go down. If they land on a blank square, they stay there until their next turn. If they land on a square with a sentence starter they should complete the sentence correctly. Their partner(s) should decide if they are right.

C You should monitor and help if they don't agree. If they get it right, they move forward two squares. If not, they move back two squares. The students all take turns throwing the die and working through the board until one student reaches the FINISH square. The first player to reach FINISH wins.

14A Crossword

Aim

To revise vocabulary related to technology.

Before class

Make enough copies of the A part of the crossword for half the class and enough copies of the B part for the other half.

In class

A Explain to the students that they are going to do a crossword. Half the class have the across clues filled in and the other half have the down clues filled in.

B Put students in same clues pairs first and ask them to check their words / abbreviations together and help each other to think of ways to define them. They can ask for your help at this stage if they need to.

C Put students in AB pairs and ask them to take turns giving each other clues for the words / abbreviations they have and filling in the crossword as they go along.

D Check meanings and pronunciation as a class.

Answers

1A				2C		3M		aP	D	4F
BU	P	G	R	A	D	E				A
T				B		N		5U		Q
O		6C		L		U		R		
cM	O	U	S	E			DP	L	U	7G
A		R								A
T		eS	A	T	U	R	A	T	E	D
I		O								G
fC	D	R	O	M						E
A					GM	8A	R	9K	E	T
HL	I	G	H	T		S		E		
L						A		Y		10I
Y		ID	V	D		jP	C	S		T

14B Grammar *-ing* forms and *to*-infinitives

Aim

To revise structures with gerunds and infinitives.

Before class

Make one copy for each student.

In class

A Give out the sentence starters. Explain to students that they are to complete them with a suitable ending, which should be grammatically correct and also something they would like to ask other students.

B Individually students complete the questions. Monitor and check their questions are correct.

C In pairs students ask and answer each other's questions. They should note their partners' answers.

D Conduct brief feedback at the end by asking a few students what their partners said.

Answers

1 *to*-infinitive / *to*-infinitive
2 *-ing* form
3 *-ing* form
4 *to*-infinitive
5 *-ing* form
6 *-ing* form
7 *to*-infinitive
8 *to*-infinitive

15A Doctors and patients

Aim
To revise vocabulary related to illnesses, accidents and remedies.

Before class
Make enough copies of set A for half the class and of set B for the other half.

In class
A Explain to the class that they have a list of illnesses, injuries and accidents. They are going to mime these to each other. Their partner should be the doctor, guess the problem and suggest a remedy e.g. *Ah, I see you have a rash. Try this ointment.*
B Put them in AB pairs and hand out the lists. Give them time to think about how to mime the problems.
C Check meanings and pronunciation as a class.

15B Reported speech – matching dictation

Aim
To revise reported speech.

Before class
Make enough copies of set A for half the class and of set B for the other half.
A Explain to the class that they are going to do a dictation / matching exercise. They must not show their sentences to each other.
B Divide the class into AB pairs and give out the sets of pairs of sentences according to their letters. Give them time to read their sentences.
C Tell students to take turns to read out their sentences in the top half of their worksheet. Their partner should look at the sentences in the lower half of their worksheet and choose the one which is most similar to that sentence. They should read it out to their partner to check it is correct. If it is not correct, they should suggest another possibility. They should write the matching sentence in the correct space.
D Check with the whole group at the end. Get students to suggest a 'scenario' for each sentence.

Answers
A 1b He promised not to leave her.
2b He offered to carry my bag.
3a I am definitely paying the bill.
4a I really love you.
B 1b She told me to phone him.
2b She said I was an idiot.
3a Please don't shout.
4a Oh, please come with me.

16A Vocabulary – newspapers, famous people

Aim
To revise vocabulary related to newspapers, the news and celebrity.

Before class
Make enough copies of set A for half the class and of set B for the other half.

In class
A Tell students they are going to work on their own to complete the words about newspapers and famous people, from the definitions and initial letter.
B Give out set A to half the class and set B to the other half.
C When they have finished students work in pairs to mark each others answers.
D Check with the whole group at the end.

16B Grammar – defining game

Aim
To revise relative clauses and review vocabulary from the whole book.

Before class
Make enough copies of set A for half the class and of set B for the other half.

In class
A Explain to students that they are going to practise relative clauses by playing a defining game. Demonstrate the activity by putting this language on the board and asking students to define the words:
stitches: X is / are something that / which Ys.
a bilingual person: X is someone that / who Ys.

Answers
Stitches are something that / which join together a person's skin after it is cut.

Answers
A bilingual person is someone that / who speaks two languages perfectly.

B Give out set A to half the class and set B to the other half. Tell them to check they understand their words and to think about how to define them.
C In AB pairs students take turns defining and guessing. Monitor and help if necessary.
D Ask students if they have any questions before you close the activity.

1A English outside of the classroom

There are a lot of opportunities to learn English outside of the classroom. Are you taking them? Try this questionnaire and see. Tick (✓) the box that is you.

I read: 1 stuff in English: books, magazines, comics, etc.
2 English in my job and/or at college.
3 things on the Internet: blogs, Wikipedia, Facebook, etc.

1 2 3
☐ ☐ ☐ I do this.
☐ ☐ ☐ I don't do this and I'm not interested in it.
☐ ☐ ☐ I don't do this but I'd like to try it.

I write: 1 emails or texts in English.
2 write essays in English.
3 write to friends online, e.g. Facebook.

1 2 3
☐ ☐ ☐ I do this.
☐ ☐ ☐ I don't do this and I'm not interested in it.
☐ ☐ ☐ I don't do this but I'd like to try it.

I listen to and/or watch: 1 music in English.
2 things on YouTube or other sites.
3 TV or films in English.

1 2 3
☐ ☐ ☐ I do this.
☐ ☐ ☐ I don't do this and I'm not interested in it.
☐ ☐ ☐ I don't do this but I'd like to try it.

I talk to: 1 people in English socially.
2 people in English professionally.
3 people in English on the Internet.

1 2 3
☐ ☐ ☐ I do this.
☐ ☐ ☐ I don't do this and I'm not interested in it.
☐ ☐ ☐ I don't do this but I'd like to try it.

Results
0–9: What are you waiting for? Don't wait for tomorrow, start today!
10–18: Not bad. Can you do better?
19–27: Good work. Your English is improving!
28–36: Excellent. You're learning fast!

There are a lot of opportunities to learn English outside of the classroom. Are you taking them? Try this questionnaire and see. Tick (✓) the box that is you.

I read: 1 stuff in English: books, magazines, comics, etc.
2 English in my job and/or at college.
3 things on the Internet: blogs, Wikipedia, Facebook, etc.

1 2 3
☐ ☐ ☐ I do this.
☐ ☐ ☐ I don't do this and I'm not interested in it.
☐ ☐ ☐ I don't do this but I'd like to try it.

I write: 1 emails or texts in English.
2 write essays in English.
3 write to friends online, e.g. Facebook.

1 2 3
☐ ☐ ☐ I do this.
☐ ☐ ☐ I don't do this and I'm not interested in it.
☐ ☐ ☐ I don't do this but I'd like to try it.

I listen to and/or watch: 1 music in English.
2 things on YouTube or other sites.
3 TV or films in English.

1 2 3
☐ ☐ ☐ I do this.
☐ ☐ ☐ I don't do this and I'm not interested in it.
☐ ☐ ☐ I don't do this but I'd like to try it.

I talk to: 1 people in English socially.
2 people in English professionally.
3 people in English on the Internet.

1 2 3
☐ ☐ ☐ I do this.
☐ ☐ ☐ I don't do this and I'm not interested in it.
☐ ☐ ☐ I don't do this but I'd like to try it.

Results
0–9: What are you waiting for? Don't wait for tomorrow, start today!
10–18: Not bad. Can you do better?
19–27: Good work. Your English is improving!
28–36: Excellent. You're learning fast!

There are a lot of opportunities to learn English outside of the classroom. Are you taking them? Try this questionnaire and see. Tick (✓) the box that is you.

I read: 1 stuff in English: books, magazines, comics, etc.
2 English in my job and/or at college.
3 things on the Internet: blogs, Wikipedia, Facebook, etc.

1 2 3
☐ ☐ ☐ I do this.
☐ ☐ ☐ I don't do this and I'm not interested in it.
☐ ☐ ☐ I don't do this but I'd like to try it.

I write: 1 emails or texts in English.
2 write essays in English.
3 write to friends online, e.g. Facebook.

1 2 3
☐ ☐ ☐ I do this.
☐ ☐ ☐ I don't do this and I'm not interested in it.
☐ ☐ ☐ I don't do this but I'd like to try it.

I listen to and/or watch: 1 music in English.
2 things on YouTube or other sites.
3 TV or films in English.

1 2 3
☐ ☐ ☐ I do this.
☐ ☐ ☐ I don't do this and I'm not interested in it.
☐ ☐ ☐ I don't do this but I'd like to try it.

I talk to: 1 people in English socially.
2 people in English professionally.
3 people in English on the Internet.

1 2 3
☐ ☐ ☐ I do this.
☐ ☐ ☐ I don't do this and I'm not interested in it.
☐ ☐ ☐ I don't do this but I'd like to try it.

Results
0–9: What are you waiting for? Don't wait for tomorrow, start today!
10–18: Not bad. Can you do better?
19–27: Good work. Your English is improving!
28–36: Excellent. You're learning fast!

There are a lot of opportunities to learn English outside of the classroom. Are you taking them? Try this questionnaire and see. Tick (✓) the box that is you.

I read: 1 stuff in English: books, magazines, comics, etc.
2 English in my job and/or at college.
3 things on the Internet: blogs, Wikipedia, Facebook, etc.

1 2 3
☐ ☐ ☐ I do this.
☐ ☐ ☐ I don't do this and I'm not interested in it.
☐ ☐ ☐ I don't do this but I'd like to try it.

I write: 1 emails or texts in English.
2 write essays in English.
3 write to friends online, e.g. Facebook.

1 2 3
☐ ☐ ☐ I do this.
☐ ☐ ☐ I don't do this and I'm not interested in it.
☐ ☐ ☐ I don't do this but I'd like to try it.

I listen to and/or watch: 1 music in English.
2 things on YouTube or other sites.
3 TV or films in English.

1 2 3
☐ ☐ ☐ I do this.
☐ ☐ ☐ I don't do this and I'm not interested in it.
☐ ☐ ☐ I don't do this but I'd like to try it.

I talk to: 1 people in English socially.
2 people in English professionally.
3 people in English on the Internet.

1 2 3
☐ ☐ ☐ I do this.
☐ ☐ ☐ I don't do this and I'm not interested in it.
☐ ☐ ☐ I don't do this but I'd like to try it.

Results
0–9: What are you waiting for? Don't wait for tomorrow, start today!
10–18: Not bad. Can you do better?
19–27: Good work. Your English is improving!
28–36: Excellent. You're learning fast!

1B Narrative tenses

Story A

A man 1 .... (give) a presentation on learning language at an educational conference at a famous university. Everything 2 .... (go) well until about halfway through his talk, when he 3 .... (notice) that everyone in the room 4 .... (laugh) at him. He 5 .... (not give) this talk before, so he 6 .... (be) surprised that they 7 .... (enjoy) it so much. When he 8 .... finish), everyone 9 .... (clap) politely but someone at the front 10 .... (point) at his trousers. He 11 .... (look) down and 12 .... (realise), to his horror, that he 13 .... (forget) to do them up.

Story A

A man 1 .... (give) a presentation on learning language at an educational conference at a famous university. Everything 2 .... (go) well until about halfway through his talk, when he 3 .... (notice) that everyone in the room 4 .... (laugh) at him. He 5 .... (not give) this talk before, so he 6 .... (be) surprised that they 7 .... (enjoy) it so much. When he 8 .... finish), everyone 9 .... (clap) politely but someone at the front 10 .... (point) at his trousers. He 11 .... (look) down and 12 .... (realise), to his horror, that he 13 .... (forget) to do them up.

Story B

A female professor was invited by a famous university to give a talk on language learning. Everything 1 .... (go) well until halfway through her talk. She 2 .... (notice) that a lot of people in the audience 3 .... (move) about in their seats and looking uncomfortable. When she 4 .... (finish) everyone 5 .... (clap) politely but without enthusiasm. She 6 .... (ask) if there 7 .... (be) a problem. There was silence until a woman 8 .... (tell) her: they 9 .... (not be) from this university. They 10 .... (visit) from another college, where she 11 .... (give) the same talk six months earlier!

Story B

A female professor was invited by a famous university to give a talk on language learning. Everything 1 .... (go) well until halfway through her talk. She 2 .... (notice) that a lot of people in the audience 3 .... (move) about in their seats and looking uncomfortable. When she 4 .... (finish) everyone 5 .... (clap) politely but without enthusiasm. She 6 .... (ask) if there 7 .... (be) a problem. There was silence until a woman 8 .... (tell) her: they 9 .... (not be) from this university. They 10 .... (visit) from another college, where she 11 .... (give) the same talk six months earlier!

2A Mime the sentence

Set 1

1 I felt guilty because I ate all the chocolate cake.
2 I'm in a bad mood because I lost my car keys.
3 The music was so relaxing that I fell asleep.
4 I'm fed up because I have too much homework.
5 I was exhausted because I didn't sleep for 24 hours.
6 We lost the football game 10-0 and that was really disappointing!

Set 2

1 I'm not scared of spiders or snakes.
2 I'm very worried about this job interview tomorrow.
3 I was furious because a dog stole my sandwich.
4 I was annoyed because people didn't listen to me.
5 That new film *Kiss of Dracula* is really scary.
6 I'm feeling down because I failed my driving test.

Set 1

1 I felt guilty because I ate all the chocolate cake.
2 I'm in a bad mood because I lost my car keys.
3 The music was so relaxing that I fell asleep.
4 I'm fed up because I have too much homework.
5 I was exhausted because I didn't sleep for 24 hours.
6 We lost the football game 10-0 and that was really disappointing!

Set 2

1 I'm not scared of spiders or snakes.
2 I'm very worried about this job interview tomorrow.
3 I was furious because a dog stole my sandwich.
4 I was annoyed because people didn't listen to me.
5 That new film *Kiss of Dracula* is really scary.
6 I'm feeling down because I failed my driving test.

Set 1

1 I felt guilty because I ate all the chocolate cake.
2 I'm in a bad mood because I lost my car keys.
3 The music was so relaxing that I fell asleep.
4 I'm fed up because I have too much homework.
5 I was exhausted because I didn't sleep for 24 hours.
6 We lost the football game 10-0 and that was really disappointing!

Set 2

1 I'm not scared of spiders or snakes.
2 I'm very worried about this job interview tomorrow.
3 I was furious because a dog stole my sandwich.
4 I was annoyed because people didn't listen to me.
5 That new film *Kiss of Dracula* is really scary.
6 I'm feeling down because I failed my driving test.

2B MAKE A BID!

MAKE A BID! In pairs, discuss the grammar of the sentences. If the sentence is correct, put a tick (✓) in the box. If it's incorrect, put a cross (✗) in the box.

1a He lives with his parents. ☐
1b He's living with his parents. ☐

2a I'm really liking this music ☐
2b I really like this music. ☐

3a Next weekend I go to the cinema. ☐
3b Next weekend I'm going to the cinema. ☐

4a You are seeming really fed up. ☐
4b You seem really fed up. ☐

5a I'm never wearing jeans. ☐
5b I never wear jeans ☐

MAKE A BID! In pairs, discuss the grammar of the sentences. If the sentence is correct, put a tick (✓) in the box. If it's incorrect, put a cross (✗) in the box.

1a He lives with his parents. ☐
1b He's living with his parents. ☐

2a I'm really liking this music ☐
2b I really like this music. ☐

3a Next weekend I go to the cinema. ☐
3b Next weekend I'm going to the cinema. ☐

4a You are seeming really fed up. ☐
4b You seem really fed up. ☐

5a I'm never wearing jeans. ☐
5b I never wear jeans. ☐

MAKE A BID! In pairs, discuss the grammar of the sentences. If the sentence is correct, put a tick (✓) in the box. If it's incorrect, put a cross (✗) in the box.

1a He lives with his parents. ☐
1b He's living with his parents. ☐

2a I'm really liking this music ☐
2b I really like this music. ☐

3a Next weekend I go to the cinema. ☐
3b Next weekend I'm going to the cinema. ☐

4a You are seeming really fed up. ☐
4b You seem really fed up. ☐

5a I'm never wearing jeans. ☐
5b I never wear jeans. ☐

MAKE A BID! In pairs, discuss the grammar of the sentences. If the sentence is correct, put a tick (✓) in the box. If it's incorrect, put a cross (✗) in the box.

1a He lives with his parents. ☐
1b He's living with his parents. ☐

2a I'm really liking this music ☐
2b I really like this music. ☐

3a Next weekend I go to the cinema. ☐
3b Next weekend I'm going to the cinema. ☐

4a You are seeming really fed up. ☐
4b You seem really fed up. ☐

5a I'm never wearing jeans. ☐
5b I never wear jeans. ☐

3A Guess the word

1 pour down	2 gallery	3 ripped off	4 crowded
5 ruins	6 bank holiday	7 boiling hot	8 market
9 stuck	10 threw up	11 cloudy	12 mosque
13 humid	14 lake	15 freezing cold	16 arguing
17 windy	18 theme park	19 square	20 palace

1 pour down	2 gallery	3 ripped off	4 crowded
5 ruins	6 bank holiday	7 boiling hot	8 market
9 stuck	10 threw up	11 cloudy	12 mosque
13 humid	14 lake	15 freezing cold	16 arguing
17 windy	18 theme park	19 square	20 palace

3B Snakes and ladders – the future

20 FINISH!	**19** The school's got a new swimming pool last year.	**18** She's moving to Mexico next year.	**17** I might go out for a bite later.	**16**
11 We're thinking of painting the bedroom red.	**12**	**13** Are you seeing Rachel and the kids this weekend?	**14**	**15** Are you got to work on Saturday?
10	**9** It probably rains later.	**8**	**7** Flying is expensive so we'll probably drive.	**6** I've got to see the doctor yesterday.
1 START	**2** I'm think of going to Japan next summer.	**3**	**4** They're not going on holiday this year	**5**

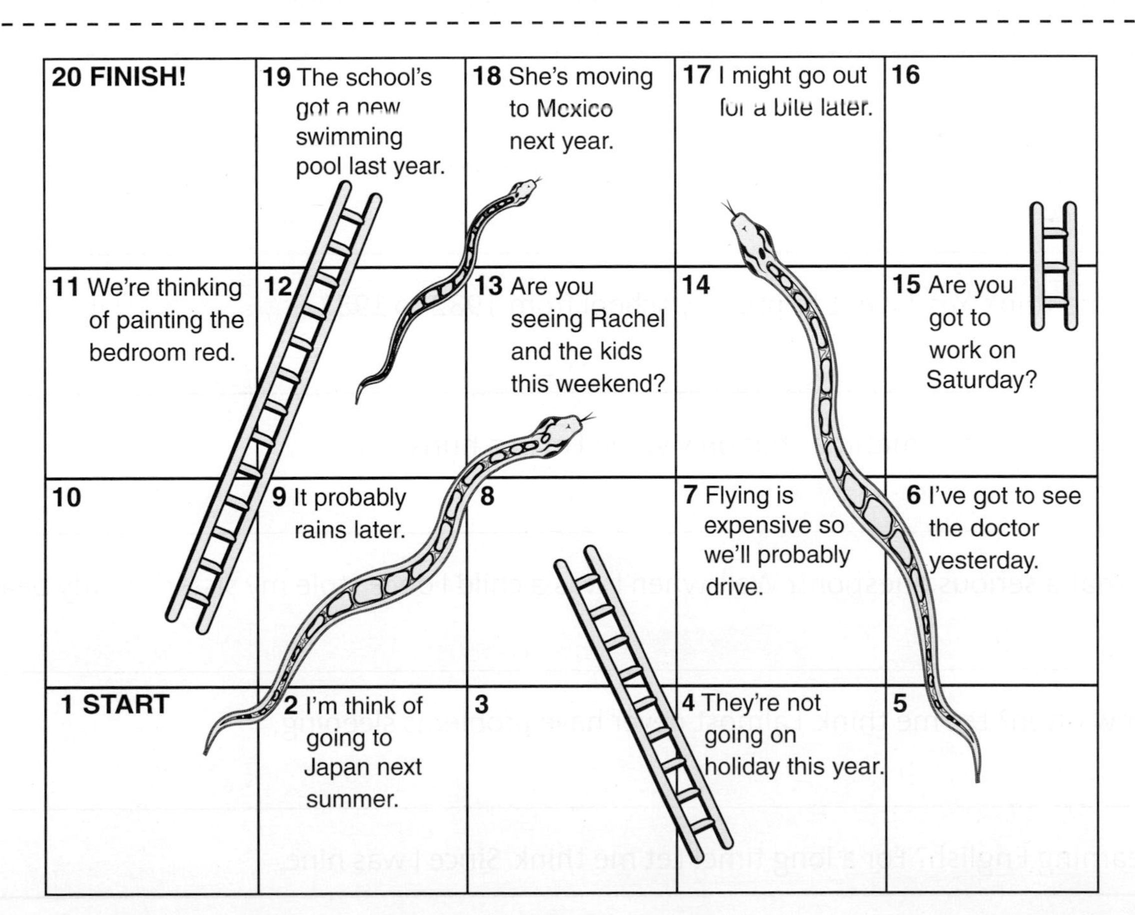

4A Frequency and duration

1 ____?

In my present home? I've been living there for three years.

2 ____?

Let me think. Yes, I went to primary school from 1982 to 1987.

3 ____?

Breakfast? Yes, sometimes but only when I'm in a hurry.

4 ____?

Is that a serious question!? Well, when I was a child I once stole my sister's teddy bear!

5 ____?

How often? Let me think. I almost never have problems sleeping.

6 ____?

Learning English? For a long time! Let me think. Since I was nine.

1 ____?

In my present home? I've been living there for three years.

2 ____?

Let me think. Yes, I went to primary school from 1982 to 1987.

3 ____?

Breakfast? Yes, sometimes but only when I'm in a hurry.

4 ____?

Is that a serious question!? Well, when I was a child I once stole my sister's teddy bear!

5 ____?

How often? Let me think. I almost never have problems sleeping.

6 ____?

Learning English? For a long time! Let me think. Since I was nine.

4B Vocabulary mix and match

go ....

play

go for

go to

listen to

the supermarket
a football match
a walk home CDs tennis
swimming the radio shopping
a meal a restaurant jazz clubbing
heavy metal a concert a coffee
the guitar pop music
a bike ride

---

go ....

play

go for

go to

listen to

the supermarket
a football match
a walk home CDs tennis
swimming the radio shopping
a meal a restaurant jazz clubbing
heavy metal a concert a coffee
the guitar pop music
a bike ride

---

go ....

play

go for

go to

listen to

the supermarket
a football match
a walk home CDs tennis
swimming the radio shopping
a meal a restaurant jazz clubbing
heavy metal a concert a coffee
the guitar pop music
a bike ride

5A What's my job?

Set A

civil servant	engineer	surgeon	estate agent
HR manager	sales rep	student	computer programmer

Set B

electrician	labourer	graphic designer	security guard
plumber	lawyer	accountant	teacher

Set A

civil servant	engineer	surgeon	estate agent
HR manager	sales rep	student	computer programmer

Set B

electrician	labourer	graphic designer	security guard
plumber	lawyer	accountant	teacher

Set A

civil servant	engineer	surgeon	estate agent
HR manager	sales rep	student	computer programmer

Set B

electrician	labourer	graphic designer	security guard
plumber	lawyer	accountant	teacher

Set A

civil servant	engineer	surgeon	estate agent
HR manager	sales rep	student	computer programmer

Set B

electrician	labourer	graphic designer	security guard
plumber	lawyer	accountant	teacher

5B Rules matching

Set A	Set B
1 You should really wear a suit.	a You must arrive on time.
2 You shouldn't smoke here.	b It's necessary to speak English.
3 You have to arrive on time.	c You must drive on the left.
4 You have to wear a uniform.	d It's all right to smoke here.
5 You don't have to wear a uniform.	e You're not supposed to smoke here.
6 You have to speak English.	f It isn't necessary to wear a uniform.
7 You have to drive on the left.	g You're really supposed to wear a suit.
8 You're allowed to smoke here.	h It's necessary to wear a uniform.

Set A	Set B
1 You should really wear a suit.	a You must arrive on time.
2 You shouldn't smoke here.	b It's necessary to speak English.
3 You have to arrive on time.	c You must drive on the left.
4 You have to wear a uniform.	d It's all right to smoke here.
5 You don't have to wear a uniform.	e You're not supposed to smoke here.
6 You have to speak English.	f It isn't necessary to wear a uniform.
7 You have to drive on the left.	g You're really supposed to wear a suit.
8 You're allowed to smoke here.	h It's necessary to wear a uniform.

6A Spot the difference

6B Must

7A Wordsearch

s	t	u	t	o	r	s	u	n	e	e	e
y	t	h	g	i	r	b	g	r	e	t	e
o	e	u	i	r	e	v	e	n	i	n	g
d	s	r	d	d	s	v	i	o	p	y	a
s	t	h	p	e	e	l	d	s	t	p	f
r	s	e	m	i	n	a	r	e	y	a	e
s	c	a	h	o	o	t	d	d	i	t	r
u	x	c	p	l	e	u	u	l	e	i	u
e	a	t	k	t	c	t	o	n	i	e	t
g	o	r	y	a	s	s	e	t	n	n	c
p	o	s	t	g	r	a	d	u	a	t	e
w	o	e	l	u	d	o	m	e	a	a	l

achieve	bright	deadline
educate	essay	evening
exam	fail	lecture
module	online	pass
patient	postgraduate	seminar
student	study	test
top	tutor	workload

s	t	u	t	o	r	s	u	n	e	e	e
y	t	h	g	i	r	b	g	r	e	t	e
o	e	u	i	r	e	v	e	n	i	n	g
d	s	r	d	d	s	v	i	o	p	y	a
s	t	h	p	e	e	l	d	s	t	p	f
r	s	e	m	i	n	a	r	e	y	a	e
s	c	a	h	o	o	t	d	d	i	t	r
u	x	c	p	l	e	u	u	l	e	i	u
e	a	t	k	t	c	t	o	n	i	e	t
g	o	r	y	a	s	s	e	t	n	n	c
p	o	s	t	g	r	a	d	u	a	t	e
w	o	e	l	u	d	o	m	e	a	a	l

achieve	bright	deadline
educate	essay	evening
exam	fail	lecture
module	online	pass
patient	postgraduate	seminar
student	study	test
top	tutor	workload

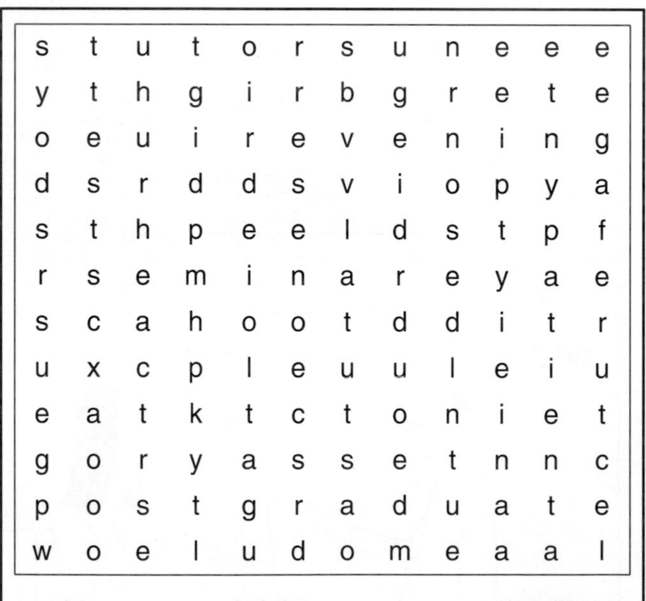

s	t	u	t	o	r	s	u	n	e	e	e
y	t	h	g	i	r	b	g	r	e	t	e
o	e	u	i	r	e	v	e	n	i	n	g
d	s	r	d	d	s	v	i	o	p	y	a
s	t	h	p	e	e	l	d	s	t	p	f
r	s	e	m	i	n	a	r	e	y	a	e
s	c	a	h	o	o	t	d	d	i	t	r
u	x	c	p	l	e	u	u	l	e	i	u
e	a	t	k	t	c	t	o	n	i	e	t
g	o	r	y	a	s	s	e	t	n	n	c
p	o	s	t	g	r	a	d	u	a	t	e
w	o	e	l	u	d	o	m	e	a	a	l

achieve	bright	deadline
educate	essay	evening
exam	fail	lecture
module	online	pass
patient	postgraduate	seminar
student	study	test
top	tutor	workload

s	t	u	t	o	r	s	u	n	e	e	e
y	t	h	g	i	r	b	g	r	e	t	e
o	e	u	i	r	e	v	e	n	i	n	g
d	s	r	d	d	s	v	i	o	p	y	a
s	t	h	p	e	e	l	d	s	t	p	f
r	s	e	m	i	n	a	r	e	y	a	e
s	c	a	h	o	o	t	d	d	i	t	r
u	x	c	p	l	e	u	u	l	e	i	u
e	a	t	k	t	c	t	o	n	i	e	t
g	o	r	y	a	s	s	e	t	n	n	c
p	o	s	t	g	r	a	d	u	a	t	e
w	o	e	l	u	d	o	m	e	a	a	l

achieve	bright	deadline
educate	essay	evening
exam	fail	lecture
module	online	pass
patient	postgraduate	seminar
student	study	test
top	tutor	workload

7B Conditionals matching

Set A

1 *If I study harder*, I'll get my degree.
2 *Unless I revise*, I won't pass the exam.
3 *If a teacher is patient*, her students learn better.
4 *If you don't understand something*, just ask.
5 *If you only speak English in class*, you learn faster.
6 *You can't apply for the job* unless you speak English.
7 *You can go to evening class* if you can't attend during the day.
8 *Don't put your hand up* unless you know the answer.

a .... I might be able to study medicine.
b .... I won't get a mark.
c .... unless I find one at university.
d .... you have a better chance of getting a job.
e .... they can't go to the next class.
f .... you'll get punished!
g .... you need to copy the notes from a classmate.
h .... if you are going to miss a tutorial.

Set A

1 *If I study harder*, I'll get my degree.
2 *Unless I revise*, I won't pass the exam.
3 *If a teacher is patient*, her students learn better.
4 *If you don't understand something*, just ask.
5 *If you only speak English in class*, you learn faster.
6 *You can't apply for the job* unless you speak English.
7 *You can go to evening class* if you can't attend during the day.
8 *Don't put your hand up* unless you know the answer.

a .... I might be able to study medicine.
b .... I won't get a mark.
c .... unless I find one at university.
d .... you have a better chance of getting a job.
e .... they can't go to the next class.
f .... you'll get punished!
g .... you need to copy the notes from a classmate.
h .... if you are going to miss a tutorial.

Set B

1 *I'll do the online course* unless I find one at university.
2 *Unless they pass the final exams*, they can't go on to the next class.
3 *If you miss lectures* you need to copy the notes from a classmate.
4 *If I improve in physics*, I might be able to study medicine.
5 *Once you have a degree* you have a better chance of getting a job.
6 *If you copy*, you'll get punished!
7 *You need to tell your tutor* if you are going to miss a tutorial.
8 *If I miss the deadline*, I won't get a mark.

a .... just ask.
b .... I won't pass the exam.
c .... her students learn better,
d .... if you can't attend during the day.
e .... unless you speak English.
f .... unless you know the answer.
g .... you learn faster.
h .... I'll get my degree.

Set B

1 *I'll do the online course* unless I find one at university.
2 *Unless they pass the final exams*, they can't go on to the next class.
3 *If you miss lectures* you need to copy the notes from a classmate.
4 *If I improve in physics*, I might be able to study medicine.
5 *Once you have a degree* you have a better chance of getting a job.
6 *If you copy*, you'll get punished!
7 *You need to tell your tutor* if you are going to miss a tutorial.
8 *If I miss the deadline*, I won't get a mark.

a .... just ask.
b .... I won't pass the exam.
c .... her students learn better,
d .... if you can't attend during the day.
e .... unless you speak English.
f .... unless you know the answer.
g .... you learn faster.
h .... I'll get my degree.

8A Cooking vocabulary

Ways of cooking	Words to describe foods

ystat	labnd	ilob
stoar	taftningae	sham
pede-ryf	thealyh	rist-yrf
seargy	inglilf	clise
lirgl	picsy	

Ways of cooking	Words to describe foods

ystat	labnd	ilob
stoar	taftningae	sham
pede-ryf	thealyh	rist-yrf
seargy	inglilf	clise
lirgl	picsy	

Ways of cooking	Words to describe foods

ystat	labnd	ilob
stoar	taftningae	sham
pede-ryf	thealyh	rist-yrf
seargy	inglilf	clise
lirgl	picsy	

Ways of cooking	Words to describe foods

ystat	labnd	ilob
stoar	taftningae	sham
pede-ryf	thealyh	rist-yrf
seargy	inglilf	clise
lirgl	picsy	

8B What would you do if … ?

If you booked a table in a restaurant and when you arrived you were told it was full, what would you do?

What would you do if you saw another guest putting food in their handbag?

If you found a cockroach swimming in your soup, what would you do?

If you had won the lottery and you were at an expensive restaurant, what would you do?

What would you do if the bill arrived and you realised you didn't have any money?

If you were in a restaurant and all the lights went out, what would you do?

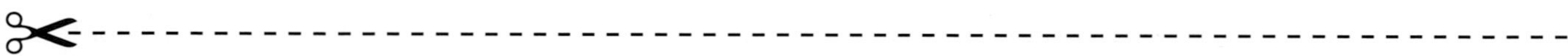

If you booked a table in a restaurant and when you arrived you were told it was full, what would you do?

What would you do if you saw another guest putting food in their handbag?

If you found a cockroach swimming in your soup, what would you do?

If you had won the lottery and you were at an expensive restaurant, what would you do?

What would you do if the bill arrived and you realised you didn't have any money?

If you were in a restaurant and all the lights went out, what would you do?

If you booked a table in a restaurant and when you arrived you were told it was full, what would you do?

What would you do if you saw another guest putting food in their handbag?

If you found a cockroach swimming in your soup, what would you do?

If you had won the lottery and you were at an expensive restaurant, what would you do?

What would you do if the bill arrived and you realised you didn't have any money?

If you were in a restaurant and all the lights went out, what would you do?

9A Guess my word – housing and areas

Set A

courtyard	central heating	loft
bright	run-down	green
lively	cramped	isolated

Set B

open fire	patio	basement
a shared flat	affordable	conveniently located
spacious	garage	posh residential

Set A

courtyard	central heating	loft
bright	run-down	green
lively	cramped	isolated

Set B

open fire	patio	basement
a shared flat	affordable	conveniently located
spacious	garage	posh residential

Set A

courtyard	central heating	loft
bright	run-down	green
lively	cramped	isolated

Set B

open fire	patio	basement
a shared flat	affordable	conveniently located
spacious	garage	posh residential

9B Now and then

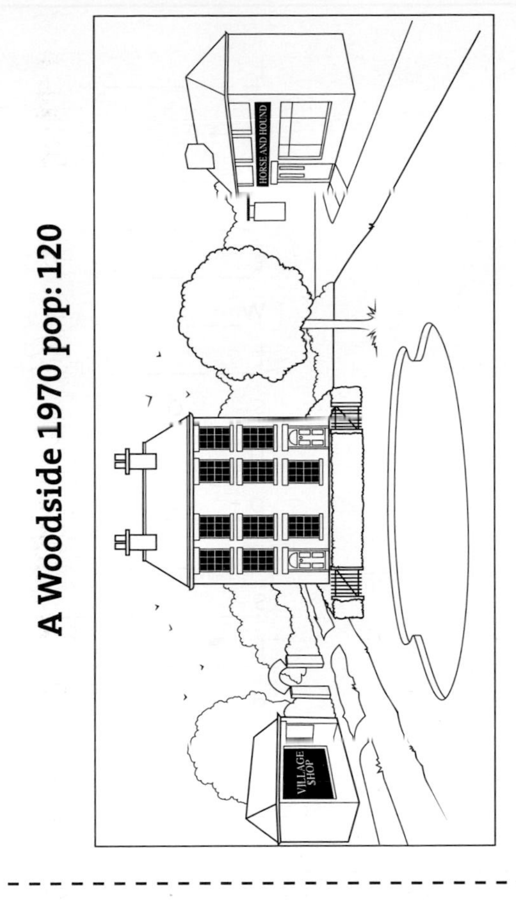

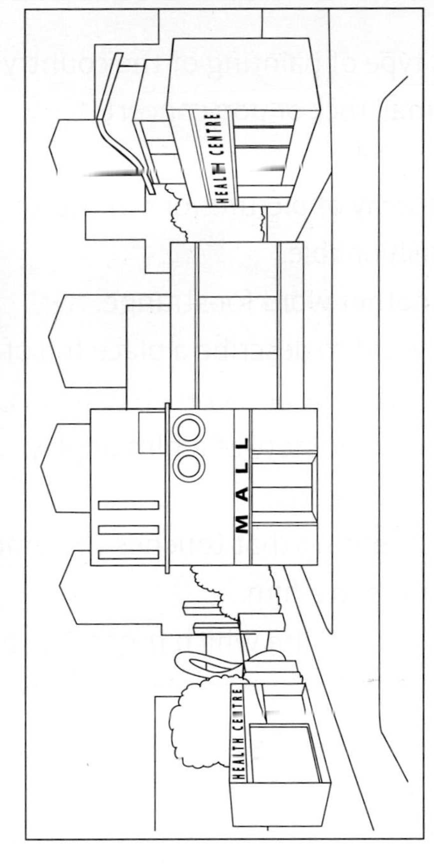

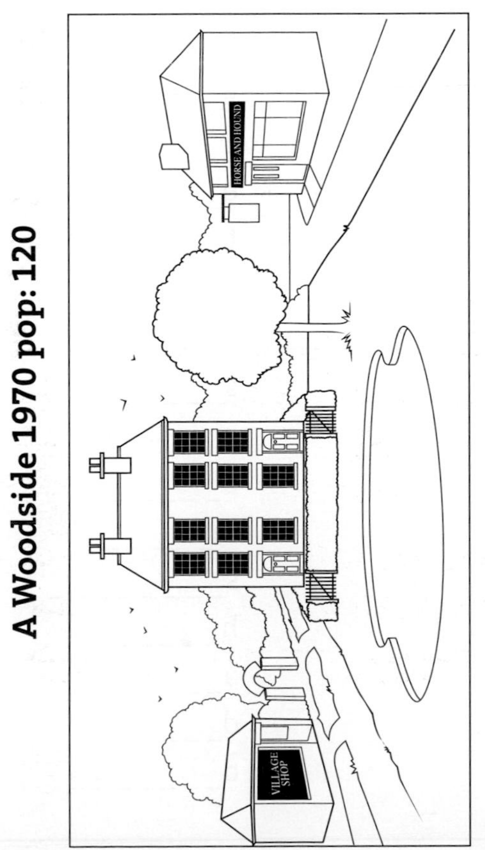

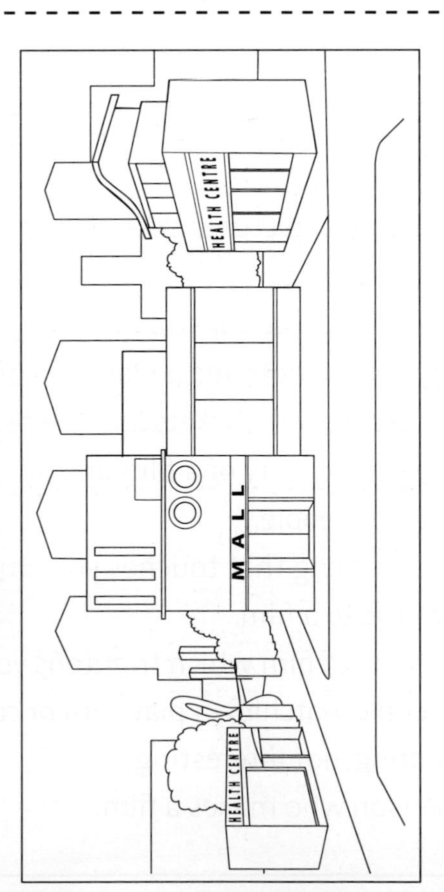

10A Vocabulary race

1 A type of painting of the countryside. l________
2 Small rock or pop concert. g__
3 A sad play. t______
4 Display of pictures or sculptures. e_________
5 Fashionable. t_____
6 Another word for strange. w____
7 A word to describe a place full of visitors. t_______
8 There were no tickets left. It was... s___o__
9 The basic story of a film or play. p___
10 Full of people. p_____
11 Something that touches you emotionally is... m_____
12 Music to a film. s_________
13 A type of film which frightens you. h_____
14 People watching a play, film or concert. a_______
15 Boring, not interesting. d___
16 Person who makes a film. d_______

1 A type of painting of the countryside. l________
2 Small rock or pop concert. g__
3 A sad play. t______
4 Display of pictures or sculptures. e_________
5 Fashionable. t_____
6 Another word for strange. w____
7 A word to describe a place full of visitors. t_______
8 There were no tickets left. It was... s___o__
9 The basic story of a film or play. p___
10 Full of people. p_____
11 Something that touches you emotionally is... m_____
12 Music to a film. s_________
13 A type of film which frightens you. h_____
14 People watching a play, film or concert. a_______
15 Boring, not interesting. d___
16 Person who makes a film. d_______

10B Future in the past

Set A

1 *I was going to invite you* but I forgot.

2 *I'm annoyed with you. You promised* you'd clean the house.

3 *He thought he'd* never leave her.

4 *We were so in love we believed* we'd stay together forever.

a .... would be so disgusting.

b .... would win the match.

c .... you were going to marry me.

d .... they thought they would rule the world.

Set A

1 *I was going to invite you* but I forgot.

2 *I'm annoyed with you. You promised* you'd clean the house.

3 *He thought he'd* never leave her.

4 *We were so in love we believed* we'd stay together forever.

a .... would be so disgusting.

b .... would win the match.

c .... you were going to marry me.

d .... they thought they would rule the world

Set B

1 *They expected they* would win the match.

2 *You said* you were going to marry me.

3 *When they were young* they thought they would rule the world.

4 *I never knew it* would be so disgusting.

a .... but I forgot.

b .... never leave her.

c .... we'd stay together forever.

d .... you'd clean the house.

Set B

1 *They expected they* would win the match.

2 *You said* you were going to marry me.

3 *When they were young* they thought they would rule the world.

4 *I never knew it* would be so disgusting.

a .... but I forgot.

b .... never leave her.

c .... we'd stay together forever.

d .... you'd clean the house.

Set A

1 *I was going to invite you* but I forgot.

2 *I'm annoyed with you. You promised* you'd clean the house.

3 *He thought he'd* never leave her.

4 *We were so in love we believed* we'd stay together forever.

a .... would be so disgusting.

b .... would win the match.

c .... you were going to marry me.

d .... they thought they would rule the world.

Set A

1 *I was going to invite you* but I forgot.

2 *I'm annoyed with you. You promised* you'd clean the house.

3 *He thought he'd* never leave her.

4 *We were so in love we believed* we'd stay together forever.

a .... would be so disgusting.

b .... would win the match.

c .... you were going to marry me.

d .... they thought they would rule the world.

Set B

1 *They expected they* would win the match.

2 *You said* you were going to marry me.

3 *When they were young* they thought they would rule the world.

4 *I never knew it* would be so disgusting.

a .... but I forgot.

b .... never leave her.

c .... we'd stay together forever.

d .... you'd clean the house.

Set B

1 *They expected they* would win the match.

2 *You said* you were going to marry me.

3 *When they were young* they thought they would rule the world.

4 *I never knew it* would be so disgusting.

a .... but I forgot.

b .... never leave her.

c .... we'd stay together forever.

d .... you'd clean the house.

11A Passives

1 The drugs were smuggling into the country.

2 The horses were badly treated by their owner.

3 The man was arrest as he tried to leave the country.

4 The prisoner is been released tomorrow.

5 These pills should not be taking by children.

6 I've been offered a new job.

7 They've never be involved in anything like that.

8 Her handbag was stolen.

1 The drugs were smuggling into the country.

2 The horses were badly treated by their owner.

3 The man was arrest as he tried to leave the country.

4 The prisoner is been released tomorrow.

5 These pills should not be taking by children.

6 I've been offered a new job.

7 They've never be involved in anything like that.

8 Her handbag was stolen.

1 The drugs were smuggling into the country.

2 The horses were badly treated by their owner.

3 The man was arrest as he tried to leave the country.

4 The prisoner is been released tomorrow.

5 These pills should not be taking by children.

6 I've been offered a new job.

7 They've never be involved in anything like that.

8 Her handbag was stolen.

1 The drugs were smuggling into the country.

2 The horses were badly treated by their owner.

3 The man was arrest as he tried to leave the country.

4 The prisoner is been released tomorrow.

5 These pills should not be taking by children.

6 I've been offered a new job.

7 They've never be involved in anything like that.

8 Her handbag was stolen.

11B What animal am I?

ape	kitten
bear	lizard
cockroach	parrot
crocodile	puppy
crow	rhino
dolphin	snake
eagle	squirrel
fox	tiger
gorilla	whale
horse	wolf

ape	kitten
bear	lizard
cockroach	parrot
crocodile	puppy
crow	rhino
dolphin	snake
eagle	squirrel
fox	tiger
gorilla	whale
horse	wolf

12A When I was a kid

1 you were a child? / be your favourite game / What / in the / used to / playground when

2 Did / stay up / your parents / late sometimes? / use to let you / What was the latest you ever stayed up?

3 would you / eat when you /were a kid? / food / refuse to / What

4 with your / always use / What did you / brothers and sisters? / to fight about/

5 when you were little? / What / you always go to bed with / cuddly toy would

6 your favourite teacher / to be / when you were 12? / Who used

1 you were a child? / be your favourite game / What / in the / used to / playground when

2 Did / stay up / your parents / late sometimes? / use to let you / What was the latest you ever stayed up?

3 would you / eat when you /were a kid? / food / refuse to / What

4 with your / always use / What did you / brothers and sisters? / to fight about/

5 when you were little? / What / you always go to bed with / cuddly toy would

6 your favourite teacher / to be / when you were 12? / Who used

1 you were a child? / be your favourite game / What / in the / used to / playground when

2 Did / stay up / your parents / late sometimes? / use to let you / What was the latest you ever stayed up?

3 would you / eat when you /were a kid? / food / refuse to / What

4 with your / always use / What did you / brothers and sisters? / to fight about/

5 when you were little? / What / you always go to bed with / cuddly toy would

6 your favourite teacher / to be / when you were 12? / Who used

12B I WISH...

Write a subject you wish you hadn't studied at school.

Write a place you wish you'd been to.

Write a skill you wish you'd learnt.

Write something you wish you hadn't eaten.

Write something you wish you'd invented.

Write a subject you wish you hadn't studied at school.

Write a place you wish you'd been to.

Write a skill you wish you'd learnt.

Write something you wish you hadn't eaten.

Write something you wish you'd invented.

Write a subject you wish you hadn't studied at school.

Write a place you wish you'd been to.

Write a skill you wish you'd learnt.

Write something you wish you hadn't eaten.

Write something you wish you'd invented.

Write a subject you wish you hadn't studied at school.

Write a place you wish you'd been to.

Write a skill you wish you'd learnt.

Write something you wish you hadn't eaten.

Write something you wish you'd invented.

13A Guess my word – travel, travel problems and strong adjectives

Set A

1 business trip	2 travel light
3 harbour	4 security
5 check-in desk	6 emigrate
7 visa	8 boiling
9 soaked	10 delicious

Set B

1 take-off	2 carriage
3 shopping trip	4 journey
5 day trip	6 traffic lights
7 ferry	8 refugee
9 freezing	10 starving

Set A

1 business trip	2 travel light
3 harbour	4 security
5 check-in desk	6 emigrate
7 visa	8 boiling
9 soaked	10 delicious

Set B

1 take-off	2 carriage
3 shopping trip	4 journey
5 day trip	6 traffic lights
7 ferry	8 refugee
9 freezing	10 starving

Set A

1 business trip	2 travel light
3 harbour	4 security
5 check-in desk	6 emigrate
7 visa	8 boiling
9 soaked	10 delicious

Set B

1 take-off	2 carriage
3 shopping trip	4 journey
5 day trip	6 traffic lights
7 ferry	8 refugee
9 freezing	10 starving

Set A

1 business trip	2 travel light
3 harbour	4 security
5 check-in desk	6 emigrate
7 visa	8 boiling
9 soaked	10 delicious

Set B

1 take-off	2 carriage
3 shopping trip	4 journey
5 day trip	6 traffic lights
7 ferry	8 refugee
9 freezing	10 starving

13B Snakes and ladders – should've / third conditional

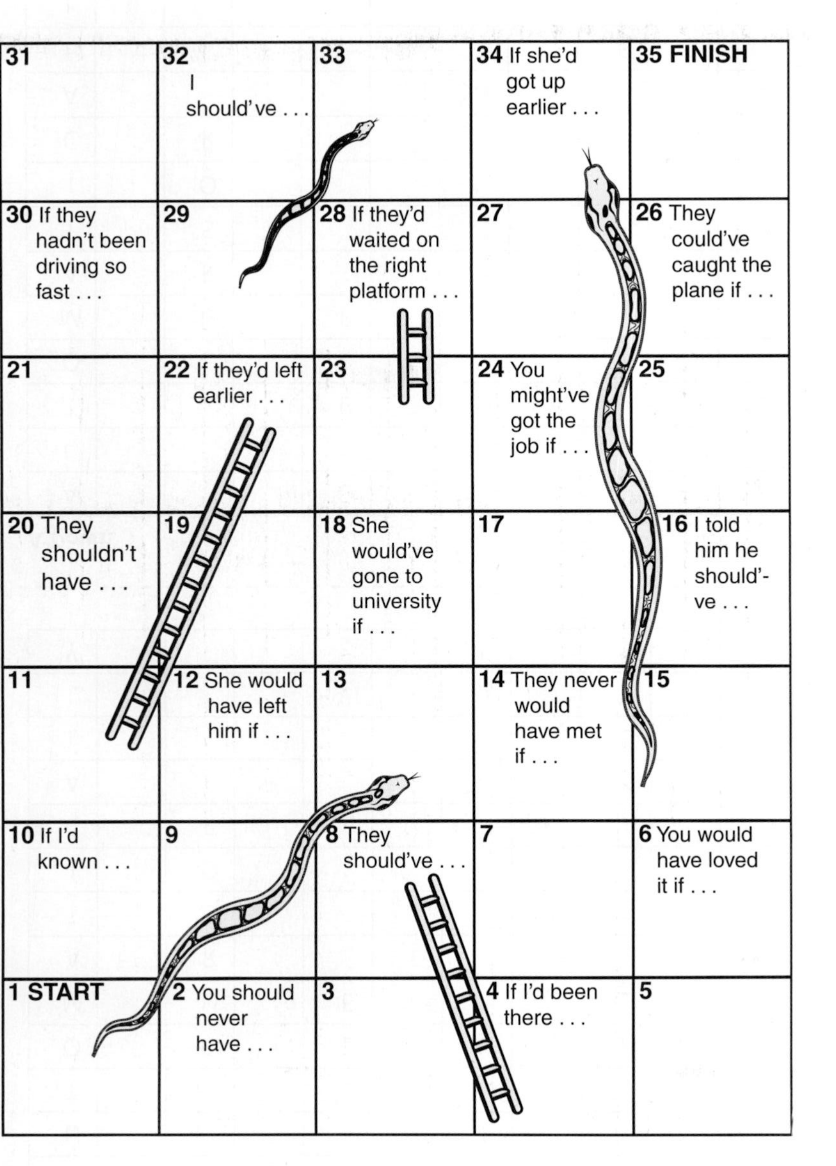

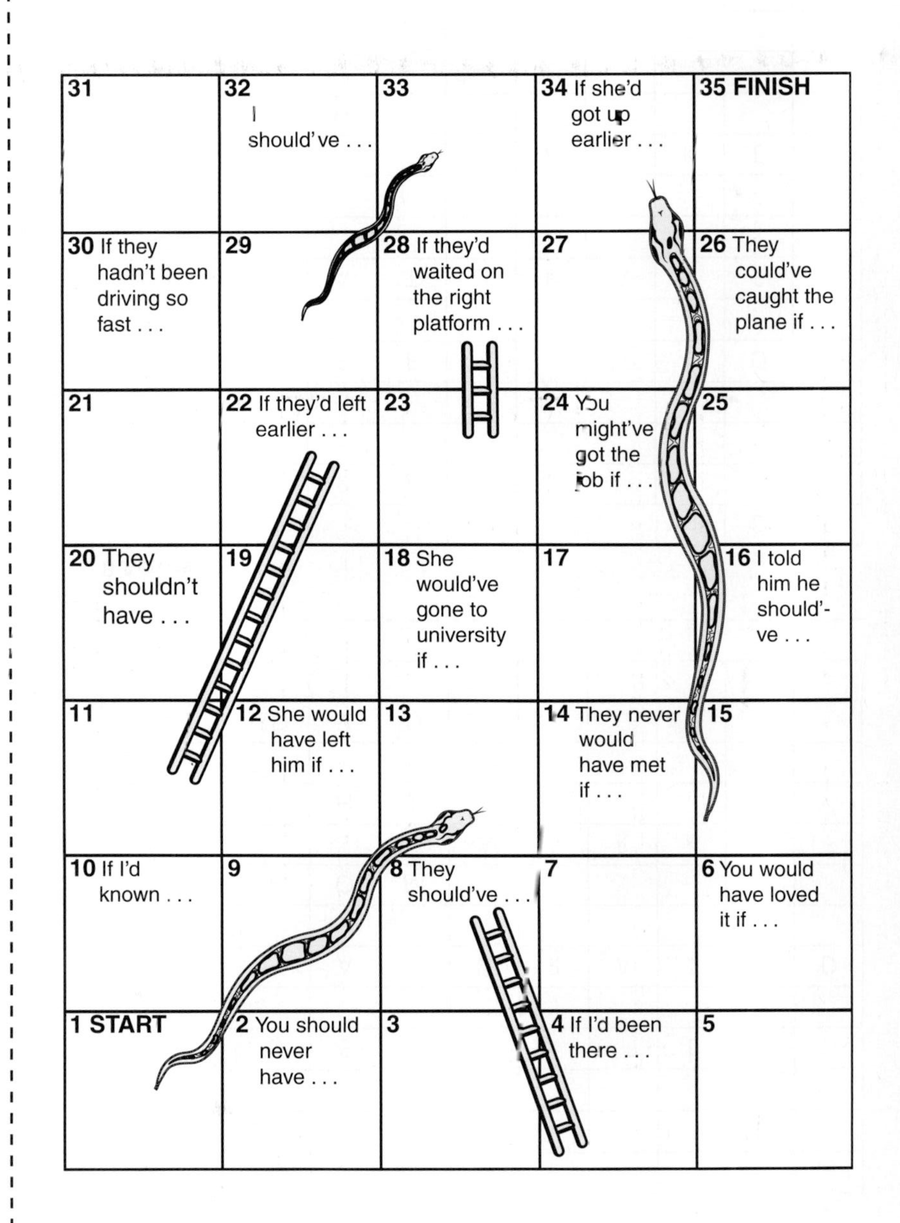

14A Crossword

A Down

[1]A				[2]C		[3]M				[4]F
U				A		E				A
T				B		N		[5]U		Q
O		[6]C		L		U		R		
M		U		E				L		[7]G
A		R								A
T		S								D
I		O								G
C		R								E
A						[8]A		[9]K		T
L						S		E		
L						A		Y		[10]I
Y						P		S		T

B Across

								[a]P	D	F
[b]U	P	G	R	A	D	E				
[c]M	O	U	S	E			[d]P	L	U	G
		[e]S	A	T	U	R	A	T	E	D
[f]C	D	R	O	M						
					[g]M	A	R	K	E	T
[h]L	I	G	H	T						
		[i]D	V	D			[j]P	C	S	

A Down

[1]A				[2]C		[3]M				[4]F
U				A		E				A
T				B		N		[5]U		Q
O		[6]C		L		U		R		
M		U		E				L		[7]G
A		R								A
T		S								D
I		O								G
C		R								E
A						[8]A		[9]K		T
L						S		E		
L						A		Y		[10]I
Y						P		S		T

B Across

								[a]P	D	F
[b]U	P	G	R	A	D	E				
[c]M	O	U	S	E			[d]P	L	U	G
		[e]S	A	T	U	R	A	T	E	D
[f]C	D	R	O	M						
					[g]M	A	R	K	E	T
[h]L	I	G	H	T						
		[i]D	V	D			[j]P	C	S	

14B Grammar *-ing* forms and *to-* infinitives

1 Do you want to improve your English __________ or __________ ?

2 Do you think __________ is good for people?

3 Would you ever consider __________ ?

4 Can you afford __________?

5 Do you spend any of your free time __________ ?

6 Do you think you could ever get used to __________ ?

7 Are you hoping __________?

8 Would you like to work in a job where you have __________ English?

1 Do you want to improve your English __________ or __________ ?

2 Do you think __________ is good for people?

3 Would you ever consider __________ ?

4 Can you afford __________?

5 Do you spend any of your free time __________ ?

6 Do you think you could ever get used to __________ ?

7 Are you hoping __________?

8 Would you like to work in a job where you have __________ English?

1 Do you want to improve your English __________ or __________ ?

2 Do you think __________ is good for people?

3 Would you ever consider __________ ?

4 Can you afford __________?

5 Do you spend any of your free time __________ ?

6 Do you think you could ever get used to __________ ?

7 Are you hoping __________?

8 Would you like to work in a job where you have __________ English?

1 Do you want to improve your English __________ or __________ ?

2 Do you think __________ is good for people?

3 Would you ever consider __________ ?

4 Can you afford __________?

5 Do you spend any of your free time __________ ?

6 Do you think you could ever get used to __________ ?

7 Are you hoping __________?

8 Would you like to work in a job where you have __________ English?

15A Doctors and patients

Set A

I can't stop coughing.

I feel a bit faint.

I've got an upset stomach.

I've got a strange rash on my arm.

I've got a migraine.

Set A

I can't stop coughing.

I feel a bit faint.

I've got an upset stomach.

I've got a strange rash on my arm.

I've got a migraine.

Set B

I think I've got high blood pressure.

My hands are really itchy.

My ankle is swollen.

I've got a temperature.

I've hurt my knee.

Set B

I think I've got high blood pressure.

My hands are really itchy.

My ankle is swollen.

I've got a temperature.

I've hurt my knee.

Set A

I can't stop coughing.

I feel a bit faint.

I've got an upset stomach.

I've got a strange rash on my arm.

I've got a migraine.

Set A

I can't stop coughing.

I feel a bit faint.

I've got an upset stomach.

I've got a strange rash on my arm.

I've got a migraine.

Set B

I think I've got high blood pressure.

My hands are really itchy.

My ankle is swollen.

I've got a temperature.

I've hurt my knee.

Set B

I think I've got high blood pressure.

My hands are really itchy.

My ankle is swollen.

I've got a temperature.

I've hurt my knee.

15B Reported speech – matching dictation

Set A

1a I will never leave you.

1b ____________________

2a Would you like me to carry that for you?

2b ____________________

3a ____________________

3b He insisted on paying the bill.

4a ____________________

4b He told me he really loved me.

Please don't shout!

She told me to phone him.

She said I was an idiot.

Oh, please come with me!

Set B

1a Don't forget to call him.

1b ____________________

2a You are an idiot.

2b ____________________

3a ____________________

3b She asked me not to shout.

4a ____________________

4b He persuaded me to go with him.

I am definitely paying the bill.

I really love you.

He promised not to leave her.

He offered to carry my bag.

Set A

1a I will never leave you.

1b ____________________

2a Would you like me to carry that for you?

2b ____________________

3a ____________________

3b He insisted on paying the bill.

4a ____________________

4b He told me he really loved me.

Please don't shout!

She told me to phone him.

She said I was an idiot.

Oh, please come with me!

Set B

1a Don't forget to call him.

1b ____________________

2a You are an idiot.

2b ____________________

3a ____________________

3b She asked me not to shout.

4a ____________________

4b He persuaded me to go with him.

I am definitely paying the bill.

I really love you.

He promised not to leave her.

He offered to carry my bag.

Set A

1a I will never leave you.

1b ____________________

2a Would you like me to carry that for you?

2b ____________________

3a ____________________

3b He insisted on paying the bill.

4a ____________________

4b He told me he really loved me.

Please don't shout!

She told me to phone him.

She said I was an idiot.

Oh, please come with me!

Set B

1a Don't forget to call him.

1b ____________________

2a You are an idiot.

2b ____________________

3a ____________________

3b She asked me not to shout.

4a ____________________

4b He persuaded me to go with him.

I am definitely paying the bill.

I really love you.

He promised not to leave her.

He offered to carry my bag.

Set A

1	Someone who fights or campaigns for political change	Activist
2	Person who runs, jumps or similar professionally	Athlete
3	Section of newspaper about the economy	Business pages
4	Agreement to stop fighting	Ceasefire
5	Person who has complete control over a country	Dictator
6	Person in charge of a newspaper	Editor
7	Value of one currency against another	Exchange rate
8	Someone who establishes a new organisation	Founder
9	Information about celebrities, their personal life, etc.	Gossip pages
10	Predictions based on star signs	Horoscope
11	Section of newspaper about other countries	I____________ p____
12	Where readers express their views	L______ p____
13	Person who is very good with figures	M____________
14	Section of newspaper about your country	N_______ n___
15	First showing of film	P_______
16	Criticisms of films, books, plays, restaurants, etc.	R_____
17	Someone who works in the field of physics or chemistry	S________
18	Present or final result in a sports game	S____
19	Section of newspaper about sport	S_____ p____
20	Someone who suffers from an accident or crime	V_____

Set B

1	Someone who fights or campaigns for political change	A_______
2	Person who runs, jumps or similar professionally	A______
3	Section of newspaper about the economy	B_______ p____
4	Agreement to stop fighting	C________
5	Person who has complete control over a country	D_______
6	Person in charge of a newspaper	E_____
7	Value of one currency against another	E_______ r___
8	Someone who establishes a new organisation	F______
9	Information about celebrities, their personal life etc.	G_____
10	Predictions based on star signs	H________
11	Section of newspaper about other countries	International pages
12	Where readers express their views	Letters pages
13	Person who is very good with figures	Mathematician
14	Section of newspaper about your country	National News
15	First showing of film	Premiere
16	Criticisms of films, books, plays, restaurants, etc.	Review
17	Someone who works in the field of physics or chemistry	Scientist
18	Present or final result in sports game	Score
19	Section of newspaper about sports	Sports pages
20	Someone who suffers from an accident or crime	Victim

Set A

1	Someone who fights or campaigns for political change	Activist
2	Person who runs, jumps or similar professionally	Athlete
3	Section of newspaper about the economy	Business pages
4	Agreement to stop fighting	Ceasefire
5	Person who has complete control over a country	Dictator
6	Person in charge of a newspaper	Editor
7	Value of one currency against another	Exchange rate
8	Someone who establishes a new organisation	Founder
9	Information about celebrities, their personal life, etc.	Gossip pages
10	Predictions based on star signs	Horoscope
11	Section of newspaper about other countries	I____________ p____
12	Where readers express their views	L______ p____
13	Person who is very good with figures	M____________
14	Section of newspaper about your country	N_______ n___
15	First showing of film	P_______
16	Criticisms of films, books, plays, restaurants, etc.	R_____
17	Someone who works in the field of physics or chemistry	S________
18	Present or final result in a sports game	S____
19	Section of newspaper about sport	S_____ p____
20	Someone who suffers from an accident or crime	V_____

Set B

1	Someone who fights or campaigns for political change	A_______
2	Person who runs, jumps or similar professionally	A______
3	Section of newspaper about the economy	B_______ p____
4	Agreement to stop fighting	C________
5	Person who has complete control over a country	D_______
6	Person in charge of a newspaper	E_____
7	Value of one currency against another	E_______ r___
8	Someone who establishes a new organisation	F______
9	Information about celebrities, their personal life etc.	G_____
10	Predictions based on star signs	H________
11	Section of newspaper about other countries	International pages
12	Where readers express their views	Letters pages
13	Person who is very good with figures	Mathematician
14	Section of newspaper about your country	National News
15	First showing of film	Premiere
16	Criticisms of films, books, plays, restaurants, etc.	Review
17	Someone who works in the field of physics or chemistry	Scientist
18	Present or final result in sports game	Score
19	Section of newspaper about sports	Sports pages
20	Someone who suffers from an accident or crime	Victim

16B Grammar – defining game

Set A

1 online course
2 hip hop
3 estate agent
4 day trip
5 sculptor
6 ferry
7 spoilt child
8 parrot

Set A

1 online course
2 hip hop
3 estate agent
4 day trip
5 sculptor
6 ferry
7 spoilt child
8 parrot

Set A

1 online course
2 hip hop
3 estate agent
4 day trip
5 sculptor
6 ferry
7 spoilt child
8 parrot

Set A

1 online course
2 hip hop
3 estate agent
4 day trip
5 sculptor
6 ferry
7 spoilt child
8 parrot

Set B

1 plumber
2 HR manager
3 platform
4 bracelet
5 audience
6 postgraduate
7 central heating
8 easy-going person

Set B

1 plumber
2 HR manager
3 platform
4 bracelet
5 audience
6 postgraduate
7 central heating
8 easy-going person

Set B

1 plumber
2 HR manager
3 platform
4 bracelet
5 audience
6 postgraduate
7 central heating
8 easy-going person

GRAMMAR REFERENCE

01 MY FIRST CLASS

Question formation

Exercise 1

1 Where
2 Why
3 What
4 Who
5 Whose
6 How often
7 What time
8 How much
9 How long

Exercise 2

1 i	4 f	7 b
2 d	5 e	8 c
3 a	6 h	9 g

Exercise 3

1 What kind of films **do** you like?
2 How's your part-time job **going** at the moment?
3 **Have** you **played** before?
4 **Are** you **working** on any projects at the moment?
5 **Have** you decided where you're going on holiday?
6 How long **has he been** learning Chinese, then?
7 How did you **first meet your wife**?

Narrative tenses

Exercise 1

1b 4e 5/ 6a 8f 10d 12c

Exercise 2

1 happened
2 went
3 had never
4 were watching
5 tried
6 grabbed
7 was walking
8 saw
9 stared
10 I was going
11 walked
12 had left
13 fell over
14 hit
15 stopped
26 started

02 EMOTIONS

be, *look*, *seem*, etc.

Exercise 1

1 correct
2 looked as if he'd seen
3 She sounded quite upset
4 I felt terrible
5 correct
6 It tastes disgusting
7 correct
8 makes me look fat?

-ed / *-ing* adjectives

Exercise 1

1a confused	1b confusing
2a annoying	2b annoyed
3a depressing	3b depressed
4a scary	4b scared
5a worried	5b worrying
6a surprised	6b surprising
7a frustrated	7b frustrating
8a boring	8b bored

The present continuous / present simple and present continuous

Exercise 1

1 I usually just work, I'm doing, I'm working
2 I normally work, I'm working, are doing up
3 I answer, make, we're holding, I'm sorting out

Exercise 2

1 I'm having dinner
2 correct
3 correct
4 He still owes
5 I'm just looking
6 I'm going
7 I prefer
8 correct

Exercise 3

1 Generally I have / I generally have, really hard this month
2 doing these days? Are you still
3 home at the moment, normally does
4 we're currently experiencing
5 office at the moment
6 usually go, miss it this week

03 TIME OFF

Present perfect questions

Exercise 1

1B supposed to **be** good
2B **he** actually rang me
3B I **went** shopping there yesterday
4B No, but I**'d** like to
5B No, (**I haven't**), **what's it** like?
6B I've always **wanted** to
7B **I've been** there
8B I'm **going** there

Exercise 2

1A Have you been there?
B I've been there lots of times
2A Did you tell Agnes we're going out? / Have you told Agnes we're going out?
B I spoke to her this afternoon
3A Have you ever eaten wild boar?
B have you?
A I think I'll order / I'm going to order it for ... It's supposed to be nice
4A Have you seen the new Bond film?
4B I'm actually going to see it on Sunday.

The future

Exercise 1

1 going
2 might
3 will
4 depends
5 are
6 got
7 going
8 will
9 might

04 INTERESTS

Frequency

Exercise 1

1 No, hardly **ever**
2 Not **very** often / Not much
3 once or **twice** a week
4 **once or twice** a year
5 **I always go**
6 Whenever **I get** the chance.
7 Not as much **as** I should
8 I used **to**.

Exercise 2

1 never let
2 goes
3 don't see
4 studied, don't need
5 used to spend, go

for, during, since, till

Exercise 1

1 How long did you live there?
2 How long has he been driving?
3 How long have they been married?
4 How long have you worked there? / been working there?
5 How long was she married?
6 How long have you known each other?
7 Yeah? Why, how long have we been talking?
8 How long has she been learning it?
9 How long did it take you to get there?

Exercise 2

1 for a couple of minutes
2 for fifty years
3 since his heart attack
4 for over six hundred years
5 for most of my adult life
6 for a few weeks now
7 since I last wrote to you
8 since 2004

05 WORKING LIFE

have to, don't have to, can

Exercise 1

1 you can't leave your car
2 correct
3 she has to work
4 I don't usually spend more
5 I couldn't go out...I had to start
6 I had to travel
7 correct
8 correct
9 Do you have to wear any

Talking about rules

Exercise 1

1 Are
2 allowed / permitted
3 should
4 allowed / permitted
5 to
6 really
7 're/ are
8 allowed

06 GOING SHOPPING

must

Exercise 1

1 visit
2 get
3 ask
4 reply
5 remember
6 forget
7 keep
8 let
9 buy
10 tell

Exercise 2

2 Don't pay the first price they ask.
3 If I were you, I would take out travel insurance.
4 I'm afraid you have to pay in cash.
5 You're not allowed to smoke in the building.
6 You're not supposed to make any personal calls from the office.
7 You'd be better off wearing a suit to the meeting instead of those old jeans.
8 You'd be better off changing some money before you go. The rates are much better.

07 SCHOOL AND STUDYING

After, *once* and *when*

Exercise 1

1 if
2 when
3 once
4 as soon as
5 as long as
6 finish
7 start
8 has finished

First conditionals

Exercise 1

1 correct
2 If he finds a job
3 you don't have
4 correct
5 won't behave better
6 What will you do if
7 I won't finish this essay
8 if you don't revise

Other conditional sentences with present tenses

Exercise 1

1 borrow + need
2 feeling + miss
3 fail + re-take
4 be + cheat
5 should stop + finding
6 be + working
7 become + leave
8 make sure + share

08 EATING

tend to

Exercise 1

1 tend to
2 tend not to / don't tend to
3 have tended to
4 didn't tend to / tended not to
5 have tended not to
6 tended to eat (a)

Second conditionals

Exercise 1

1 would really
2 correct
3 if you paid me
4 correct
5 would make more
6 If I were better at
7 correct
8 correct
9 I didn't really need
10 If I were / was you

Exercise 2

1 was / were, would cancel
2 was / were, might enjoy
3 would come, wasn't / weren't
4 would be, was
5 wasn't / weren't, would try
6 wasn't / weren't working, would love

09 HOUSES

Comparing the past with now

Exercise 1

1 greener **than** it is
2 **as** nice
3 as **many** people
4 far **more** multicultural
5 there are (**far**) more... than **there** were
6 working class as **it**
7 as **much** pollution
8 there **never used** to be

Exercise 2

2 more and more
3 fewer and fewer
4 more and more expensive
5 more and more sophisticated
6 less and less

10 GOING OUT

Exercise 1

1 f
2 d
3 g
4 h
5 e
6 c
7 b
8 a

Exercise 2

1 He said he would help me later.
2 We wanted to stay longer, but we ran out of money.
3 I was just about to phone him when he called me.
4 His performance was much better than I thought it would be.
5 I wasn't expecting it to cost so much.
6 They said it was going to rain, but it's turned out really nice.

11 THE NATURAL WORLD

Exercise 1

1 chasing
2 staring
3 eating
4 jump
5 making
6 looking for
7 circling
8 crawl / crawling

Passives

Exercise 1

1 was searched
2 be smuggled
3 was arrested
4 was released
5 are being created
6 were being kept
7 be seen
8 was given

12 PEOPLE I KNOW

Used to, *would* and the past simple

Exercise 1

1 have
2 would
3 is / was
4 never / didn't
5 go
6 went
7 used
8 did
9 to
10 would

Regrets and wishes

Exercise 1

1 had
2 hadn't
3 hadn't
4 had
5 hadn't
6 had
7 hadn't
8 had

Exercise 2

1 I hadn't started smoking
2 I had asked her
3 you had told me
4 I hadn't been so hard on my children
5 I hadn't lost touch with them
6 I'd moved when I had the chance

13 TRAVEL

Third conditionals

Exercise 1

1 I could **have** come
2 If we **had**
3 If she **hadn't been wearing**
4 I would've **done**
5 correct
6 If there **hadn't been**
7 If we'd **been given**
8 correct

Exercise 2

1 would have called, I'd had
2 would have come, I'd known
3 hadn't left, wouldn't have tripped
4 had paid, wouldn't have crashed
5 would have caught, wouldn't be

Should have

Exercise 1

1 should never have
2 should've
3 should've
4 shouldn't have
5 should've told
6 shouldn't have

Exercise 2

1 should've set off
2 shouldn't have left it
3 should've got here earlier
4 should've gone
5 should've told
6 shouldn't have been

14 TECHNOLOGY

-ing forms

Exercise 1

1 in letting
2 in setting up
3 of flying
4 into studying
5 of giving up
6 for shouting
7 of storing
8 with working
9 for being
10 with organising
11 at talking
12 about having to

Exercise 2

1 travelling
2 going
3 to meet
4 going
5 to pay
6 to lose
7 to email
8 talking
9 losing
10 to fire

15 INJURIES AND ILLNESSES

Exercise 1

1 suffers / suffered
2 had had
3 would take
4 had taken
5 would be
6 shouldn't take

Exercise 2

1 warn
2 agreed
3 told
4 recommended
5 persuade
6 threatened
7 promised
8 refused

16 NEWS AND EVENTS

Defining relative clauses

Exercise 1

1d 2f 3b 4e 5a 6c

Exercise 2

1 which / that
2 whose
3 who / that
4 which / that
5 where
6 which / that
7 which / that
8 when / (can be left out)